Praise for *Gods of Ground Zero*

Carl Gallups has done it again! If your desire is to achieve a much deeper understanding of the tumultuous times in which we live, I could not recommend a better book that will put everything in perspective from a biblical point of view. *Gods of Ground Zero* is a must read! It will blow you away!

—GREGG JACKSON, national bestselling author of *Conservative Comebacks to Liberal Lies, 40 Things to Teach Your Children Before You Die, & 40 Rules to Help Boys Become Men.*

Carl Gallups very rightly points us to Jerusalem as the epicenter and the eye of the storm of emerging geopolitical and spiritual controversy. Like a divine magnet, the whole world is currently being pulled into the raging storms of controversy and warfare that are increasingly swirling over this city. The closer we get to the Day of the Lord and the culmination of God's plan of redemption, the more the attention of the world will become focused on the City of the Great King. Spot on!

—JOEL RICHARDSON, *New York Times* bestselling author of *The Mid-East Beast*

Mysteries and treasures revealed! A stunning e

—MESSIANIC RABBI ZEV PORAT, Tel Aviv, Israel

So many renowned biblical scholars have been trying to tell us these truths—but their findings have been largely ignored and often disconnected from conventional theological understanding. Carl Gallups has pulled the facts and the answers to myriad tough theological questions together into a single, page-turning, captivating resource. If you don't read this book, you'll forever miss the central theme and understanding of the entire Word of God. This book is that important!

—DR. TOM HORN, CEO, Skywatch TV

ALSO BY CARL GALLUPS

Gods and Thrones: Nachash, Forgotten Prophecy, and the Return of the Elohim

When the Lion Roars: Understanding the Implications of Ancient Prophecies for Our Time

Be Thou Prepared: Equipping the Church for Persecution and Times of Trouble

The Rabbi Who Found Messiah: The Story of Yitzhak Kaduri

Final Warning: Understanding the Trumpet Days of Revelation

The Magic Man in the Sky: Effectively Defending the Christian Faith

★★★★★ *ASTONISHING! A page-turning, captivating revelation that peels back the lid on forgotten knowledge from the dawn of time!*
– DR. THOMAS R. HORN

GODS OF GROUND ZERO

THE TRUTH OF EDEN'S INIQUITY, WHY IT STILL MATTERS, AND THE MYSTERY SURROUNDING WHAT'S COMING NEXT

CARL GALLUPS

Best-selling author of *GODS & THRONES*

DEFENDER

CRANE, MO

Gods of Ground Zero: The Truth of Eden's Iniquity, Why It Still Matters, and What's Coming Next
By Carl Gallups

© Copyright 2018 Defender Publishing. All rights reserved.

Printed in the United States of America.

Unless otherwise noted, all Scripture quotations are from The Holy Bible, New International Version®, NIV®, Copyright © 1973, 1978, 1984, 2011 by Biblica, Inc. ™ Used by permission. All rights reserved worldwide.

Cover design by Jeffrey Mardis.

ISBN: 9781948014052

For Brandon.
My son and my friend. A husband to an amazing wife,
a dad to my beloved grandson,
and a partner in the ministry of the Kingdom work of Jesus Christ.
What more could a father desire?

ACKNOWLEDGMENTS

To my wife, Pam. You are the reason life is still sweet.

To the people of Hickory Hammock Baptist Church. Since 1987, you have stood by my side in advancing the Kingdom of Jesus Christ. Thank you for your encouragement and love.

To Tom and Nita Horn and the entire team at Defender Publishing and Skywatch TV—Joe Horn, Katherine Horn, Derek Gilbert, Sharon Gilbert, Josh Peck, Christina Peck, Donna Howell, Allie Anderson, Angie Peters (an absolutely amazing editor—the kind that makes me look much smarter than I am!), Pamela McGrew, and Jeffrey Mardis. You're the greatest! Thank you for your assistance, tenacity, excellence, and friendship. What a blessing you are to my life, ministry, and family.

To my fellow academic biblical researchers of years past. You blazed the way in much of the scholarly research endeavors associated with this topic. You dared to stand in divergence from some of the safer and more acceptable traditions of interpretation. You endured the initial scorn, which is always the hardest to withstand. You did a lot of the heavy lifting that enabled this book to eventually come forward with a stamp of genuine academic integrity. I am indebted to you.

To Brooke and Sidney. You know why. Pam and I love you both so very much.

CONTENTS

PART THREE

THE OBJECTIONS

PART FOUR

THE CONNECTIONS

FOREWORD

To the materialist, the conspiratorial view of history is pathological paranoia. However, this elemental question of whether history unfolds as either mere happenstance or is willed into being, planned and manufactured by some unseen hand, should be of paramount importance to the Bible-believing Christian.

For anyone who truly desires to discover how our violent and depraved human history is shaped, and by whom, the quest must begin in the Old Testament and chapter 3 of the book of Genesis.

In *The Gods of Ground Zero*, Carl Gallups tackles the foundational question of how a single profane act of betrayal is the root cause of the entire bloody and tragic saga of humankind. As he so thoroughly demonstrates, when it comes to understanding our past, present, and future, all roads ultimately lead back to the garden.

—RICHARD SYRETT, broadcaster and regular guest host of *Coast to Coast AM*

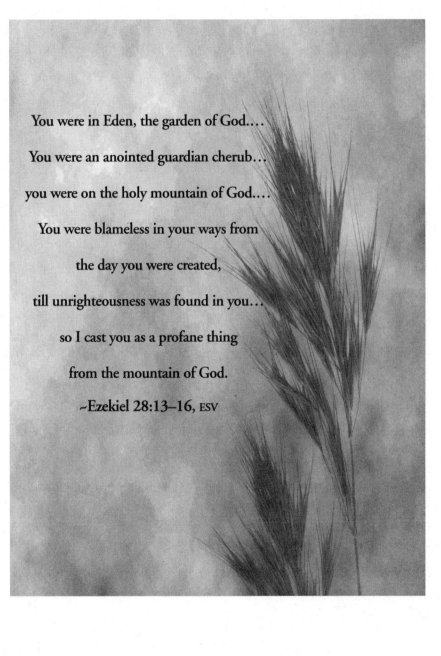

You were in Eden, the garden of God....

You were an anointed guardian cherub...

you were on the holy mountain of God....

You were blameless in your ways from

the day you were created,

till unrighteousness was found in you...

so I cast you as a profane thing

from the mountain of God.

~Ezekiel 28:13–16, ESV

DID GOD REALLY SAY?

> But God expressly forbids us to eat the fruit
> from the Tree of Knowledge. Ah *yessssss*,
> God.... But God gave us life, did He not?
> And God gave us desire, did He not? And
> God gave us taste, did He not? And who else
> but God made the apples in the first place? So
> what else is life for but to *tassste* the fruit we
> desire?
>
> ~David Mitchell, *Ghostwritten*[1]

Do you want to know a dirty little secret?

Here it is. Much of the real message of the Garden of Eden has been "adjusted" over time. Surprised? If you are, you'll soon discover why you shouldn't be.

Of course, this adjustment of truth is exactly what the enemy desires, because uncovering the reality of Eden's iniquity exposes Satan's diabolical scheme of the ages, and it will give you more insight into the Word of God than you have ever before possessed.

By the time you have finished this book, you will be stunned to see how deep the obfuscation process has plunged.

THE QUESTION

Right out of the box, let's begin by asking a foundational question.

Is it an academically sound practice to read a passage of Scripture and stop there, assuming you've gleaned the most accurate interpretation of it without doing an extensive comparison of related passages? Of course not. But, it happens more often than it should.

However, the Bible isn't simply a random collection of individual passages. It is a cohesive and inspired unit. The Old Testament must always be interpreted by the greater revelations of the New Testament, and vice versa. Therefore, the entirety of the Word of God ought to be contextually plumbed to its depths before declaring a particular interpretation of a single passage of Scripture to be a solid one. Most scholars apply that type of methodology to practically every challenging passage except, it seems, for one biblical episode in particular: the Garden of Eden. We will correct that travesty through the following pages.

THE SIGNIFICANCE

The plain truth is that the third chapter of Genesis happens to be the foundational platform for the entire biblical message, including the Gospel itself. This is why it is so important that we get this matter correct. In fact, right up to some of the very last words of the book of Revelation, the Word of God has a number of shocking things to say about Eden. As you uncover what the Bible communicates about the subject, you might find yourself asking aloud, "*Why haven't I been told this before?*"

Think of the eternal ramifications. Literally everything wrong with the world, as well as with our personal lives, is directly linked to the Garden of Eden. Why is it, then, that we so frequently insist upon turning that vital chapter into a childlike bedtime story? How can the Garden account so often be glossed over with a few winks and nods, as well as cryptic and cartoonish interpretations, without appealing to a deeply academic study of contextual biblical comparisons? You'll soon find the answers to these questions. But be forewarned: The truth is not very pretty, nor is it always comfortable. I have a feeling you're going to be shocked by what you see—and probably more than once—as we move forward.

CONTEMPLATIONS

Have you ever wondered about the following?

Why was the Garden of Eden created in the first place? Was God alone in the Garden when He created Adam and Eve? Did God have divine "assistance" in the creation process? Was the "serpent" alone with Adam and Eve in the Garden when the Fall occurred? When were the angels created? When was Satan's original fall?

Where was the original *region* of Eden? Does the Bible give us any clues as to the location of the Garden within that region? Did Jesus say anything specific about the Garden of Eden? Do any of the New Testament writers mention the Garden? Will the Garden ever be restored?

Did you know that Jesus Himself indisputably links Satan with a tree, a garden, and fruit? And did you know that He also directly connects Himself with a specific tree of the Garden of Eden? It's true! Those two facts alone begin to shed a different light on the traditional interpretation of the Garden of Eden, don't they? But there's much more. I promise. I'm just trying to whet your appetite for everything else that lies ahead.

Here are a few more considerations: How does what happened in the Garden directly relate to today's world, our personal lives, our walk with the Lord, and where eternity is headed? And this is probably the most important question regarding Genesis 3: *Does the Bible tell us exactly what happened in the Garden—what was the actual "sin" of Adam and Eve?*

Think of the gravity of that question. Are we truly meant to believe that a real-life, walking, talking snake manipulatively convinced humanity's first couple to eat a single piece of literal fruit? Is that really the scenario that plunged the entire human race, and creation itself, into an eternal course of destruction and indescribable depravity? Or is there a more specific message that is, somehow, infinitely deeper than the text appears to indicate? Once you see the truth, so many other answers about life, spiritual warfare, and our world's current ills will be laid bare before the eyes of your soul.

IMPACT

Each of the foregoing questions and a number of others like them will be explored to their depths in the pages that follow. And when those clear revelations are linked together in their proper context, the disclosures are jaw-dropping. Trust me.

In response to innumerable requests to investigate the topic of the Garden of Eden more thoroughly, this book became the natural sequel to my previous work, *Gods and Thrones*. And while it is essential to briefly revisit several defining themes from that first book, I can assure you that the book you now hold contains a treasure trove of brand-new material and fresh biblical revelation. It is not necessary for you to have read *Gods and Thrones* to thoroughly understand and enjoy this work.

Warning! In the pages that follow are many startling disclosures that will forever change the way you read the Bible, as well as the way you understand the times in which we live. What might once have been considered "unknowable" biblical mysteries are about to be unfurled onto your lap. By the time you reach the end of this book, you might even hear angels singing. In short, expect the unexpected.

[The LORD said] Call to Me and I will answer you, and I will tell you great and mighty things, which you do not know. (Jeremiah 33:3, NAS)

Now, if you're up for a journey like the one I just described, *let's dig in.*

PART ONE

....

THE PRIMORDIAL

Do you, good people, believe that Adam and Eve
were created in the Garden of Eden
and that they were forbidden to eat
from the tree of knowledge?
I do. The church has always been afraid of that tree.
It still is afraid of knowledge.
~Clarence Darrow[2]

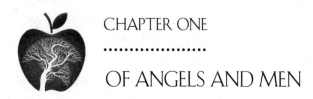

CHAPTER ONE

OF ANGELS AND MEN

And the sunlight was coming from what
certainly did look like a different world—what
they could see of it.

~C. S. Lewis, *The Silver Chair*[3]

There are those rare instances upon the path of life's brief journey
that contain an extraordinary potential to forever change a person's
perspective.

The transformation might come through the turning of a significant
life corner. Perhaps it comes through an unexpected epiphany. Or, it
could involve one of those exceptional moments when one brushes right
up next to the supernatural.

One such day delivered all three of those components into the lives
of several unsuspecting people. In the following several pages is the
account of that true story.

LIFE AND DEATH

The funeral chapel was already at capacity attendance. The crowd had
long ago extended into the vestibule and spilled over to the parking lot.

The deceased was a well-known, local woman in her early twenties.

The pastor who was about to preach her funeral had only met her within the last few weeks. She had been the mother of a 4-year-old girl, and she had been the wife of her longtime sweetheart. At the time of her emergency hospitalization, the young mom had been pregnant with the couple's second child—another girl. Mercifully, the doctors were able to save the newborn through a Cesarean procedure shortly before the baby's mother tragically passed away.

Just a few days before, in the hospital, the pastor had led the young wife to a born-again faith in Jesus Christ. Very soon thereafter, she was gone from this world. The young couple's first daughter now had a new sister. But, that heartbroken 4-year-old had also just lost her mommy on a day that should have been full of joy and celebration.

All these realities raced through the pastor's mind as he began presenting his message to the somber crowd. He silently prayed: *Lord please give me your strength. Assist me with your supernatural presence.*

The father-in-law of the deceased sat in the front row of the family section, snuggling his granddaughter as he held her in his lap. For the last few minutes, she had been whispering into her Pawpaw's ear, and every few moments, she had pointed in the pastor's direction. Suddenly, Granddaddy's mouth dropped open, and he looked directly at the pastor with an expression of utter shock.

The preacher thought to himself, *Oh my word! Have I said something inappropriate?* He could feel the sweat begin to trickle down his temples. He continued the message along with his silent plea for divine help.

THE DIVINE

After the final prayer was delivered and the attendees were beginning to disperse from the chapel, the pastor eased over to stand with the family. He went straight to the grandfather. "What happened?" he murmured. "Is everything okay?"

The man explained in a whispered voice, "Pastor, when you went to the pulpit to preach—my granddaughter leaned over and asked, 'Pawpaw, who's that man dressed *all in white* standing beside the preacher?'"

Now the *pastor's* mouth was gaping in shock. "*Wha…?*" He tried to speak but couldn't.

The grandfather resumed the explanation, "I asked her: 'Baby, what man are you talking about? Do you *see* a man dressed in white up there at the pulpit right now?'"

She told me, "*Yes* Pawpaw, he's there right now; he's standing right beside the preacher. Don't you see him?" The pastor stood dumbstruck, listening to the incredible account.

Pawpaw continued, "I asked her what she knew about the 'man in white.' I asked her if she had ever seen him before. She told me that she didn't know anything about him and had never seen him before this moment."

Granddaddy momentarily paused the story to regain his composure. "She kept pointing in your direction," he said to the pastor. "I didn't see anyone there, of course."

He continued, "And there was not a single person in the crowd dressed all in white, either. But she insisted the man was standing right there beside you the entire time you were preaching!"

The shaken grandfather added, "Pastor, she was as sincere as any child could be. But that's not all; she also said the man had even spoken to her! She said that he came over to her just as the funeral began and told her that her mommy was going to be okay and she didn't need to be afraid."

He swallowed hard and said, "Pastor, I can tell you—this little girl knows very little about angels or the deep things of the Lord at this point in her life."

When the grandfather had finished the account, the child gazed directly into the pastor's eyes with a look on her face that said, "My Pawpaw's telling you the truth, Mister!"

THE REALITY

It has now been well over two decades since I preached that difficult funeral. The event forever changed the perspective by which I currently view my life and ministry—as well as my perception of the world around me. All these years later, "Pawpaw" and I still reminisce about that day—a day when, while she was walking through the valley of the shadow of death, a grieving little girl was lovingly visited by the benevolent side of the unseen realm.

In instances of a reported "supernatural experience," I am careful to measure the account through the contextual Word of God. However, in that particular event, I could find nothing biblically out of bounds about what that innocent preschooler related to us. On the contrary, everything she asserted squared perfectly with well-known assurances revealed in the Scriptures—assurances of which she had no prior knowledge....

> See that you don't look down on one of these little ones, because I tell you that in heaven their angels continually view the face of My Father in heaven. (Matthew 18:10, HCSB)

> You have taught children and infants to tell of your strength, silencing your enemies and all who oppose you. (Psalm 8:2, NLT)

> [The angel said to me] I am a fellow servant with you and with your fellow prophets and with all who keep the words of this scroll. Worship God! (Revelation 22:9)

> An angel from heaven appeared to him and strengthened him. (Luke 22:43)

> Are not all angels ministering spirits sent to serve those who will inherit salvation? (Hebrews 1:14)

GLIMPSES OF GLORY

The truth is that there was once a time when humanity and divine beings dwelt together. There was no veil of separation or "unseen realm" during those ages. There was nothing incredulous about seeing and talking to a celestial being—one that came straight from the throne of God.

That marvelous place was one of ultimate delight, and it was designed specifically for the placement of humanity's first generation. That garden paradise was in a specific region of our primordial planet: the region known as Eden.

A heavy veil between the divine abode of the original Garden of Eden and our earthly existence has since been erected. We have been cut off from that direct heavenly fellowship. However, on occasion, certain mere mortals are briefly allowed to have a peek at the divine realm, even in the midst of our unholy world and our own personal iniquity.

Through those glimpses, and through the promises of the Word of God, we are reminded that our Creator has not abandoned us. He is not finished with us, and He will reinstate our original divine nature at the final restitution of all things.

And, most thrillingly, in the midst of our ever-darkening, sin-stained world, our Creator vows that we will once again dwell among our heavenly counterparts in a restored paradise…in the *Garden of God.*

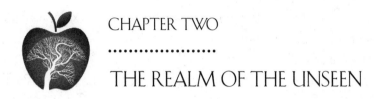

CHAPTER TWO

· ·

THE REALM OF THE UNSEEN

All I have seen teaches me to trust the Creator
for all I have not seen.

~Ralph Waldo Emerson[4]

Even a number of sincere believers still have difficulty imagining the possibility of the existence of unseen dimensions—especially realms that might be inhabited by intelligent beings who sometimes interact in our earthly domain.

To those skeptics, the topic sounds like the stuff of science fiction or a tale from ancient mythology. To others, talk of the angelic and demonic realms are merely discussions of theological fascination. The mention of the idea serves only as a point of amusing conversation over a cup of coffee and holds little relevance to the daily cares of this mortal life.

I understand.

At one time, I too shared some of those same apprehensions.

However, regardless of the various objections, the disclosure of the existence of the unseen realm is one of the most prominent communications of God's Word. From cover to cover, the Bible assures us that the "other side" exists, and that the reality of its existence is crucial to understanding the overall biblical message as well as our own earthly existence and purpose.

NEMO'S DILEMMA

Over the years, I have illustrated these great truths with examples straight from our own mortal realm. Perhaps you will find these simple illustrations helpful as well.

For instance, a goldfish that spends its life in a bowl on a shelf, in a specific room inside a house, has no idea of what exists just outside its bowl. That little fish is incapable of comprehending the enormous cosmos on the other side of the front door of the house. The fish's concept of reality consists only of whatever is in that room, and only of that which it can at least faintly comprehend. That's it. That's the entire known world, as far as our fishy little friend is concerned.

Think of it: That goldfish can't even come close to fathoming the reality of seven billion creatures called *humans*, or of twenty-plus million other species of living things that exist all around it, unseen by its eyes. If that goldfish were somehow told by another goldfish that we truly did exist, and the first goldfish then exclaimed "I don't believe it! That's impossible! That's a crazy fairytale!" well, that little unconvinced fish would be entirely mistaken. Even its most ardent disbelief would be irrelevant regarding the reality of what truly exists just outside that door.

ATOM ANT

Similarly, ants cannot fully experience the world that surrounds their mound of dirt. They have no idea that their little tunneled kingdom is situated on a planet called earth, a globe that revolves around the sun and hangs on nothing in the middle of an endless universe. As a matter of fact, ants don't even know humans exist. Yet, here we are, billions upon billions of us, and so are all the other realities around us that the ant will never be able to comprehend. But the reality of our world is simply not predicated upon what the ant *believes* or *doesn't believe* about its own world, or upon what it can or cannot see. We are here whether the ants understand it or not.

SORRY, CHARLIE

The same is true of certain sea creatures destined to live their entire existences at the bottom of the deepest levels of the ocean's vast, circumnavigating expanses. How could they know of the universe of other living things that exist miles above them and at the same time surrounding their very presence? They cannot. But, it's all there. The ocean-bottom dwellers simply cannot experience the other world of reality in which their world is immersed; therefore, they don't "believe" in it. But little do they know…

On and on the illustrations go, right in our own world. Like the goldfish, the ants, and the ocean-bottom sea creatures, we too are surrounded by intelligent life created by Yahweh and existing in physical realms of reality that we are not yet equipped to fully experience. From the first book of the Bible to the last, we are assured of this incomprehensible fact.

But, from time to time, some of us are allowed a peek at the "other side"—just like what happened to the precious little girl at her mother's funeral and to those of us who were directly affected by that incident. Those kinds of moments often change a person's perspective…forever. As you traverse the remaining pages of this book with me, I pray you will receive at least a small glimpse of similar divine revelations. When you do experience them, they are truly exhilarating.

THE DAY THAT LIVES IN INFAMY

It was in the Garden of Eden that a certain diabolical portion of the *other side* first made its ugly mark upon our earthly existence. That ominous day started just like every other day before it. But, after the sun set, the color-drenched landscape of the brand-new paradise had already faded into a mere façade of the beauty it once displayed. Shamefully, humanity eventually grew to prefer the resulting darkness, rather than the light in which it had previously basked. Their deeds became increasingly evil as their hearts blackened and turned into hard stone.

So they concealed the most intimate parts of their bodies, then quietly hid themselves under the silky gray skirts of the loathsome darkness. They thought to themselves: *Surely, our Creator can't find us here.*

They were mistaken. He *could* find them. In fact, He had never lost sight of them. Little did they know that even the cover of darkness could not hide them from the crime they had committed. As a result, a heavy veil of separation descended upon the land of Eden.

The trees of the Garden drooped their mighty heads…and wept.

They knew.

Death had arrived, and humanity was enslaved by its dread.

But, because of the Creator's great love for His creation, they had not been abandoned. God had a plan. There would come a day of restitution. Everything would be made new.

But not yet.

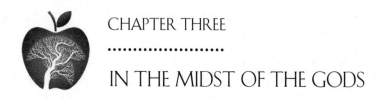

CHAPTER THREE

....

IN THE MIDST OF THE GODS

> The secret things belong to the LORD our God,
> but the things revealed belong to us and to
> our sons forever.
>
> ~Deuteronomy 29:29, NAS

A certain mystical term found in the Old Testament is essential for us to properly understand before we proceed any farther. That vital concept is directly tied to the Garden of Eden, and it is one of the Garden's most shocking revelations.

Some Bible translations identify the expression as the "heavenly court." Others list it as "God's assembly." Still other versions render the Hebrew phrase by terms like these: the "multitudes of heaven," the "divine assembly," the "great assembly," "His own congregation," the "heavenly host," or the "congregation of the mighty."[5]

But probably one of the most recognized translations within a modern discussion of the topic is the "divine council."[6]

Following are only a few examples of the various ways the concept of God's heavenly assemblage is rendered in familiar passages:

- "God has taken his place in the divine council; in the midst of the gods he holds judgment" (Psalm 82:1, ESV).

- "Micaiah continued, 'Therefore hear the word of the Lord: I saw the Lord sitting on his throne with all the multitudes of heaven standing around him on his right and on his left'" (1 Kings 22:19).
- "You alone are the LORD; You have made heaven, the heaven of heavens, with all their host, the earth and everything on it, the seas and all that is in them, and You preserve them all. The host of heaven worships You" (Nehemiah 9:5–6, NKJV).

THE DIVINE GATHERING[7]

The assembling of God's created beings of the unseen realm is a rather frequent theme in the Scriptures. A few of the most recognizable glimpses of those gatherings are found in Job 1–2, Daniel 7, and even in Revelation 4–5. However, the phenomenon is also spoken of in many other passages as well (i.e., Psalm 89:5–8; Isaiah 14:12–17; Jeremiah 23:16–18, 21–22; Daniel 4:17, 23–25; Hebrews 12:22–24).

Obviously, Yahweh does not surround Himself with this heavenly council to seek direction concerning His divine decision making. In fact, the Bible informs us that the very opposite is true:

- "Who has directed the Spirit of the LORD, Or as His counselor has informed Him? With whom did He consult and who gave Him understanding? And who taught Him in the path of justice and taught Him knowledge and informed Him of the way of understanding?" (Isaiah 40:13–14, NAS).
- "O, the depth of the riches of the wisdom and knowledge of God! How unsearchable His judgments, and untraceable His ways! 'Who has known the mind of the Lord? Or who has been His counselor?'" (Romans 11:33–34, Berean Study Bible).

- "Who has known the mind of the Lord so as to instruct him?" (1 Corinthians 2:16).
- "In the same way no one knows the thoughts of God except the Spirit of God" (1 Corinthians 2:11).

Nor does the divine council exist to give Yahweh information that He doesn't already possess. Rather, we discover through scriptural revelation that it is primarily assembled as the heavenly guardians of His righteousness, holiness, and glory—especially as He prepares to intercede in the affairs of humanity (Deuteronomy 33:2).

However, when Yahweh asks the divine council, "What is *your* opinion in this matter?" or "In what way should my decree be carried out?" the members respond accordingly and become active participants in God's ultimate will (1 Kings 22:16–23; Daniel 4:13–17).

We also discover from Scripture that the heavenly host is always ready to be "sent out" by Yahweh to the ends of the cosmos to do His holy bidding:

And suddenly there was with the angel a multitude of the heavenly host praising God, and saying, Glory to God in the highest, and on earth peace, good will toward men. And it came to pass, as the angels were gone away from them into heaven. (Luke 2:13–15, KJV)

And he will send his angels and gather his elect from the four winds, from the ends of the earth to the ends of the heavens. (Mark 13:27)

Bless the LORD, you angels who belong to him, you mighty warriors who carry out his commands, who are obedient to the sound of his words. (Psalm 103:20, ISV)

WITNESSES

The Scripture also tells us the divine council appeared with Yahweh at the giving of the Law at Mt. Sinai. The angelic realm came with Him as witnesses of that event. Both the Old and New Testaments bear out this truth:

- "He said: 'The LORD came from Sinai.... He came with myriads of holy ones from the south, from his mountain slopes" (Deuteronomy 33:2).
- "The law was given through angels and entrusted to a mediator" (Galatians 3:19).
- "You who have received the law that was given through angels but have not obeyed it" (Acts 7:53).

The obedient divine beings serve as ambassadors of God's heavenly Kingdom. When the angels represent God's truth before humanity, the inhabitants of the earth are without excuse. They can never say, "I didn't know."

REGENTS

Like the obedient and faithful angelic realm, born-again humans are not designated as God's ambassadors because we somehow *deserve* to be used in that way (2 Corinthians 5:18–20), nor are we, in and of ourselves, even capable of rightly representing the Lord's perfect glory. Rather, He *allows* us to do so. He chooses to use us because He created us and He loves us—and because we have returned His great love by willingly serving His Son.

So, what is it that God is ultimately up to; what is His ultimate game plan?

Here is the biblical answer. Yahweh is in the process of returning fallen humanity to Eden. In the middle of that process, you and I are His representatives on this earth. Sometimes we are aided by the angels of God's divine council as they occasionally enter our realm in order to minister alongside us, or in order to minister *to us*.

In that moment, you will be moving and ministering squarely in the midst of the unseen realm, just like it was in the beginning, before the dawn of Eden's iniquity. That moment is a gift from Heaven sent especially for you. It is a divine *glimpse of glory*.

Do not forget to show hospitality to strangers, for by so doing some people have shown hospitality to angels without knowing it. (Hebrews 13:2)

Now there's a sobering thought!
But wait—there's still more…

....

CHAPTER FOUR

ALLEGIANCES

> He...cannot say: I will not think about it, but
> will go on just as I did before. There was one
> road, now there are two, and he must make
> his choice.
>
> ~Leo Tolstoy,
> *The Kingdom of God Is Within You*[8]

W hy does the Bible use the term "gods" in the first place? Couldn't that term be confused with the specific designation of *God* Himself?

Have another look at this verse, quoted in the previous chapter:

God has taken his place in the divine council; in the midst of the gods he holds judgment. (Psalm 82:1, ESV)

You probably noticed right away that the word "God" appears twice in the same verse. The first time, the word is represented in singular form, upper case. The second time, the word is rendered in lower case, in plural form. What gives?

ELOHIM[9]

The word translated "God" or "gods" is the Hebrew word *elohim*.[10]

Elohim happens to be one of the most prolific words our Creator uses to identify Himself. In fact, it is the very *first word* we find in Scripture representing His Holy Name:

> In the beginning God [*Elohim*] created the heavens and the earth. (Genesis 1:1)

However, when the context is correct, *elohim* can also mean Yahweh's created beings (those existing in the divine realm)—the gods. It is for this reason that various translations of Psalm 82 and other passages like it often render the term *elohim* as: "angels," "divine beings," "heavenly beings," "the heavenly host,"—or, in a number of cases, as simply "the gods."

Elohim is always spelled the same, whether designating the singular Yahweh or the plural/divine beings created by Him. In that manner, *elohim* is like the English words "deer" and "buffalo." Both are either singular or plural, depending on the other qualifiers within context.

For example, if someone says "Look at the deer!" do you think he is looking at a single deer standing in a field, or at an entire herd of deer? It depends. We need more information. The surrounding words and the immediate context would have to be closely examined. Only then can we determine what the exclamation meant.[11]

John Eadie's Commentary addresses the biblical use of the word "gods" as a divine title for the angelic beings: "No wonder that those beings, so sublimely commissioned by God, and burning in the reflection of His majesty, command human reverence, and are therefore themselves called 'gods.'"[12]

ANGELS, DEMONS, IDOLS

The term *elohim* can apply to both the obedient heavenly angels, which do the bidding of their Creator, and the rebellious demonic realm. In the same sense, sacrificing to the *elohim* can apply to the worship of idols, which God says is really the worship of demons, or fallen *elohim*, the gods.

Consider several examples of these biblical truths:

Obedient Angelic Beings

You made him [humanity] a little lower than the heavenly beings [*elohim*] and crowned him with glory and honor. (Psalm 8:5)

Demons and Idols

They sacrificed to demons that were no gods [*elohim*], to gods [*elohim*] they had never known, to new gods [*elohim*] that had come recently, whom your fathers had never dreaded. (Deuteronomy 32:17, ESV)

Notice the phrase: "to *new gods* that had come recently."

Here is what *Gill's Exposition of the Entire Bible* says about these words: "To gods that came newly up; such as angels, into the worship of which they fell, as their writings testify, and to which the apostle seems to have respect."[13]

Adam Clarke's Commentary agrees: "Rebellious angels appear to be intended.... And it is likely that these fallen spirits, having utterly lost the empire at which they aimed, got themselves worshipped under various forms and names in different places."[14]

The people of Yahweh understood that the recalcitrant *elohim* were behind the evil influences upon fallen humanity. They were well aware that the heathen nations around them served other *gods,* and that those *gods* posed as supreme deities in order to be worshipped. They also knew that those *gods* possessed very real supernatural authority, not equal to Yahweh, yet well beyond mere human ability or understanding.

The various man-made idols, or graven images, erected in the worship of fallen *elohim*, had no power in and of themselves. Rather, those idols served as meeting points or platforms by which the fallen *elohim* would connect with the people in much the same way the Tent of Meeting (Exodus 33:7) served as the holy gathering place between Yahweh and His people.

Thus, Yahweh gave stern warnings against attempting to connect with the fallen *elohim*:

> You shall fear only the LORD your God [*Elohim*]; and you shall worship Him and swear by His name. You shall not follow other gods [*elohim*], any of the gods [*elohim*] of the peoples who surround you, for the LORD your God in the midst of you is a jealous God; otherwise the anger of the LORD your God will be kindled against you, and He will wipe you off the face of the earth. (Deuteronomy 6:13–15, NASB)

By the time we get to the New Testament, we find the very same warnings regarding pagan "rituals" and the reality of the demonic infestation they bring:

> No, but the sacrifices of pagans are offered to demons, not to God, and I do not want you to be participants with demons. (1 Corinthians 10:20)

We find a similar understanding in the warning the apostle Paul delivered to the church at Colossi:

Do not let anyone who delights in false humility and the worship of angels disqualify you. Such a person also goes into great detail about what they have seen; they are puffed up with idle notions by their unspiritual mind. (Colossians 2:18)

The *Forerunner Commentary* entry for the Colossians passage agrees that the subject of Paul's admonition ultimately involves that of demon worship—through fallen angels: "The subject of Paul's teaching does not involve God's laws at all but worldly, pagan teachings that involve asceticism and demon worship."[15]

Calvin's Commentary on the Bible defines the worship of angels as nothing less than a purposed deception of Satan: "The Devil has always endeavored to set off his impostures under this title."[16]

The *Thomas Coke Commentary on the Holy Bible* says regarding the declaration of Colossians 2:18:

It is uncertain whether the heathens began so early as this to call those celestial spirits angels whom they before had called good demons; but it is evident that very soon after the Apostle's days, they speak of angels, and archangels, and recommend the worship of them, under those names. (accessed at Studylight.org)

Whedon's Commentary on the Bible also addresses the matter of Paul's admonition to the church at Colossi:

Notwithstanding the apostle's labour and caution, this evil took so deep root in Phrygia and Pisidia, that three centuries later the Council of Laodicea forbade the practice by a special decree, condemning it as idolatry and an abandonment of Christ.[17]

Here is the long and short of the matter. The worship of the fallen *elohim*, or erecting idols in their honor, was declared by Yahweh to be a deadly crime, one against the person and holiness of God Himself. In fact, the first two of the Ten Commandments speak directly to this offense (Exodus 20:1–6).

From the most primitive days of the Old Testament, right up through the days of the early church and into our current time, humanity's infatuation with the fallen *elohim* has been a global curse. The infusion of this infatuation was a part of Satan's plan since the creation of the first humans. And the *gods* are still up to their diabolical scheming. According to the Word of God, the scourge will only grow worse as we draw closer to the return of Jesus Christ and His ultimate reign.

> The Spirit clearly says that in later times some will abandon the faith and follow deceiving spirits and things taught by demons. (1 Timothy 4:1)

I hope the pieces of the puzzle are beginning to fall into place and the bigger picture is coming into focus. Yet, there's much more to the overall understanding, and there are several amazing Garden connections still to be made.

CHAPTER FIVE

·····················

THE YEARNING

Freely they stood who stood, and fell who fell.
~John Milton, *Paradise Lost*[18]

D
r. Richard Gallagher says that "demonic possession is real." He also claims that on more than one occasion he has personally witnessed evidence of it.

Gallagher is an Ivy League-educated, board-certified psychiatrist who teaches at Columbia University and New York Medical College, and his acknowledgment of the reality of the demonic realm shocked the world when he was interviewed in a 2017 CNN story.

Dr. Gallagher claims he has personally witnessed victims under demonic control who suddenly speak with different voices and languages, even perfect Latin. He said he has seen them displaying hidden knowledge or even secrets about people—information they could not possibly have known—as well as exhibiting feats of super-human strength. The doctor ardently maintains that he has also witnessed "sacred objects" flying off the shelves when a demonically possessed person is in the room.[19]

Recounting Dr. Gallagher's experience with the reality of the "other side," the same CNN story also claimed:

Fighting Satan's minions wasn't part of Gallagher's career plan while he was studying medicine at Yale. He knew about biblical accounts of demonic possession but thought they were an ancient culture's attempt to grapple with mental disorders like epilepsy. He proudly calls himself a "man of science."[20]

According to that news piece, Dr. Gallagher is now in high demand among the expansive, quickly growing network of exorcists operating in the United States.

Also speaking to the expanding global uptick in demonic possession and infestations, Father Vincent Lampert, a renowned Catholic exorcist, claims, "The problem isn't that the devil has upped his game, but more people are willing to play it." Lampert points to epidemic pornography, illegal drug use, and the occult. "Where there is demonic activity, there is always an entry point," Dr. Lampert said.[21]

Hmm. Sexual perversion, rampant pornography, drug abuse, and immersion in the occult—all bringing about an increase in worldwide demonic infestation, as well as opening doors leading to the domain of darkness. Can you guess who might be the "father" of that diabolical mess?

THE DELUGE

There should be no real surprise that an ever-expanding network of professionals is dealing with the reality of the demonic realm among us. The Bible is clear that the days just before the ushering in of the return of Jesus Christ will be accompanied by an unprecedented demonic outpouring:

- "The Spirit clearly says that in later times some will abandon the faith and follow deceiving spirits and things taught by demons" (1 Timothy 4:1).

- "The rest of mankind, who were not killed by these plagues, did not repent of the works of their hands, so as not to worship demons" (Revelation 9:20–21).
- "The great dragon was hurled down—that ancient serpent called the devil, or Satan, who leads the whole world astray. He was hurled to the earth, and his angels with him…. But woe to the earth and the sea, because the devil has gone down to you! He is filled with fury, because he knows that his time is short" (Revelation 12:9, 12).
- "They are demonic spirits that perform signs, and they go out to the kings of the whole world, to gather them for the battle on the great day of God Almighty" (Revelation 16:14).

ADORATION

Even those of the earliest tribes of fallen humanity soon learned that the powers of the fallen angelic realm could be "summoned." They had no doubt that the demonic powers they were experiencing were very real indeed. That diabolical empire, led by the prince of the fallen ones, was all too happy to oblige the tribute given to them in exchange for a bit of supernatural intervention in the affairs of humanity.

After all, this kind of devotion was what Satan had desired from the time he first laid his eyes upon the Garden of Eden—and especially as he longingly gazed upon Adam and Eve, whom he perceived to be his nearest rivals in creation.[22]

Satan yearned for their allegiance. He desired their adoration. He coveted the "nations" that would eventually come through their offspring. He hungered for the unbridled allegiance of their souls. He knew he had to bring them down. He knew he had to somehow profane Adam and Eve to the extent that they would no longer be under the special protection of Yahweh's holiness. And he had a plan.

DIVINING THE FUTURE

Satan was plotting ahead—way ahead. In the vanity of his prideful arrogance, if his strategy worked, he imagined himself ascending to the very throne of Yahweh.

> You said in your heart, "I will ascend to heaven; I will raise my throne above the stars of God; I will sit enthroned on the mount of assembly, on the utmost heights of the sacred mountain. I will ascend above the tops of the clouds; I will make myself like the Most High." (Isaiah 14:13–14)

The Garden tempter's first promise to Eve should be making more sense, because you now understand a little more about the power behind that promise:

> And the serpent said unto the woman, Ye shall not surely die: For God doth know that in the day ye eat thereof, then your eyes shall be opened, and ye shall be *as gods* [the *elohim*—or even Elohim Himself], knowing good and evil. (Genesis 3:4–5, KJV, emphasis added)

So, in effect, Satan said to the first couple: "You can be exactly like the *elohim*, if you so desire. But you must relinquish your complete fidelity to me! You were created a little lower than us, but I can raise you up to our status. You can be just like us—even like God himself! He has done you a severe injustice. I can correct this horrible wrong! Just eat this nice little piece of fruit...*there you go!* Now, doesn't that taste *sssso ssssweet?*"

Think about it. What has sparked practically every war since that fateful day in the Garden? Is it not the continual hunger for power, control, and dominance over the nations—the seed of man? Is it not also humanity's internal yearning to be its own *god?* Isn't the entirety of life all about allegiances—either to the father of lies, or to the Father of our very souls? Sure it is. It has been so from the very beginning.

Ever since that fateful day of original iniquity, the demonic realm has been about the business of influencing and corrupting the foundational powers of the earth. They fancy themselves to be the *new gods* behind the thrones of earth's powers.

Our ancient ancestors ate from the fruit of corruption, and because of that rebellion, Satan is now officially our "father" (John 8:44). He is the "prince [god] of this world" (2 Corinthians 4:4; John 14:30)… unless, of course, we are under the blood of Jesus. Then, and only then, can we be called the true "children of God" (John 1:12). And only then can we also be declared "no longer of this world" (John 15:19; 17:16).

The foregoing biblical revelations also raise several other very important questions: Where was Eden located? Is there anything significant about its original location that might have a connection to today's global geography and geopolitical wranglings?

And why was Eden even created in the first place?

Let's find out the answers…

CHAPTER SIX

....

LOCATION, LOCATION, LOCATION

Now the Lord God had planted a garden in
the east, in Eden.

~Genesis 2:8

The search for Eden's original location has been a fascination for humanity for thousands of years. But, does the Bible hold the keys of discovery that might satiate our desire for this knowledge?

The second chapter of Genesis is clear: Humanity had its beginnings in Eden. The Hebrew word *Eden* (ay'-den) means: "delicate," "delight," "pleasure." In other words, Eden means "paradise."[23]

Sometimes "Eden" and the "Garden of Eden" are used synonymously. However, they are not the same. Eden was an entire region of the newly created planet, while the Garden of Eden was located within that region:

Now the Lord God had planted a garden in the east, in Eden;
and there he put the man he had formed. (Genesis 2:8)

One of the biggest problems for identifying the *region of Eden* in today's geography is that, in ages past, there was a global deluge (Genesis 7). Surely the entire landscape of the planet—including mountains, river locations, ocean borders, and perhaps even continent locations and sizes, are drastically different now than they were before the Flood of Noah's day.

The *International Standard Bible Encyclopedia* (ISBE) addresses a popular theory asserting that the location of the larger "region of Eden" could therefore be almost anywhere on the planet:

> It is doubtful whether the phrase "eastward, in Eden" refers to the position with reference to the writer or simply with reference to Eden itself. So far as that phrase is concerned, therefore, speculation is left free to *range over the whole earth*, and *this it has done*.[24] (Emphasis added)

However, that same *ISBE* article draws this conclusion:

> If we are compelled to choose between these theories it would seem that the one which locates Eden near the head of the Persian Gulf combines the greater number of probabilities of every kind.[25]

Most of the leading commentaries tend to agree with the general assessment, expressed by the *ISBE*, regarding the location of the region of Eden.

But here's the question most people want answered regarding this subject: While we may be uncertain of the borders of the original region of Eden, is it still possible to pinpoint where the actual Garden of Eden might have been?

Believe it or not, for that question some reliable biblical/historical/archeological evidence might exist, regardless of the Flood's potential destruction of the original borders of the land of Eden. Here is where the study gets fascinating—and very pertinent to our times.

We begin by examining the scholarly research that first homes in on the region of Eden. Then we will narrow the focus to the Garden itself.

THE LAND OF PROMISE

Dr. Keith Krell, who has a PhD from the University of Bristol, is an associate professor of biblical exposition at the Moody Bible Institute in Spokane, Washington. Dr. Krell holds the view that the Garden's original location was at least specific to the *region* of the Promised Land:

> The Tigris and Euphrates are now in Babylonia. Eden (meaning delight, pleasure, or perhaps place of abundant waters) therefore appears to have lain in the general area of the Promised Land.
>
> It can hardly be a coincidence that two of these rivers are exactly the ones that God uses to explain to Abraham where the Promised Land will be (15:18).[26]

Rabbi Avraham Arieh Trugman, director of Ohr Chadash Torah Institute, confirms the ancient Jewish beliefs. Those early Hebrew scholars also believed the Garden was somewhere in what we now know as the ancient land of Israel:

> According to Jewish tradition, the Garden of Eden is associated with the Land of Israel, according to the big borders—from the river of Egypt to the Euphrates.[27]

The *Benson Commentary*, addressing Genesis 2:8, says:

> A place peculiarly pleasant, a paradise, separated, it seems, from the rest of the earth, and enclosed, but in what way, we are not

informed; eastward—from the place where Moses wrote, and from the place where the Israelites afterward dwelt—In Eden.[28]

Likewise, the *Pulpit Commentary* declares the original location of the region of Eden to have been in the Promised Land:

Israel, *like Adam*, had been *settled by God in Palestine*, the *glory of all lands*; but, ungrateful for God's great bounty and gracious gift, they broke the covenant of their God, the condition of which, as in the case of the Adamic covenant, was obedience.[29] (Emphasis added)

The preceding scholarly assertions are backed by numerous scriptural hints. For example, we find that in both Ezekiel 36 and Joel 2, passages that ultimately deal with the return of the Lord and the establishment of His earthly Kingdom, the current land of Israel is said, in that day, to finally be restored "like the Garden of Eden."

- "This is what the Sovereign Lord says: On the day I cleanse you from all your sins.... They will say, 'This land that was laid waste has become like the garden of Eden'" (Ezekiel 36: 33, 35).
- "Blow ye the trumpet in Zion, and sound an alarm in my holy mountain: let all the inhabitants of the land tremble: for the day of the LORD cometh, for it is nigh at hand...the land is as the garden of Eden before them" (Joel 2:1, 3, KJV).

An interesting academic proposition is already taking place concerning the land of Eden.

If the Promised Land truly is the location of the original *land of Eden*, then is it possible to at least approximate the area of the original Garden of Eden? Does the Bible offer foundational clues?

As a matter of fact, it does.

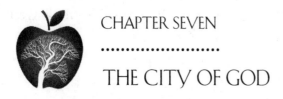

••••••••••••••••••••••

CHAPTER SEVEN

THE CITY OF GOD

This is Jerusalem, which I have set in the
center of the nations, with countries all
around her.

~Ezekiel 5:5

A number of scholars believe they have narrowed down the location of the actual Garden of Eden even further. They insist it was originally located not only in Israel, but perhaps on Mt. Zion itself—in the very center of Jerusalem, the city of God.[30]

According to ancient Jewish tradition, the Temple Mount in Jerusalem is the location of the foundation stone upon which God created the world. In Hebrew, the stone is called the *Even HaShtiya*. The Jews claim this is the place of the original Garden of Eden, as well as the site of Abraham's intended sacrifice of Isaac (Genesis 22). According to Scripture, this was also where Solomon built the Temple and where the "Lord appeared" to King David (2 Chronicles 3:1).

The Hebrew word *Even* means "rock." This is also the reason for the name "Dome of the Rock," the Islamic Mosque now located on the site of the original temple.[31]

The western facade of the Dome of the Rock features the following Arabic inscription: "The Rock of the Temple from the Garden of Eden."

The northern gate of the mosque, facing the foundation stone, is named the Gate of Paradise, *Bab ej-Jinah*. On the floor in front of this gate is a stone of green jasper about half a meter square that the Muslims call "the Stone of Eden."[32]

SPIRITUAL GROUND ZERO

Given the laser-focused attention of certain international powers aimed directly at Israel, particularly the Temple Mount in Jerusalem, it would make perfect spiritual sense that this is, in fact, the angelic/demonic battleground of the ages. The fallen *elohim* behind the global thrones of power, both political and religious, certainly appear to be fixated upon this one site more than any other in all the earth. It is the divine Ground Zero.[33]

This phenomenon is foretold in Scripture:

- "On that day, when all the nations of the earth are gathered against her, I will make Jerusalem an immovable rock for all the nations. All who try to move it will injure themselves" (Zechariah 12:3).
- [Jesus said, in reference to His Second Coming], "When you see Jerusalem being surrounded by armies, you will know that its desolation is near" (Luke 21:20).

Another attestation that the Garden of Eden was in Jerusalem is expressed in an article at *The Israel Bible* website:

Eden and its rivers may signify the real Jerusalem, the Temple of Solomon, or the Promised Land. It may also represent the divine garden on Zion, and the mountain of God, which was also Jerusalem. The imagery of the Garden, with its serpent and cherubs, has been compared to the images of the Solomonic

Temple with its copper serpent (the nehushtan) and guardian cherubs.[34]

An additional work, published in 2012, titled *Kingdom through Covenant: A Biblical-Theological Understanding of the Covenants*, also sets forth the Jerusalem/Temple area as a potential location for the Garden of Eden. Following is a small portion of its lengthier observations:

> According to Genesis 2:10, "A river flows out of Eden to water the garden." This river brings fertility and life to the entire world, as we see in verses 11–14. Similarly, in Psalm 46:5 we read of "A river whose streams make glad the city of God," and Ezekiel 47 describes a great river flowing out of the temple in the New Jerusalem to sweeten the Dead Sea. Such a source of fertility and life is an indication that the divine presence is there.[35]

That source further points out that the Garden was the place where Yahweh announced His decrees to His newly created humanity and where He fellowshipped with man. The comparison of the Garden is then made with the wilderness Tabernacle (and later Solomon's Temple in Jerusalem) and with Exodus 25:8: "Then make for me a sanctuary so that I might dwell among them."[36]

The implication of that work is that the wilderness Tabernacle, and ultimately the Jerusalem Temple, were designated by the LORD as a temporary substitute for Eden's fellowship until Yeshua reestablishes the original Eden fellowship in Jerusalem at the restitution of all things.[37]

TABERNACLE-TEMPLE SYMBOLISM

A strong case can be made that the Wilderness Tabernacle, as well as the eventual Jerusalem Temple, were indeed earthly representations of the

Garden of Eden. The Tabernacle was called the Tent of Meeting. God called the later Jerusalem Temple the place where He would meet with His people.

Within the tent/temple there was a shielding curtain (Exodus 39:34, 40:21) that prevented unwarranted entrance into the Holy of Holies. Just outside that veil stood a stylized, golden almond tree with buds, blossoms, almond flowers, and fruit, all on the same "tree" (Exodus 25:31–36), symbolizing the fullness of life lost in the Fall. The lampstand-tree also appears as a reminder of the Lord's visit to Moses, as was His presence in Eden, as well as upon the mountain of God (Exodus 3:1ff.).[38]

The symbols of the veiled Eden are unmistakable. David installed the Tabernacle in Jerusalem, along with the returned Ark of the Covenant, and declared Jerusalem the place where God would meet with the people of Israel. Also in Jerusalem, on Zion, Solomon built the first Temple of the Lord.

THE SUPREMACY OF JERUSALEM

Think of it. Why else would Yahweh have declared that Jerusalem was to be the center of the nations, as well as the place where He had established His Name?

- "This is what the Sovereign LORD says: This is Jerusalem, which I have set in the center of the nations, with countries all around her" (Ezekiel 5:5).
- "But you shall seek the LORD at the place which the LORD your God will choose from all your tribes, *to establish His name there for His dwelling*, and there you shall come" (Deuteronomy 12:5, emphasis added).

Additionally, a reestablished earthly Garden of Eden is exactly what Revelation 22:1–3 pictures for the believer in the day of final bliss and the restitution of all things. In fact, the picture is so obvious that in the NIV translation, the very last chapter of the Bible is subtitled "Eden Restored."[39]

Notice the Eden-like words of that passage, complete with a river of life, the tree of life, and Yahweh's eternal fellowship with believers. The passage also speaks of a heavenly city in which the throne of God is located:

> Then the angel showed me the river of the water of life, as clear as crystal, flowing from the throne of God and of the Lamb down the middle of the great street of the city. On each side of the river stood the tree of life, bearing twelve crops of fruit, yielding its fruit every month. And the leaves of the tree are for the healing of the nations. No longer will there be any curse. The throne of God and of the Lamb will be in the city, and his servants will serve him. (Revelation 22:1–3)

THE ROCKS CRY OUT

In November 2017, Israeli mainstream media source *Haaretz* reported that "mounting evidence from around the world" challenged the standard evolutionary model that Homo sapiens first appeared in Africa.[40]

Even though the *Haaretz* article is decidedly steeped in the typical evolutionary assumptions of scientifically dubious periods of time, the conclusion of the piece is still quite telling.

Because of those very latest archeological findings, researchers now admit a strikingly inconvenient truth. The oldest known remains of certifiably "real" human beings have been unearthed in a completely different location than what was previously proclaimed as "fact." You guessed it—those remains were found in Israel.

The artifacts were not found just anywhere in Israel, but just a little more than forty miles northeast of Jerusalem. This, of course, is the vicinity so many Bible scholars claim is in or near the original location of the Garden of Eden—and where genuine humanity, according to the Bible, did indeed make its debut.

I told you the discovery was inconvenient.

Then, in January 2018, the *Jerusalem Post* ran yet another story reporting that even more evidence had been unearthed. An ancient human jawbone, with teeth, was exhumed in a cave on Mt. Carmel.

"This finding *completely changes* our view on modern human dispersal and the history of modern human evolution," said Prof. Israel Hershkovitz of Tel Aviv University Sackler Faculty of Medicine's Department of Anatomy and Anthropology.[41]

Apparently, archeological research is just now beginning to unveil what the Bible has asserted all along: Verifiably genuine humanity had its earliest beginnings from the area in and around Jerusalem and throughout the land of Israel, the original location of Eden and Eden's Garden. The Bible first declared it. Secularists rejected it. But now, in only our generation, archeology confirms it. Imagine that.

STRIKING BIBLICAL CONNECTIONS

Think of the biblical connections. Jerusalem is where Abraham offered up Isaac as a sacrifice and where, in the Spirit of prophecy, Abraham was certain that on that mountain, "God himself will provide the lamb" (Genesis 22:14).

Jerusalem was where Jesus was dedicated at the Temple, spent the last week of His life, ate the Passover Last Supper with His disciples, was put on trial by the religious elite, and was tempted by Satan in the Garden of Gethsemane. It is where Jesus was crucified and resurrected, and where He ascended into Heaven at the Mount of Olives.

Jerusalem is also where Jesus will return at His Second Coming (Zechariah 14:4; Revelation 14:1), and it is the place from where He will rule and reign during the millennial kingdom (Jeremiah 3:17; Psalm 2:6–9; Isaiah 2:1–4).

Yahweh originally fellowshipped with humanity in the Garden of Eden, and that is where Yahweh brought His first word of judgment against Satan. It is also Jerusalem where God promises to *reestablish* His fellowship with humanity as well as the place where He will mete out His punishment upon Satan, the fallen *elohim*, and the wicked kings of the earth (Isaiah 24:21–23).

Yahweh even promises a restored garden paradise in the New Jerusalem during the Kingdom reign (Ezekiel 43:7; 34:26–29; Isaiah 51:3).

Jerusalem certainly sounds like spiritual *Ground Zero* to me. How about you?

There's little room for serious doubt at this point. The scriptural indications, as well as the declarations of ancient Jewish understanding and even modern archeological attestation concerning Jerusalem as Eden's original site, are plenteous.

However, there is yet another important consideration: Why is there apparently nothing said in the Bible about a *mountain* being related to the Garden of Eden? After all, Mount Zion is the undeniable focal point of Jerusalem. Wouldn't that geographical feature have also been the focal point of the Garden as well?

Prepare for a surprise.

CHAPTER EIGHT

....

THE GARDEN MOUNTAIN

You were in Eden, the garden of God.... You
were on the holy mount of God.

~Ezekiel 28:13–14

In the ancient biblical lands, temples were often strategically located
upon mountaintops or the high places. The idea was that, in this way,
worship would be nearer to the *gods*. However, the practice most likely
owes its origins to more direct biblical truth, especially as the matter
relates to the Garden of Eden. Don't forget, Satan is always in the business
of perverting, or attempting to counterfeit, what God has originated.

Most scholars attest that Ezekiel 28:11–19 clearly relates that Satan
was in the Garden of Eden. If this is so, then the passage concurrently
declares that Satan was on "the holy mountain of God." Satan was in
both places—in the Garden *and* on God's mountain. Were the two
places different locations, or were they one and the same? Following are
several scholarly observations:

The Bible Exposition Commentary:

The use of the word "cherub" (Ezek[iel] 28:4–6) suggests that
we're dealing here with an angelic creature, also the fact that he
had been "upon the holy mountain of God" (v. 14). This sounds

49

a great deal like the description in Isa[iah] 14:12 ff. Satan began as an obedient angel but rebelled against God and led a revolt to secure God's throne.[42]

The Cambridge Bible for Schools and Colleges:

Different representations of the abode of God were current; it was sometimes spoken of as a mountain and sometimes as a garden. *The mountain here is the same as the garden* of Ezekiel 28:13, cf. Ezekiel 28:16 [The Garden of Eden]. It is the abode of God.[43] (Emphasis added)

The Pulpit Commentary:

In that earthly Paradise [Garden of Eden] the prophet saw the "holy mountain of God," the Olympus, so to speak, of the Hebrews, the throne of the Eternal. Isaiah's words as to the King of Babylon (Isaiah 14:13–14) present a suggestive parallel.[44]

Dr. Michael Heiser, a renowned modern day biblical languages expert, contends that "a tradition preserved in Ezekiel 28:13–16 equates the 'mountain of God' with Eden, the 'garden of God.'"[45]

Dr. Heiser goes on to assert, "We naturally think of God's mountain as Mount Sinai or Mount Zion. When it comes to garden imagery, *the latter [Zion in Jerusalem] is spoken of in Edenic terms.* Like Eden, Mount Zion is also described as a watery habitation (Isa[iah] 33:20–22; Ezek[iel] 47:1–12; Zech[ariah] 14:8; Joel 3:18)."[46] (Emphasis and brackets added)

The Bible Exposition Commentary directly correlates Satan and the Garden of Eden, as well as the Jerusalem Temple and the holy mountain of God:

All of these jewels [that adorned Satan, the cherub] were also found in the breastplate of the Jewish high priest (Ex[odus] 28:17–20). This suggests that in "Eden, the garden of God" and upon "God's holy mountain" this person had special priestly functions to perform for the Lord.... While the original description refers to the ruler of Tyre, it certainly applies to the god of this age. Satan, the enemy of the Lord.[47] (Bracketed words added)

CONCLUDING CONNECTIONS

The *Jewish Virtual Library* offers additional insight tying together everything we have examined thus far:

Ezekiel (28:11–19; 31:8–9, 16–18) in his description *introduces new and variant details not present in the Genesis narrative* of the Garden of Eden.

Thus, in Genesis there is no trace of the "holy mountain" of Ezekiel 28:14 and no mention of the "stones of fire" of Ezekiel 28:14, 16.[48] (Emphasis added)

Following is another verification regarding ancient Jewish thought on Eden. The entry is from the *Encyclopedia Judaica*:

Talmudic and Midrashic sources know of two Gardens of Eden: the terrestrial, of abundant fertility and vegetation, and the celestial, which serves as the habitation of souls of the righteous. The location of the earthly Eden is traced by the boundaries delineated in Genesis 2:11–14.... The boundary line between the earthly and heavenly Garden of Eden is barely discernible in rabbinic literature. In fact, "The Garden of Eden and heaven were created by one word [of God], and the chambers of the Garden of Eden are constructed as those of heaven."[49]

It appears that the more we gaze into the matter of the Garden of Eden, the more the Lord reveals: Jerusalem was the central location of that paradise, and Mount Zion was its epicenter.

In addition to everything we've just laid out, the New Testament also tells us that the divine council of Yahweh *continues* to assemble themselves in the unseen realm, in Jerusalem, and on Mount Zion:

> But you have come to Mount Zion, to the city of the living God, the heavenly Jerusalem. You have come to thousands upon thousands of angels in joyful assembly, to the church of the firstborn, whose names are written in heaven. You have come to God, the Judge of all, to the spirits of the righteous made perfect, to Jesus the mediator of a new covenant. (Hebrews 12:22–24)

I assure you, there are additional revelations to come. Thus far, we have only peeled back the first of many more exciting layers.

CHAPTER NINE

....

GUARDIAN OF THE GARDEN

These were the living creatures I had seen by
the Kebar River.

~Ezekiel 10:20

Now for another huge biblical connection. In Ezekiel 28 we discover that Satan was called the "anointed cherub." We also learn in Ezekiel that the cherubim were called "the living creatures." An example of this is found in Ezekiel 10:15:

Then the cherubim rose upward. These were the living creatures
I had seen by the Kebar River.

By the time we get to the fourth chapter of Revelation, we run right into the cherubim again. They are encircling the throne of God as guardians of His holiness and majesty:

"Holy, holy, holy is the Lord God Almighty, who was, and is,
and is to come." Whenever the living creatures give glory, honor
and thanks to him who sits on the throne and who lives for
ever and ever, the twenty-four elders fall down before him who
sits on the throne and worship him who lives for ever and ever.
(Revelation 4:8–9)

The New Testament designation of Satan as sometimes appearing as an "angel of light" (2 Corinthians 11:14) now makes much more sense, doesn't it? So does his diabolical use of his beauty, majesty, and knowledge. He came straight from the throne of God. His understanding of creation and humanity is second only to that of God Himself. Satan certainly is not the "ordinary" angelic creature.

THE HOLY CUSTODIAN

The Bible is clear: Satan the cherub was chosen from among the entire heavenly realm to be the *divine regent* of God's new creation. The assignment was the highest place of honor to which any of God's creation could have been appointed. And, as we shall see, that very honor eventually became Satan's prideful undoing.

The *Expositor's Bible Commentary* confirms Satan's position in the Garden, as that truth relates to the Ezekiel 28 narrative: "The cherub is the warden of the 'holy mountain of God,' and no doubt also the symbol and bearer of the divine glory."[50]

The *Pulpit Commentary* attests to the same truth: "The splendor of the King of Tyre had suggested the idea of Eden the garden of God. This, in its turn, led on to that of the cherub that was the warder of that garden (Genesis 3:24)."[51]

SUMMARY

By this time in our study, we can safely make the following biblical claims with a great degree of academically-backed certainty:

- The Garden of Eden and God's holy mountain are the same place.

- The original Garden most likely corresponds with Jerusalem, specifically the area of Mount Zion.
- Satan's holy assignment was guardian of the Garden of Eden.
- Adam was created just *outside* the Garden, but was eventually brought there by Yahweh (Genesis 2:7–8, 15).
- Eve was created in the Garden, out of Adam (Genesis 2:20–22).
- The boundary lines between the earthly Garden of Eden, the heavenly Garden of Eden yet to come, and the Garden of Eden that exists right this moment in God's unseen realm are thin indeed. The ancient Jews understood these biblical truths. The word "Eden" was synonymous with "paradise" or "heaven."[52]

There are yet additional great truths that apply to our understanding of the Garden of Eden, especially to the eternal tragedy that eventually emanated from that place.

In fact, the next revelation might prove to be a real eye-opener.

CHAPTER TEN

....

GARDEN OF THE GODS

The Garden of Eden was where Yahweh established the center of personal fellowship. This divine communion was not only to be between humanity and Himself, but also between humanity and the entire heavenly realm. It is this same heavenly fellowship that the Lord will restore at the culmination of His celestial plan.

- "For this reason I kneel before the Father, from whom every family in heaven and on earth derives its name" (Ephesians 3:14–15).
- "[God] made known unto us the mystery of his will, according to his good pleasure which he hath purposed in himself: That in the dispensation of the fullness of times he might gather together in one all things in Christ, both which are in heaven, and which are on earth; even in [Christ]" (Ephesians 1:9–10, KJV).
- "Heaven must receive [Jesus Christ] until the time comes for God to restore everything, as he promised long ago through his holy prophets" (Acts 3:21).

In other words, everything will eventually revert to the way it was meant to be from the beginning—in the restored Garden of Eden. God's two "families" will be reunited and completely redeemed.

GODS IN THE GARDEN

There are several things about the presence of the divine realm in the Garden of Eden that we already know from Scripture. For example, we know that God Himself was there and that He "walked with man" and communicated with him (Genesis 3:8).

Obviously, God chose to appear in human/angel form as He presented Himself to Adam. That shouldn't surprise us in the least. Yahweh also appeared as a human to Abraham and several other Old Testament personalities (Genesis 16:7–13, 17:1, 18:1–33; Exodus 3:2–6, 6:2–3, 24:9–11; Numbers 12:6–8; Joshua 5:14; Judges 2:1–5, 6:11).

We know, of course, that Yahweh appeared to the entire first-century world in the person of Yeshua/Jesus (Matthew 1:23). And, in that form, Jesus was declared to be representing the "image" of God, who is normally not visible to humanity in His complete fullness (Colossians 1:15–16).

THE ONLY BEGOTTEN

This is why Jesus was also declared the "unique" manifestation of Yahweh (the only begotten), because appearing in this form required Him to come into the human realm the way that the rest of us do— "begotten" from the womb of a woman (Genesis 3:15; Galatians 4:4). Elohim would never again make an entrance into the world in this way. This was His "one and only" presentation of Himself in this manner. Therefore, Jesus truly was God's "only begotten."

Not only was His "presentation" of Himself unique in the human form of Jesus Christ, but it was also Elohim's only appearance in which He would be willing take the sin of the world upon His own person. Thus, Jesus was the unique manifestation of God's divine mission to restore paradise. Yahweh was covertly among us, in the flesh, for a one-time-only undertaking (Zechariah 12:10; Hebrews 9:27).[53]

JESUS, OUR CREATOR

The Bible also tells us that God was manifest "in the person of Jesus" when He created the heavens, the earth, and humanity:

> The Son is the image of the invisible God, the firstborn over all creation. For in him all things were created: things in heaven and on earth, visible and invisible, whether thrones or powers or rulers or authorities; all things have been created through him and for him. He is before all things, and in him all things hold together. (Colossians 1:15–17; see also John 1:1–14; Hebrews 1:1–5)

The point is our Creator has no problem presenting Himself in the image of humanity and/or in the image of the angelic realm whenever He so desires. Both realms of intelligent beings were, in the first place, made in His image. Yahweh is Lord of all realms.

THE HEAVENLY HOST

We also know that a specific "anointed cherub" was in the Garden (Ezekiel 28:13–14). He came straight from the divine realm. Additionally, we have learned that the "mount of God," the meeting place of the entire Divine Council, was also located in the Garden of Eden (Ezekiel 28:14).

So, when Satan lied to Eve and said, in effect, "If you will do this thing—if you will eat this fruit—you can be like the gods," Adam and Eve knew the offer held real potential—that is, if the shimmering, slick-talking cherub could actually pull off this amazing feat as he had promised.

The first human couple knew full well that they had been created "just a little lower" than the divine realm (Psalm 8). They also enjoyed personal fellowship with that realm. They were all in the Garden together; that's why it was created.

WERE YOU THERE?

We also know the Divine Council was with God when He created the earth and the universe sometime *before* He created humanity. An important statement of this comes from the book of Job:

> [God said] Brace yourself like a man; I will question you, and you shall answer me. Where were you when I laid the earth's foundation? Tell me, if you understand. Who marked off its dimensions? Surely you know! Who stretched a measuring line across it? On what were its footings set, or who laid its cornerstone—while the morning stars sang together and all the angels [Hebrew, *bene Elohim,* "sons of God"] shouted for joy? (Job 38:3–7)

There it is! The *bene elohim* were present before and during the time the earth was made. This declaration also tells us the angels were created, obviously, sometime before any of what we know as the "Creation event" took place. Beyond that huge clue, we are told nothing else about the exact timing of when the angels themselves were created.

However, we also know the angelic realm was present in the Garden for yet another amazing display of God's power and glory.

CHAPTER ELEVEN

....

FROM THE DUST OF THE EARTH

For he knows our frame; he remembers that
we are dust.

~Psalm 104:14, ESV

The angels were also in attendance in Eden at the moment Elohim
breathed life into the nostrils of Adam and Eve. The revelation of
this is exposed in the first page of the Bible, in Genesis 1:26:

> Then God said, "Let *us* make mankind in *our* image, in *our*
> likeness, so that they may rule over the fish in the sea and the
> birds in the sky, over the livestock and all the wild animals, and
> over all the creatures that move along the ground." (Genesis
> 1:26, emphasis added)

In my previous book, *Gods and Thrones,* I explore this topic in just
about every scriptural way possible, examining each place in the Word of
God where Yahweh refers to "us" and "our"—as though the Lord might
somehow be referring to "others" around Him. This is a hugely important truth to settle before we go any further with our study, because in
so doing, we establish one of the most important reasons Eden's iniquity
was so hideous, deserving of eternal death.[54]

"LET US"

Dr. Michael Heiser is one of the world's foremost experts in this matter, especially regarding the Hebrew language nuances concerning this passage and others like it. Following is an example of his explanation:

> The most likely explanation for the plurality in Gen[esis] 1:26 is that God, the lone speaker, is announcing to the members of his heavenly host, his divine council (Psa[lm] 82; 89:5–8), his intention to create humankind.... God among his heavenly host is a familiar biblical description (Deut[eronomy] 33:1–2; Psa[lm] 68:17; 1 Kings 22:19–23).[55]

Dr. Heiser reminds us that we use this same language style (inclusiveness, yet without actual assistance) quite regularly. For example, a mother might say: "*Let's* make supper!" Obviously, she does not intend for the entire family to gather in the kitchen and engage in the process of "making supper." She will accomplish the task while her family enjoys the resulting feast. Heiser asserts this is the same way the inclusive language is used in this verse.[56]

The Cambridge Bible for Schools and Colleges affirms that this is what is meant by God's inclusive language:

> [This passage involves the] Jewish explanation that God is here addressing the inhabitants of heaven. In the thought of the devout Israelite, God was One, but not isolated. He was surrounded by the heavenly host (1 Kings 22:19); attended by the Seraphim (Isaiah 6:1–6); holding His court with "the sons of God" (Job 1:6; Job 2:1).[57]

The International Standard Bible Encyclopedia has this to say regarding what is meant by "us": "Genesis 1:26 has the plural 'us,'...most probably [it refers] to the angels or mighty ones which surrounded the throne of God as servants or counselors; compare Job 38:7."[58]

At this point, the question is often asked whether the presence of the Divine Council at Creation means the angels helped God form Adam and Eve. The answer is: *No, they did not.* The clue is given through the clear grammatical construct of the text. The Hebrew verbs in the original text are singular, as are the singular qualifying words, "So God created man *in His own image.*"

We also know from the entirety of biblical revelation that God alone did the actual creating. So, when it is recorded that God said, "let us make," there is no incongruity in the textual meaning. God was inviting the heavenly host to accompany Him to witness the divine act He was about to accomplish. They would share in the joy of that day, and they would be Yahweh's witnesses of it.

"IN OUR IMAGE"

Here is the next logical question: "Were the angels created in God's image as well, since God said, 'Let us make man in *our* image'?" The answer is yes, the angels were also created in God's image. They also were to be unique representatives of God's glory and person. Humans and angels are distinct from every other living thing God has made. Humanity and the angelic realm alone possess something of His "image" within their being and form. They alone are called *His family* (Ephesians 1:9–10, 3:14–15).

The *Cambridge Bible for Schools and Colleges* succinctly addresses both foregoing questions concerning God's proclamation, "Let **us** make a man in **our image**":

The picture which it suggests is in harmony with the religious thought of the Israelites; and…the work of creating man is neither delegated to, nor shared with, others. God "created man in his own image" (Genesis 1:27); but, before creating him, He had associated with Himself all those [the angels] who, through participation *in image and likeness with Himself,* would henceforth be allied to man.[59] (Emphasis and bracketed words added)

Cambridge also states:

It is claimed that, at the climax of the work of Creation, when man is about to be formed, the Almighty admits into the confidence of his Divine Purpose the angelic beings whose nature, in part, man will be privileged to share (Psalm 8:4–5, cf. Hebrews 2:7).[60]

Barnes' Notes on the Bible further reinforces the truth that the angels also share something of God's "image:" "The sons of God—Angels—called the sons of God from their resemblance to him, or their being created by him."[61]

Matthew Poole's Commentary concurs: "These are called the sons of God, partly because they had their whole being from him, and partly because they were made partakers of his Divine and glorious image."[62]

John W. Schoenheit, who authored a 2015 article for the online *Sower Magazine* titled "God's Divine Council," states:

God confers with and works together with a divine council. This explains the verses where God says, "let us." While God supplies the power for what He does, He also works in concert with His creation. Thus, in Genesis 1:26, He speaks to his divine council and says, "Let us make man in our image."[63]

The picture should now be shaping up to be much clearer. The Garden iniquity was so terrible, at least in part, because it was done within the realm of the immediate fellowship of the *elohim*, Yahweh's heavenly witnesses and representatives. Apparently, the tempter used the upper family's exalted status and direct presence with them in the Garden to invoke a sense of covetousness within the hearts of Adam and Eve.

By calling God a liar, Satan was able to convince the first human couple that they were somehow missing out on exclusive knowledge and certain understanding that only their divine counterparts possessed: *the knowledge of good and evil.* Adam and Eve succumbed to the temptation, and they "ate" the "fruit" of the "tree."

THE FALL OF SATAN

We really don't know exactly *when* Satan fell from his previously obedient state. However, following are the biblical facts about which we can be certain. The angels (this includes Satan) were created before the earth was formed (Job 38:4–7).

Also, Satan had not fallen by the end of the initial Creation event; therefore, he could not have fallen before it (Ezekiel 28:13–15). This is backed up by the declaration in Genesis 1:31 that the entire creation was "very good" at the culmination of that week.

The biblical narrative about the Garden appears to suggest that the sin occurred rather soon after the creation of humanity. However, that allusion within the narrative cannot be depended upon as fact, since the entire account is presented solely for revealing "what happened" regarding our fallen state, and not necessarily the precise timing of the event.

Because of this truth, some biblical researchers have surmised that the fall of Satan could have occurred as many as a hundred years or more after the creation of the first couple. Other scholars, however, believe that Satan fell sometime before he tempted Adam and Eve, and only a very short time after their creation.[64]

THE FIRST CRIME SCENE

But here is the most important truth of the matter: In the primordial mist of ages past, the Garden of Eden became the world's very first crime scene. The law had been laid down: "Do not eat from that tree." The Law Giver was called a "liar." The tempter asked Adam and Eve: "Did God really say?" Then he declared, "you surely shall not die.... God lied to you."

The culprit had a motive. He wanted the new creation for himself. He imagined one day being the sole ruler of the new Garden paradise. More than likely, he, in his diabolical pride, became insanely jealous that Adam, Eve, and their offspring had been appointed "rulers" of the earthly realm—royal representatives of Yahweh (Genesis 1:26). The majestic tempter obviously thought the honor should have belonged only to him.

The two key human players, initially starting out as mere victims, eventually became accomplices in the affair. They ultimately thumbed their noses at Yahweh while cuddling up to the shiny slick-meister.

But what *was* the crime, exactly? What specific deed occurred in God's Garden paradise? Was the crime of the ages simply the literal eating of a piece of fruit? Did the act occur only because a talking snake somehow convinced the first couple to do so? Or, was there more to the wrongdoing than meets the eye? Is a much deeper message meant to be received?

You will soon discover that today's church, by and large, is missing a huge piece of the overall picture and message. The piece that's missing, put in its proper light, will change everything about the way you understand in-depth biblical truths, your own life, and the headlines of today's news world.

Buckle up. Take a deep breath.

The real roller coaster ride begins...*now.*

PART TWO

THE INIQUITY

It is hardly too much to say that
[the third chapter of Genesis] is the pivot of the Bible....
With the exception of the fact of Creation,
we have here the record of the most important and
far-reaching event in the world's history—the entrance of sin.
~Dr. Thomas Constable,
Expository Notes on Genesis 3 [65]

······················

CHAPTER TWELVE

THE *SSS*ERPENT

The snake grins through his fangs, admiring
Eve's playacting. "God is a nice enough chap
in His way. I daresay He means well. But
between you and The Tree of Knowledge, He
is terribly insecure."

~David Mitchell, *Ghostwritten*[66]

How do we make biblical sense out of the utterly unbelievable?
As we begin examining each element of the mystery of Eden's iniquity, let's first deal with the opening revelation of Genesis 3 for what it plainly says. From that inspection, we'll get a good idea of what the *logical* conclusion ought to be. From that point, we'll move directly to the true scriptural revelation.

The passage begins by introducing us to a peculiarly endowed serpent. This strange snake could both walk and talk.

WHERE IN THE WORLD?

Let us ask a few obvious questions:

Where in the Bible do we ever again run into a literal, walking, talking snake? *Nowhere*.

Where in the entirety of human experience has anyone ever seen such a thing and documented it, thus enabling the world to examine the phenomenon? *Nowhere.*

Where does Jesus speak of such a thing? *Nowhere.*

And where do any of the nine writers of the New Testament documents speak of a literal creature of this sort? Again, the answer is *nowhere.*[67]

Also consider that Adam himself had named all the animals (Genesis 2:20). In so doing, did he ever run across a snake that could walk upright and talk like a man? *No.*

Did he come across any animal that was smarter than he was? *Nope.*

Besides, Adam was told that he would have dominion over all the living things God created upon the earth—not the other way around (Genesis 1:26). So, did God lie to Adam? *No. He did not.*

Think about it. If Adam and Eve had never seen an animal like this, how is it that they apparently saw nothing unusual about a snake that was now conversing with them in the Garden, walking around on two legs, and looking them in the eye? I don't know about you, but I'm already creeped out by the thing after just *talking* about it!

You might ask, "But couldn't God have done such a thing—*just once?*" Of course He could. God can do whatever He wishes. However, if He *had* created such a macabre animal, one that wound up being the downfall of all creation (the central theme of the entirety of God's Word), why do we never hear Yahweh Himself mention the creature again? Don't all these facts seem a little odd, considering that so many in today's academic world would dogmatically have us interpret the Garden serpent as a literal snake?[68]

The Garden and the Fall of humanity are mentioned *several* more times throughout Scripture. But never do we hear anyone in those Scriptures even come close to suggesting that there was a literal snake in the Garden that could communicate in human language and walk upright on hind legs. It just is not there. And there's a reason it's not there.

LET THE ADJUSTMENTS BEGIN

Since the Garden narrative commences by abruptly introducing the serpent without any further comment upon its identity, sadly, some have been satisfied to stop right there. They often declare something like: "The Scripture presents the matter in a literal format, therefore we must also interpret the entire passage from a strictly literal perspective, whether we understand it or not."

That response sounds "righteous" enough. But then those same commentators spend an inordinate amount of time and energy attempting to make the idea of such an odd thing fit the remainder of the biblical narrative, as well as real life, even though there's no evidence of such a creature in either place. The problem with this approach is that rarely do we treat any other difficult passage of the Bible in the same manner. Why is it then that so many students of the Bible take that approach with this specific passage?

To explain every element of Genesis 3 in a literal manner defies almost every modicum of logic and proper exegetical exploration, regardless of what other kind of imaginative or virtuous spin we place upon our analysis. It also places the Garden of Eden in the embarrassing and unfair category of simply reading like another piece of ancient folklore, one that blends in with those of the surrounding and earliest pagan cultures.[69]

Following are a couple of commentary assertions concerning this matter.

The Lange Commentary on the Holy Scriptures:

The comparatively stronger *symbolical* that appeared in the representation of the primeval facts...continues here [in the Garden of Eden]...since the subject is the primeval history of Adam, as it is, at the same time, the primitive history of man, or of humanity.

The fact of the first temptation is *the symbol* of every human temptation; the fact of the first fall is *the symbol* of every human transgression; the great mistake that lay in the first human sin is *the symbol* of every effect of sin.[70] (Emphasis and bracketed words added)

The Expositor's Bible Commentary:

Profound as the teaching of [the Garden of Eden] narrative is, its meaning does not lie on the surface. Literal interpretation will reach a measure of its significance, but *plainly there is more here than appears in the letter.*[71] (Emphasis added)

As you have probably surmised, I agree with *Lange, Expositor's,* and others like them. There is plainly more here than what we first read in the surface text of Genesis 3. It is a reading that clearly appears to be steeped in divine symbolism, and one that was intended for a sincere seeker of truth to investigate further through the remaining pages of God's Word.

A FANCY SNAKE COSTUME

Through centuries of theological mulling over this subject, numerous sources still have opted to interpret the Garden account in a strictly literal fashion. They declare that the serpent in the Garden was indeed a real snake, but one that was somehow "inhabited" by Satan. However, we will soon discover that even this explanation doesn't come close to cleaning up the matter. Nor does it match the more complete New Testament revelations on the topic.

To illustrate the peculiarities into which some of the commentaries venture, consider the conclusion reached by the *Adam Clarke Commen-*

tary, in which several lengthy paragraphs go through numerous hypothetical possibilities in order to rule out a walking, talking snake—which Clarke apparently (and correctly) cannot reconcile with logic or other scriptural comparisons. However, where he finally arrives takes us into the realm of an even more incredible position than that of a Satan-possessed snake.

Adam Clarke says:

> All these things considered, we are obliged to seek for some other word to designate…the word serpent, which on every view of the subject appears to me inefficient and inapplicable….
>
> It therefore appears to me that a creature of the ape or [orangutan] kind is here intended; and that Satan made use of this creature as the most proper instrument for the accomplishment of his murderous purposes against the life and soul of man. Under this creature he lay hid, and by this creature he seduced our first parents, and drew off or slunk away from every eye but the eye of God.[72]

Yes, you read that correctly: He asserts that the tempter in the Garden was Satan, who was covertly "inhabiting" an ape or an orangutan. *Satan in an ape suit!*

Just as shocking as that analysis is the number of other commentators who, with a dignified tone, refer to *Clarke's* "orangutan" as at least a potential consideration in determining a "scholarly" interpretation of the Garden narrative.[73]

So, what about this idea of human-like, walking snakes (or orangutans) that like to "chat it up" with women who are out for a leisurely stroll in their garden? What does the Bible really say about all this?

Let's dig a little deeper. This is about to get fascinating.

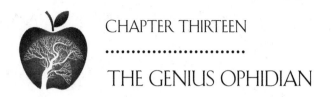

CHAPTER THIRTEEN

••••••••••••••••••••••••

THE GENIUS OPHIDIAN

Round and round they went with their
snakes, snakily...
   ~Aldous Huxley, *Brave New World*[74]

While continuing to insist upon a talking snake—one operating under the influence of Satan—a number of commentary sources find themselves in yet another uncomfortable position. They still have to explain how that especially chatty little fellow could, miraculously, walk upright, *like a human*.

Their argument is, "The judgment pronounced upon the serpent was that from now on, 'you will crawl on your belly' (Genesis 3:14). This declaration implies that before the curse, the serpent could actually walk."

The following examples reflect this vein of thought. Note that the first five examples attempt to explain how the Garden serpent used to walk erect, eye to eye with humans.

Henry Morris:

The body of the serpent, in addition, was altered even further by eliminating his ability to stand erect, eye-to-eye with man as it were. It is further possible that all these animals (other than the birds) were quadrupeds, except the serpent, who had the remarkable ability, with a strong vertebral skeleton supported by limbs, to rear and hold himself erect when talking with Adam and Eve.[75]

Matthew Henry:

The devil chose to act his part in a serpent, because it is a specious creature, has a spotted dappled skin, and then went erect.[76]

Adam Clarke:

The [serpent], whom I suppose to have been at the head of all the inferior animals, and in a sort of society and intimacy with man, is to be greatly degraded, entirely banished from human society, and deprived of the gift of speech. Cursed art thou above all cattle, and above every beast of the field—thou shalt be considered the most contemptible of animals; upon thy belly shalt thou go—thou shalt no longer walk erect, but mark the ground equally with thy hands and feet.[77]

Matthew Poole:

It seems more probable that this serpent before the fall either had feet, or rather did go with its breast erect.[78]

Martin Luther:

From this some obvious conclusions follow: that before sin the serpent was a most beautiful little animal and most pleasing to man, as little mules, sheep and puppies today; moreover, that it walked upright.[79]

Answers in Genesis:

The more logical answer is that the serpent originally had some form of legs or appendages, and these were either lost or reduced (consider how many reptiles crawl on their bellies and yet have legs, e.g., crocodiles). This seems to correlate with the plainest reading of the passage and the comparison of a curse ("on your belly you shall go") as compared with cattle and other beasts of the field, which do have legs.[80]

Institute for Creation Research:

A fallen creation full of creatures with the genetic potential to produce trait variations in offspring explains snakes losing legs over time.[81]

BibleQ (Bible Questions Answered):

The serpent was to go on its belly and (a little poetically), "eat dust." If the snake had walked before then, this comment would make perfect sense as a curse—it would lose the ability to walk and lift itself above the ground. If the snake had always travelled on its belly as snakes do now, this would have no obvious meaning as a curse since it made no change to the existing situation.[82]

TALKING WILDLIFE

As already mentioned, along with the incredulous notion of a walking snake is the additionally illogical presentation of a dazzlingly brilliant, *conversational* snake. Again, no other instance anywhere in Scripture or within the realm of known reality presents a talking reptile (or any other animal) that is somehow enabled to speak human language by the power of Satan.

We do, however, find *one example* in Scripture wherein *Yahweh* used an animal to deliver His divine word of warning. It is the well-known account of Balaam's donkey, found in Numbers 22, and confirmed in 2 Peter 2:16.

Shockingly, a few of the same scholars who insist upon a literal, talking snake empowered by Satan also go to great lengths to try to *explain away* a "talking donkey" enabled by Yahweh. I kid you not.

The *Cambridge Bible for Schools and Colleges* is one example:

> We are *not under the necessity…of believing* that the [donkey] actually spoke…. The speaking [donkey] is to be considered not as a fable—in the sense in which the word is applied, for example, to Aesop's Fables—but as a detail of a *fabulous nature* which attached itself, during the course of Israel's *early traditions*, to a narrative which *may have had* a historical basis.[83] (Emphasis added)

Yet, *Cambridge* also insists:

> The serpent is…gifted with speech and is able, by means of knowledge superior to that of the woman, to tell her what will be the results of eating of the forbidden fruit.[84]

The *Pulpit Commentary* is another example of a source with writers who can't seem to accept a talking donkey even if it was done under the power of Yahweh, and even if the Apostle Peter declared it had been a literal occurrence:

> It is truly said, however, that a passing illusion of this kind, while it testifies that the Apostle understood the words, like all his

contemporaries, in their most natural and simple sense, *does not oblige us to hold the same view....*

It would indeed seem *much more satisfactory to regard the story*, if we cannot accept it as literally true, *as a parable* which *Balaam wrote against himself*, and which Moses simply incorporated in the narrative.[85] (Emphasis added)

Similarly, the *Keil and Delitzsch OT Commentary* says:

[This consideration] leads *with certainty* to the conclusion, that the whole affair must have been a *purely internal one*, which Balaam alone experienced in *a state of ecstasy*.[86] (Emphasis added)

Cambridge Bible Commentary, Pulpit Commentary, and *Keil and Delitzsch OT Commentary* appear quite put off by a talking donkey divinely empowered by its Creator.[87] The first source explains it as a possible fable, the second as a parable, and the last as an "internal one," only brought about by *a state of ecstasy*. Yet, each of these sources completely accept a talking snake in the Garden of Eden that is ultimately enabled by Satan. *Go figure*—more theological "tweaking."

EXPLAINING THE NONEXISTENT

Several commentators, even modern ones, continue to stumble over themselves attempting to explain how Satan empowered a snake to talk. But they still aren't quite able to explain why Adam and Eve were not terrified by the freak of nature supposedly doing the diabolical jabbering.

A sampling of commentary material attempts to explain what never literally happened in the first place.

Answers in Genesis:

Because *there is no other place in Scripture that reveals Satan or demons can cause animals to speak,* it makes more sense that the serpent could make the sounds capable of speech and Satan used this to his advantage. In essence, Satan likely used this feature that the original serpent had and caused it to say what he wanted.[88, 89] (Emphasis added)

Got Questions?

Most scholars hold that it was Satan in the Garden of Eden who was speaking through the snake, not the snake itself speaking on its own. Thus, the Genesis 3 account is not suggesting that snakes were of an intellect that would have enabled them to speak coherently.

Still, why didn't Adam and Eve find it strange that an animal was speaking to them? It is unlikely that Adam and Eve had the same perspective we do on animals.[90]

Pulpit Commentary:

Not as originally endowed with speech, or gifted at this particular time with the power of articulation, but simply as used by the devil, who from this circumstance is commonly styled in Scripture "The serpent," "the old serpent," "that old serpent."[91]

Cambridge Bible for Schools and Colleges:

Vivid and picturesque as it is, the story leaves many things omitted and unexplained. The serpent is brought upon the scene without explanation, though he is gifted with speech and is able, by means of knowledge superior to that of the woman, to tell her what will be the results of eating of the forbidden fruit.[92]

Ellicott's Commentary for English Readers:

It has been remarked, [Eve] would not be surprised on finding herself spoken to by so sagacious a creature. If this be so, it follows that Eve must have dwelt in Paradise long enough to have learnt something of the habits of the animals around her, though she had never studied them so earnestly as Adam, not having felt that want of a companion which had made even his state of happiness so dull.[93]

Keil and Delitzsch OT Commentary:

The serpent…was a real serpent, perverted by Satan to be the instrument of his temptation…. When the serpent, therefore, is introduced as speaking…the speaking must have emanated… from a superior spirit, which had taken possession of the serpent for the sake of seducing man.[94]

Warren Wiersbe BE Bible Study Series

Satan used the body of a serpent, one of God's creatures that He had pronounced "good" (Gen[esis] 1:31). Eve didn't seem disturbed by the serpent's presence or its speech, so we assume that she saw nothing threatening about the encounter. Perhaps Eve hadn't been introduced to this species and concluded that it had the ability to speak.[95]

LET THE BIBLE SPEAK

When a proper exegetical study is performed, you can rest assured that nowhere in the rest of Scripture do we get close to the suggestion of a *devil-in-a-snake-costume* scenario. Neither do we find an upright, walking snake or a snake that can outtalk any human being with brilliantly deceptive banter. And most assuredly, we do not find a freaky orangutan that the Holy Spirit inspiration of Scripture somehow misidentified as a serpent.

Instead, we come face to face with the actual culprit—*the father of lies*—the one who manipulated the mind of Eve, the one who was a murderer from the beginning wrapped in the apt symbolism of *that ancient serpent.*

Yeah, that's right. *That* one!

It's time we let the Bible speak for itself and peel back the charade.

CHAPTER FOURTEEN

....

THE CHARADE

Banish me from Eden when you will; but first
let me eat of the fruit of the tree of knowledge!
~Robert G. Ingersoll[96]

This next question may be one of the most contentious and important topics of biblical argument regarding Eden. Its contextual
answer is the foundation to properly interpreting the entire account:
Does the Bible ever clearly equate the serpent in the Garden with Satan
himself? And does it assure us that no literal, conversational serpent was
there that day? If it does not, then we are left with a walking, talking
snake and all kinds of fantastical explanations, illogical conjectures, and
myriad contrived tweaking processes.

However, if Scripture does succinctly disclose that the serpent of
Genesis 3 was a mere symbol of the literal person of Satan, we then
possess a much different interpretation of the entire Garden account,
especially the nature of the sin that occurred there.

NAYSAYERS

The matter of who the real tempter was, as you will soon discover,
is in fact settled by the Bible itself in context and in more than one

passage, regardless of some of the arguments of today's commentators to the contrary.

However, for our study to remain academically honest and hold scholarly validity, we must understand the views of those holding a different persuasion. Following is an example of one such opposing opinion.

Dr. Shawna Dolansky is adjunct research professor and instructor in the religion program of the College of Humanities, Carleton University in Ottawa, Ontario. In October 2017, writing for *Bible History Daily* on the topic of our current investigation, Dr. Dolansky penned the following words as her closing argument in that article:

> When Paul re-tells the story of Adam and Eve, he places the blame on the humans (Romans 5:18; cf. 1 Corinthians 15:21–22) **and not on fallen angels, or on the serpent as Satan.**
>
> Still, the conflation begged to be made, and it **will seem natural** for later Christian authors—Justin Martyr, Tertullian, Cyprian, Irenaeus and Augustine, for example—**to assume Satan's association with Eden's talking snake.**
>
> …But this connection is not forged anywhere in the Bible.[97] (Emphasis added)

Earlier in the article, Dr. Dolansky claimed:

> The serpent in the Garden of Eden is portrayed as just that: a serpent. Satan does not make an appearance in Genesis 2–3, for the simple reason that when the story was written, **the concept of the devil had not yet been invented.**
>
> Eden's serpent is not identified with Satan anywhere in the Hebrew Bible or New Testament.[98] (Emphasis added)

However, over the next several chapters of this book, you will discover that Eden's "serpent" is, in fact, *specifically* identified in the New

Testament with the literal person of Satan. The devil was assuredly not a mere concept that needed to be "invented."

Indeed, Satan is identified either by proper name or by his *role* five times in the Old Testament (Job 1:6, 2:1; Zechariah 3:2; 1 Chronicles 21:1; Psalm 109:6).

Commenting upon the first appearance of the name "Satan," found in the book of Job, *Ellicott's Commentary for English Readers* states:

No reliance can be placed on speculations as to the late introduction of a belief in Satan among the Jews, nor, therefore, on any as to the lateness of these early chapters of Job.

Here only [in Job] and in Zechariah it is found with the definite article "the adversary." [Indicating the name Satan is derived because of the "office" or "role" he plays. *Satan* is merely the actual Hebrew word for "adversary."].

The theory of the personality of the evil one must largely depend upon the view we take of these and other passages of Scripture as containing an authoritative revelation.[99] (Emphasis and brackets added)

Also speaking to the erroneous view that "the concept of the devil had not yet been invented" until the time of the New Testament, *Barnes' Notes on the Bible* gives additional clarity:

An insuperable objection to this view is, that it does not accord with the character usually ascribed to Satan in the Bible, and especially that the disposition attributed to him in the narrative before us is wholly inconsistent with this view.[100]

Barnes' Notes on the Bible also comments upon Satan's first appearance in the book of Job, further affirming our position:

It [the word "Satan"] is then used by way of eminence, to denote the "adversary," and assumes the form of a proper name, and is applied to the great foe of God and man—the malignant spirit who seduces people to evil, and who accuses them before God.[101] (Brackets added)

The *Jamieson-Fausset-Brown Bible Commentary* not only speaks of the ancient Jewish tradition concerning Satan's identification in Job 1 and 2, but also that Satan was indeed connected directly to the Garden of Eden:

Satan—*the tradition was widely spread* that [Satan] had been the agent in *Adam's temptation.* Hence his name is given without comment. The feeling with which he looks on Job is similar to that with which he *looked on Adam* in Paradise.[102] (Emphasis added)

You will soon discover that Paul did in fact equate the symbolic serpent with the person of Satan, and specifically defined him as the "deceiver" in the Garden that led humanity astray, regardless of the "scholarly" objections to the contrary.

Additionally, you will find the Bible truly *does* forge a clear connection between Eden's symbol of a talking snake and the literal person of Satan. This fact is backed up by the attestations of the biblical language lexicons as well as documented ancient Jewish understanding. For this very reason, later Christian authors, as Dr. Dolansky notes, would indeed find the link to be a *natural one.*

Here's the plain truth: The notion that the serpent was simply "Satan in disguise" is, in fact, rather commonplace, but only in today's standard Christian scholarship. But this view wasn't even close to a self-evident truth when the New Testament was written. You'll see this fact for yourself, very shortly.[103]

Now, let's find out what God the Father, God the Son, and the Apostle John (who, by the way, got his information straight from the literal throne of God) had to say about this matter.

This should prove to be quite enlightening.

CHAPTER FIFTEEN

....

BOOM!

That ancient serpent, who is the devil, or
Satan…

~Revelation 20:2

Let's light the fuse on the first Garden bombshell.

At least five passages of Scripture—four in the New Testament and one in the Old—reveal that the serpent in the Garden was a *symbol* of the literal person of Satan himself and was not a walking, talking snake—possessed or otherwise. We will begin at the end, at the book of Revelation.

Both Revelation 12 and Revelation 20 address the matter in clear language:

The great dragon was hurled down—that ancient serpent called the devil, or Satan, who leads the whole world astray. (Revelation 12:9)

He seized the dragon, that ancient serpent, who is the devil, or Satan, and bound him for a thousand years. (Revelation 20:2)

GETTING IT CORRECT

The *Expositor's Greek Testament* confirms that the designation of that "old serpent" was merely a symbolic rabbinical expression. It is meant to be taken in much the same way we might call a fellow human being a serpent, or a "snake in the grass."

> *The old serpent* (a rabbinical *expression*, cf. Gfrörer, i. 386–389)... the opponent of God was the adversary of man.
>
> Two *characteristic traits of Satan* are blended here: (a) cunning exercised on men to lure them into ruin, cf. 2 Corinthians 2:11; 2 Corinthians 11:3), and (b) eagerness to thwart and slander them before God (Revelation 12:10, cf. En[och]. xl. 7; Zechariah 3:1 f.).[104] (Emphasis added)

The Bible calls Satan a "serpent" because he exhibits snake-like traits. The term is merely a representative comparison, an expression. It really is as simple as that.

But that's not all. Let's go back and look at that passage in Revelation 12, putting the passage in context from its beginning. Especially note the emphasized words:

> Then another *sign* appeared in heaven: an *enormous red dragon* with seven heads and ten horns and seven crowns on its heads. Its tail swept a third of the stars out of the sky and flung them to the earth. The *dragon stood in front of the woman* who was about to give birth, *so that it might devour her child* the moment he was born. She gave birth to a son, a male child, who "will rule all the nations with an iron scepter."
>
> The great *dragon* was hurled down—that ancient *serpent* called the devil, or *Satan*, who leads the whole world astray. *He*

[not "it"] was hurled to the earth, and *his* angels [serpents don't have angels within their command] with him.

Then from his mouth *the serpent spewed water like a river,* to overtake the woman and sweep her away with the torrent. (Revelation 12:1–5, 9, 15, emphasis and brackets added)

My…my. When we read that verse in its complete context, an entirely new light is shed on the matter, isn't it? I firmly believe that nothing interprets the Bible quite like the Bible itself.

Read Revelation 12 and then ask yourself whether the "dragon" or "serpent" (one and the same creature) in this chapter is being presented as a literal being. The answer is obvious. *No. It certainly is not.* How so many scholars miss this clear point is a mystery to me.

Notice Revelation 12 is identified to John as a "sign." In other words, according to the Greek word used in this verse, it is a symbolic revelation of an ultimate reality being revealed to John.[105]

How is the *sign* described in reference to the serpent? He is first called a seven-headed dragon with ten horns, and crowns on his head. He also is pictured as a "baby-eating" dragon, as well as a serpent that spews rivers of water out of his mouth to knock down a grown woman.

Does anyone believe these biblical descriptions are meant literally? Ask yourself: Where in Scripture, or otherwise, are we confronted with a literal, baby-eating and river-spewing dragon? *Nowhere.*

The truth is that the dragon, along with its heads and crowns, are symbolic of Satan's power and international prowess. Every major scholar attests to this fact. So why do we have such a hard time with the very next symbolic name given to Satan—*the serpent*—which is right there in the same sentence, and is also presented in an obvious symbolic manner throughout the entire passage? *Tweaking.*

THE LION AND THE LAMB

Also consider that at least thirty different times in the book of Revelation, the "Lamb of God" or the "Lamb" is mentioned. Additionally, in Revelation 5:5, we see the phrase "Lion of the tribe of Judah." Who, or what, are the Lamb of God and the Lion of Judah? We don't even have to guess, do we? In both cases, it is Jesus Christ.

We never assume that Jesus was a literal, talking lamb, that He embodied a lamb, or that He merely disguised Himself as a lamb. Nor do we insist that He was ever disguised as a lion, or that the lamb or lion could walk upright. We understand that the terms "lion" and "lamb" are used only as divine symbols for the person of Jesus Christ. How do we know these things? Because the Bible clearly proclaims the truth in each case, just as it does with the "serpent" and "Satan" symbol.

Why do so many overlook the lion and lamb symbolism while ignoring the serpent imagery so clearly defined as Satan, right in the same book of Revelation? *Even more tweaking.*

OPHIS

But there's more. The Greek word used for "serpent" in Revelation 12:9 is *ophis*. This word can certainly be used to describe a literal snake, but *Strong's Concordance, Thayer's Greek Lexicon,* and *Strong's Exhaustive Concordance* also assert that the word is often used in a symbolic sense for the literal person of Satan.[106]

Thayer's Greek Lexicon stresses that even the Jews of Jesus' day understood this symbolism as relating all the way back to the Garden account:

The serpent narrated to have deceived Eve (see Gen[esis] as above) was regarded by the later Jews as the devil (Sap[ientia] ii., 23f, cf. 4 Macc[abbees] 18:8); hence, he is called: Revelation 12:9, 14; Revelation 20:2.[107]

IF JESUS SAID IT...

There is still another important matter to consider. In John 8, Jesus identified Satan as the "father of all lies" and a "murderer from the beginning." Where does the Bible record the very first lie ever told, as well as the spirit of murder and death entering the world? In the Garden of Eden. Who told that lie, and who brought that spirit of death to humanity by way of his lies? The "serpent."

Obviously, Jesus directly connects the person of Satan with the Garden. He says nothing about Satan inhabiting a snake and making it talk, nor does He say anything about the serpent walking upright. The reason Jesus never mentions these elements is because Satan does not have those powers, not to mention the fact that a literal, walking, talking snake never existed in the first place. Obviously, Jesus was well aware that His audience knew this.

[Satan] was a murderer from the beginning, not holding to the truth, for there is no truth in him. When he lies, he speaks his native language, for he is a liar and the father of lies. (John 8:44)

Let's not forget that it was Jesus who first identified Satan in the New Testament. He did this in the fourth chapter of Matthew, the account of Jesus' wilderness temptation experience as He was preparing to begin His three-year earthly ministry.

Jesus said to him, "Away from me, Satan! For it is written: 'Worship the Lord your God, and serve him only.'" (Matthew 4:10)

Jesus recognized that the ancient adversary had shown up to test Him. Not only did He recognize Satan, but He also called him by that specific name. Notice also that there is no mention of Satan inhabiting the body of a snake when he showed up to tempt Jesus.

This same tempter of Jesus was the true culprit in the Garden, as well as Job's adversary—the enemy of God and God's people. How could it be any other? Jesus was not mistaken, and He assuredly didn't "invent" the name simply because He was an "enlightened later-Jew."

The *Pulpit Commentary* bears out the truth of this assertion:

> *To be tempted of the devil.* Him whose characteristic is false accusation; e.g. against men (Revelation 12:10–12); against God (Genesis 3:1–5) [in the Garden of Eden].[108] (Brackets added)

Clarke's Commentary supports this as well:

> To be tempted—The first act of the ministry of Jesus Christ was a combat with Satan. Does not this receive light from Genesis 3:17?[109]

Gill's Exposition also connects Jesus' temptation with the tempter of the Garden, that "old serpent":

> By "the devil" is meant "Satan" the prince of devils, the enemy of mankind, the old serpent.[110]

It cannot be exegetically argued otherwise. The New Testament gives us the greatest revelation on the entire Scripture. The Old Testament must ultimately be interpreted by New Testament revelations, especially by the testimony of Jesus Christ. On that score, the serpent issue is settled. The wily creature of the Garden was only a symbol of something much more diabolical: the literal person of Satan, the ancient tempter.

THE ANCIENT ONE

Just how ancient is the serpent identified in Revelation 12 and 20? We know the word "ancient" at least means "all the way back to the Garden of Eden."

And please don't forget this important theological truth: The information in Revelation was given to John from the throne of God. That's about as "inspired" as the Word of God gets! How can any true student of the Bible claim the person of Satan was not in the Garden of Eden when the declaration from the throne of God in the book of Revelation proclaims that he *was* there?

The IVP New Testament Commentary Series agrees with all we have set forth thus far regarding the identity of the serpent and Satan's link to Eden:

John identifies the dragon repeatedly (v. 9) as the ancient serpent, the devil (compare 2:10) and Satan (compare 2:9, 13, 24; 3:9)…. The dragon's remote past is defined by the term ancient serpent, *which links him to the story of Adam and Eve in the Garden of Eden.*

The assumption that the serpent in the garden is the devil in disguise is common today in popular Christianity, but was by no means self-evident in John's time. Like the serpent in Genesis, the dragon in Revelation is seen as the enemy of the woman.[111] (Emphasis added)

YAHWEH HAS SPOKEN

As we have already discovered, God Himself, through Ezekiel 28, places Satan directly in the Garden of Eden. Yahweh also defines Satan as a created being of the Heavenly Host, one of the cherubim, created even *before* humanity was fashioned:

This is what the Sovereign Lord says: "You were the seal of perfection, full of wisdom and perfect in beauty. *You were in Eden, the garden of God.*... You were anointed as a *guardian cherub*, for so I ordained you. You were on the holy mount of God." (Ezekiel 28:12, 13, 14; emphasis added)

The declaration of Ezekiel 28 settles the fact of who the original tempter turns out to be. We are assured that Satan was in the Garden—in the form in which he was first created—a guardian cherub. If he was there as a talking snake or even "inhabiting" a snake, then God missed the perfect opportunity to spill the beans. But, alas, there is no mention of these things from the mouth of Yahweh in Ezekiel 28 or elsewhere.

Satan was a cherub. The cherubim are the guardians of God's throne of glory. They are the perpetual witnesses and the declarers of Yahweh's holiness, majesty, and honor. Based upon God's description of Satan in Ezekiel 28, he was originally the regent-royal of all the cherubim.

The matter is biblically settled. The Garden tempter was not a talking, walking snake, and he wasn't a seven-headed dragon or a serpent that spit a river of water out of his mouth as a weapon against humans. He wasn't Satan dressed up like a snake. The Garden serpent wasn't a snake possessed by Satan. And, most assuredly, the Garden tempter certainly was not an orangutan.

Was Satan cunning *like* a serpent? Yes. Was he deceptive, dangerous, and deadly *like* a snake? Absolutely. Was he in the Garden of Eden? Yes. Was he expelled from God's presence because of what he did in the Garden? Most definitely.

It's all right there in Ezekiel 28 and, out of the mouth of Jesus in John 8, as well as in Revelation 12 and 20—straight from the throne of God.

But this is still not the only word on the matter.

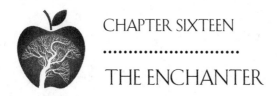

CHAPTER SIXTEEN

••••••••••••••••••••••••

THE ENCHANTER

And no wonder, for Satan himself
masquerades as an angel of light.

~2 Corinthians 11:14

In yet another reference to the Garden tempter, the Apostle Paul also pinpoints the serpent as Satan. And, as in Ezekiel 28, Paul places the "angel of light" squarely *in the Garden*:

> But I am afraid that just as *Eve was deceived by the serpent's cunning,* your minds may somehow be led astray from your sincere and pure devotion to Christ…. And no wonder, *for Satan himself masquerades* as an *angel of light.* (2 Corinthians 11:3, 14, emphasis added)

The Bible Exposition Commentary addresses the understanding of 2 Corinthians 11 and its direct link to Genesis 3 in this manner:

> The Person behind the peril *was Satan, pictured here as the serpent.* The reference is to Genesis 3. It is worth noting that Paul had a great deal to say about our adversary, the devil, when he wrote

this letter to the Corinthians He warned that Satan had several devices for attacking believers.[112] (Emphasis added)

Dr. Michael Heiser says:

Eve was not talking to a snake.... She was in the presence of one of the sons of God (*bene elohim*), beings who had free will, who were more powerful than mere angels, whom humanity was created "a little lower." She was speaking to a member of the divine council who did not share Yahweh's enthusiasm for his new creation, humankind, to whom Yahweh had just given rule over the planet. (Gen[esis] 1:26–27)[113]

Dr. John W. Ritenbaugh of the *Forerunner Commentary* declares:

Lucifer is not a snake, a serpent, or a crocodile. He is not what men like to picture him as being. He was a powerful, supremely intelligent, beautiful free-moral agent—an angelic one.[114]

For further clarification of the matter, look at the commentary of the following four additional sources.

The Expositor's Greek Commentary:

[Paul, in 2 Corinthians 11] assumes that "the serpent" is to be identified with Satan, the tempter of mankind.[115]

McLaren's Expositions:

The serpent, by its poison and its loathly form, is *the natural symbol* of such an enemy of man. The insinuating slyness of the suggestions of evil *is like* the sinuous gliding of the snake, and *truly represents* the process by which temptation found its way into the hearts of the first pair, and of all their descendants.[116] (Emphasis added)

The Jewish Encyclopedia (prepared by more than six hundred scholars and specialists):

Satan was the seducer and the paramour of Eve, and was hurled from heaven together with other angels because of his iniquity.... The chief functions of Satan are, as already noted, those of temptation, accusation, and punishment. He was an active agent in the fall of man.... The serpent of [Genesis 3] is *identified with* [symbolized by] Satan.[117] (Emphasis and bracketed words added)

The Benson Commentary:

That it was the devil who beguiled Eve, our Lord hath intimated, by calling him a murderer from the beginning, and a liar, John 8:44.

The same also St. John hath intimated, by giving *the name of the old serpent to him who is called the devil and Satan*, who deceiveth the whole world, Revelation 12:9; Revelation 20:2. Besides, in the history of the fall, the serpent is said to have been punished, as a *rational and accountable agent.*[118] (Emphasis added)

NACHASH

Another crucial grammatical consideration is that the Hebrew word for "serpent" (*nachash*, pronounced *naw'-kawsh*) also carries a well-known double meaning. Not only can *nachash* mean a literal snake (or serpent), but the Hebrew lexicon tells us that the word's root meaning is one who is an enchanter and whisperer of magic spells; or one who manipulates others by diligently observing and learning by experience the ways of its prey—a clever diviner of the future.[119]

Easton's Bible Dictionary adds another important element to the understanding of the word. *Nachash* is directly related to the Hebrew word *nehushtan*:

> Of copper; a brazen thing—a name of contempt given to the serpent Moses had made in the wilderness (Numbers 21:8), and which Hezekiah destroyed because the children of Israel began to regard it as an idol and "burn incense to it." The lapse of nearly one thousand years had invested the "brazen serpent" with a mysterious sanctity; and in order to deliver the people from their infatuation, and impress them with the idea of its worthlessness, Hezekiah called it, in contempt, "Nehushtan," a brazen thing, a mere piece of brass (2 Kings 18:4).[120]

Today, we use the word "brazen" to indicate the personality of someone who is shameless and without remorse, someone who is obscene. When we use the word in this manner, its meaning is ultimately derived from the Hebrew word *Nachash,* the same word the Bible uses for Satan.

Nachash, therefore, is a perfect Hebrew word to be used in the Garden account as the central antagonist figure. That word rounds out the divine metaphor, while at the same time identifying the exact nature of Satan himself.

THE ACCOUNTABLE ONE

This fact also lends credibility to the truth we just observed in the very last words of the previously referenced *Benson Commentary.* Read those words again: "Besides, in the history of the fall, the serpent is said to have been punished, as a rational and accountable agent."[121]

Benson asserts correctly that Satan alone—not a literal serpent or snake, and especially not the entirety of snakedom from the dawn of time until the end of the ages—was made answerable for the deed. After all, how could a talking snake be held accountable and brought to eternal judgment as a rational agent before Yahweh, one who will be ultimately destroyed and "reduced to ashes" in the last days? It couldn't be, but a guardian cherub, fallen from the realm of the Heavenly Host, could be held to an elevated measure of divine judgment...and he was.

A singular prophetic utterance is the source from which all other biblical messianic prophecy flows; that prophecy was first set forth, of all places, in the Garden of Eden by Yahweh himself.

It is the wellspring, *the fountainhead*, of all biblical understanding...

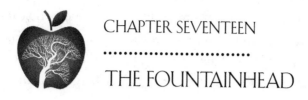

CHAPTER SEVENTEEN

························

THE FOUNTAINHEAD

One great promise respecting the Redeemer
is that He should be of the human race, but
peculiarly of the *woman's* "seed," not the
man's.

~Dr. Lehman Strauss[122]

Quick! Who uttered the very first prophetic words concerning the
coming of Messiah found in the Bible—and where are those
words located?

That first prophecy is found in Genesis 3:15. God Himself spoke
the words, making Elohim the very first "prophet." God's declaration
references the eventual coming of the Christ through the *seed* of the
woman. This Seed would be the One who would turn back the cosmic clock and set everything right, ultimately proving to be the agent
of Satan's demise. This one prophecy is the declaration upon which all
other prophecies concerning the Messiah rest:

And I will put enmity between you and the woman, and
between your offspring [seed] and hers; he [a singular person]
will crush your head, and you will strike his [a singular person]
heel. (Genesis 3:15, brackets added)

The *Benson Commentary* says of Genesis 3:15:

Serpents are, of all creatures, the most disagreeable and terrible to mankind…*but the devil, who seduced the woman, and his angels, are here meant,* who are hated and dreaded by all men, even by those that serve them, but more especially by good men.[123] (Emphasis added)

The *Benson Commentary* also affirms:

All carnal and wicked men, who, *in reference to this text,* are called *the children and seed of Satan;* and her seed—That is, her offspring, first and principally CHRIST, who, with respect to this promise, is termed, by way of eminence, her seed, (see Galatians 3:16; Galatians 3:19) whose alone work it is to bruise the serpent's head, to destroy the policy and power *of the devil.*[124] (Emphasis added)

Dr. Lehman Strauss, former professor of Old Testament history at Philadelphia Bible Institute, asserts the following:

[Genesis 3:15] *is the fountainhead of all prophecy* from which flows the ever-increasing stream of testimony to the promised Deliverer. One great promise respecting the Redeemer is that He should be of the human race, but peculiarly of the woman's "seed," not the man's. To fulfill this promise, Jesus Christ cannot, therefore, be begotten by any man. He must be born of a virgin. This is precisely what Isaiah prophesied more than 3000 years after the promise was first given: Therefore the Lord Himself shall give you a sign: Behold, a virgin shall conceive, and bear a son, and shall call His name Immanuel (Isaiah 7:14).[125]

The truth is evident. If we deny Genesis 3:15 as the origin of all messianic prophecy, then we fundamentally corrupt the rest of the biblical message.

Bob Deffinbaugh, ThD, supplies extensive commentary material for the online biblical research source *Bible.org*. In an article titled, "The Anticipation of Israel's Messiah," Dr. Deffinbaugh asserts the following regarding Genesis 3:15:

> God began *by addressing Satan* and spelling out the punishment for his sin. This is appropriate in light of the fact that Satan was the instigator, the tempter.... As the promoter of sin, his punishment rightly comes first. *The first promise of a coming Messiah in the Bible comes in God's rebuke of Satan in Genesis 3:15.* The Messiah was to come, then, both to destroy Satan and to deliver men from his dominion, a theme which continues on into the New Testament.[126] (Emphasis added)

Similarly, Dr. Don Stewart, who provides scholarly material for the online source, Blue Letter Bible, declares of Genesis 3:15:

> The ultimate seed of the woman would be Jesus Himself. Therefore, *we have in Genesis 3:15, the first promise of a Redeemer.* It is the beginning of a long line of prophecies concerning the coming Messiah. The Promised One would be from the woman's seed an indication of the eventual virgin birth of Christ.[127] (Emphasis added)

Numerous renowned commentaries draw the same conclusion; Genesis 3:15 is the first and distinctive prophecy of Jesus Christ's crushing blow that would be delivered to Satan at Calvary's cross and through the empty tomb.[128]

THE SEED

By the time we arrive at the New Testament, we find Jesus Christ clearly referred to as "the Seed" of *God's promise.*

> Why, then, was the law given at all? It was added because of transgressions until the Seed to whom the promise referred had come. (Galatians 3:19)

Although the primary context of Galatians 3:19 is a reference to God's promise to Abraham, scholars also acknowledge the obvious connection all the way back to Genesis 3:15. Have a look at the words of *The Bible Exposition Commentary (New Testament)* regarding Galatians 3:

> The Bible concept of "the seed" goes back to Gen[esis] 3:15, after the Fall of man. God states that there will be a conflict in the world between Satan's seed (children of the devil, see John 8:33–44) and the woman's seed (God's children, and, ultimately, God's Son). Satan's goal in the Old Testament was to keep the Seed (Christ) from being born into the world, for Satan knew that God's Son would one day crush his head.[129]

The first pointed affirmation we get from the New Testament regarding Genesis 3:15 and the seed is found in Romans 16:20: "The God of peace will soon *crush Satan under your feet.* The grace of our Lord Jesus be with you" (emphasis added).

The *Jamieson-Fausset-Brown Bible Commentary,* among many others, confirms that Romans 16:20 is a direct reference to the prophecy of Genesis 3:15:

Indeed this assurance is but a reproduction of the first great promise, that the Seed of the woman should bruise the Serpent's head (Ge[nesis] 3:15).[130]

Even the twelfth chapter of the book of Revelation is directly linked to the prophecy of Genesis 3:15:

The dragon [who is Satan] stood in front of the woman who was about to give birth, so that it might devour her child the moment he was born. She gave birth to a son, a male child, who "will rule all the nations with an iron scepter." (Revelation 12:4–5, bracketed words added, encapsulating Revelation 12:9)

There simply is no way to escape the fact that the Garden tempter was Satan himself, not Satan "disguised" as a snake.

We now understand, as we let the Bible contextually interpret itself, that the entire Garden account begins with symbolism. Adam and Eve are indeed literal characters; the entirety of Scripture clearly punctuates this truth. However, the *serpent* of Eden, and everything connected with it, is an unquestionable metaphor for the literal person of Satan.

THE ULTIMATE DECEPTION

If incorrectly identifying the snake in the Garden turns out to be the first *adjustment* of Genesis 3 among certain scholars, then the next set of revelations certainly stand as the greatest interpretation travesties ever leveled upon the entire Garden narrative.

Now, the investigation of the Garden crime gets deeper. Much deeper.

CHAPTER EIGHTEEN

....

THE COVERING

Well, knowledge is a fine thing, and mother
Eve thought so; but she smarted so severely
for hers, that most of her daughters have been
afraid of it since.

~Abigail Adams [131]

Once we can get past the notion of a chatty, ambulating snake—and a woman eating a literal piece of fruit—we can move on to the heart of the matter. But, this is where it gets tough for some folks, especially when we continue to let the Bible interpret itself in its proper context.

Let's begin by examining what should be one of the most obvious hints as to the foundational nature of the Garden sin. Sadly, that tip often becomes the victim of quickly glossed-over explanations in a number of commentary entries regarding that inglorious, snaky day. Let's look at our first piece of forensic evidence.

THE LOINCLOTH

Then the eyes of both were opened, and they knew that they were naked. And they sewed fig leaves together and made themselves loincloths. Then the man and his wife heard the sound of the Lord God as he was walking in the garden in the cool of the day, and they hid from the Lord God among the trees of the garden. (Genesis 3:7–8, ESV)

Let's break the scenario down in the same linear manner in which it is presented in the Genesis account. We'll paraphrase the elemental facts of the case. The process is like the beginning stages of investigating a crime scene: *Just the facts Ma'am—just the facts.*

First, Satan made an offer. The offer involved engaging in a specific act: partaking of "forbidden fruit." A conversation ensued. The manipulated couple finally gave in. What was the promised payoff for doing this thing? The assurance of being made privy to a particular, elevated "knowledge." This specific knowledge was presented as a privilege Adam and Eve had never before enjoyed. Apparently, the temptation was physically appealing, and quite overwhelming. So they "ate."

Next came the "reveal." After "eating…the fruit," Adam and Eve were immediately engulfed with shame. How did they demonstrate their remorse? First, they departed from Satan's presence. Then they covered their sex organs with a quickly crafted "loincloth." Finally, they skedaddled deep into the woods to hide themselves—and their cloaked genitals—from God. What a strange set of reactions, *unless…*

It's not a very pleasant thought, but that's exactly what the Bible says. What kind of activity could they have engaged in that would have made Adam and Eve react this way? I can only think of one reason that would be their very first recourse—that is, without going through an odd array of mental gymnastics to explain the obvious.

We are told from Scripture that prior to the Fall, Adam and Eve were naked, and they were unashamed of that nakedness: "Adam and his wife were both naked, and they felt no shame" (Genesis 2:25).

Yet, immediately after their sin, which was associated directly with

Satan's allurement, they *were* ashamed—specifically of their sexual organs. They expressed that shame by covering their genitals. This was their *first* response to their guilt.

Think of it: If those same facts and that specific reaction were recorded in any other piece of literature, or if you saw that scene playing out in a Hollywood movie, there's not a person on the planet who wouldn't have a strong idea of the nature of their failing. But since it's in the Bible, the entire matter becomes a victim of "adjustment" and the subject of children's bedtime stories.

THE EXPERTS SPEAK

Gill's Exposition of the Entire Bible is one of several sources offering the most logical explanation for Adam and Eve's actions:

> And they sewed fig leaves together, and made themselves aprons; not to cover their whole bodies, *but only those parts* which, ever since, mankind have been ashamed to expose to public view, and which they studiously conceal from sight: *the reason* of which perhaps is, *because by those members the original corruption* of human nature *has been from the beginning,* and still is propagated from parents to children.[132] (Emphasis added)

The *Guzik Commentary* on Genesis 3 sees the connection as well:

> Obviously, they covered their genital areas…because we have both received our fallenness and pass it on genetically through sexual reproduction.[133]

Matthew Poole's Commentary also appears to allude to the nature of the Garden sin:

They knew that they were naked. They knew it before, when it was their glory, but now they know it with grief and shame, from a sense both of their guilt for the sin newly past, and of that sinful *concupiscence* [overwhelming sexual lust] which they now found working in them.[134] (Emphasis and brackets added)

Dr. Thomas Constable concedes that a number of renowned biblical scholars interpret the Hebrew language of the Garden text as speaking directly to some sort of sexual sin. Dr. Constable references Dr. E. A. Speiser's commentary on Genesis 3 as one such example:[135]

Some commentators have interpreted eating the forbidden fruit as a euphemism for having sexual intercourse. [Note: E.g., E. A. Speiser, Genesis, p 26.] They say that the original sin was a sexual sin.[136] (Bracketed words in the original)

In the scholarly work written by Dr. Isaac M. Kikawada and Dr. Arthur Quinn *Before Abraham Was: The Unity of Genesis 1–11*, we find this affirmation:[137]

This helps to explain the quandary many interpreters have found themselves in when attempting to explain the "original sin." They have sensed (correctly) that the sin had to do with sexual intercourse. The sin was sexual…and hence we can agree with the general conclusion of J. L. McKenzie decades ago that the ancient Hebrews would have understood the Garden of Eden as a story about "the *perversion of the sexual life* from its primitive integrity."[138] (Emphasis added; parenthesis in original)

John Calvin's Bible Commentary for Genesis 3:6 also dives right into the apparent heart of the matter:

And when the woman saw. This impure look of Eve, infected with the poison of *concupiscence* [overwhelming sexual lust], was both the messenger and the witness of an impure heart…. But now, after the heart had declined from faith, and from obedience to the word, she *corrupted both herself* and all her senses, and depravity was diffused through all parts of her soul *as well as her body*…. For now, having shaken off the bridle, her mind wanders dissolutely and intemperately, drawing *the body with it* to the same licentiousness [promiscuous in sexual matters].[139] (Bracketed words contain dictionary definitions of the preceding italicized words.)

Additionally, we discover the following surprising attestation in a rather unexpected source. It was published by the University of Michigan Library in a work titled *The American Journal of Urology and Sexology*:

In his later work already quoted [Havelock Ellis] asks, "How has it happened that in all parts of the world the snake … has been credited with some design sinister or erotic, on women?" (Vol. 2, p. 236)…

Indeed, so obvious was this [observation] to the Jews that "In Rabbinical tradition the serpent is the symbol of sexual desire," and this led the Rabbis to think that in the Eden story "the serpent here represented the sexual passion" (Barton, SO, p.93: *Midrash Rabba to Genesis*, sec. 20)….

[Numerous] biblical exegetes recognize that the narrative in Gen. III, is a sex story euphemistically told.[140] (Bracketed words added for clarification from lengthy texts.)

Think of this. Isn't it interesting that what we are really dealing with in the Garden narrative is primarily an attempt to define the meaning of that mysterious *forbidden fruit?* Yet, we frequently use that very term in regular conversation, even in today's English; and we most often equate its meaning to something sexual. That's because the root of its meaning goes all the way back to the Garden of Eden. Following is the *Cambridge Dictionary* definition for the frequently used phrase:

> Something, *especially something sexual*, that is even more attractive because it is not allowed: [i.e.] He was always drawn to other men's wives - the forbidden fruit.[141] (Emphasis added)

SATAN, SEX, AND SALVATION

January 2018 turned a very telling corner regarding our current study. In a news piece out of the United Kingdom, prominently posted on the *Drudge Report*, appeared this title: "The Church of Satan Believes That Sex Robots Could Save Our Society."

> Yesterday, the Church of Satan started posting videos about sex robots online …
>
> Oddly, the founder of the church of Satan, Anton Lavey, predicted sex robots more than two decades ago—and today's Satanists still believe they *could save us all*. In Lavey's "Five Point Plan," drawn up in the Eighties, he recommended the use of "humanoids" as *an outlet for people's darker impulses.…*
>
> Recognizing that the *human animal often raises himself up through the denigration of another*, this would provide a safe outlet for such behavior. Have the lover of your dreams, regardless of your own prowess; *every man a king* who can *purchase his own subject*; or contrariwise, *buy the master you wish to serve.*[142] (Emphasis added)

Who better to speak to the world on behalf of Satan's diabolical plan than the "Church of Satan?"

Ironically, the so-called Church of Satan claims they do not believe in the literal person of Satan. As a matter of fact, current high priest Peter H. Gilmore identifies the church of Satan's followers as *skeptical atheists*. The church views the devil as an archetype who characterizes pride and enlightenment, and stands as a symbol of defiance against the Abrahamic faiths.[143]

Hmm. So what we really have here are atheists who hold up pride and "knowledge" as the ultimate virtues, yet at the same time stand in rebellion against the Word of God. They even use the name of Satan as the foundation for spreading their anti-God rhetoric. Sounds like Satan's people to me; how about you? I don't guess Satan cares if they "believe" in him or not, as long as they faithfully do the bidding of his lusts.

But why is it that Satan appears to be so historically infatuated with perverted sex? And why does he continually seek to devise ways whereby he might further degenerate human sexuality? And, all the while, his spokespeople are insisting that slipping ever-deeper into defiling and profane sexual activities might just turn out to be the long-awaited "savior" of all humanity. *Really?*

This sounds to me like a familiar old lie: *Eat of this forbidden fruit and you can live forever! You can be your own king. You can choose your own master! You can be like the gods.*

Surely we're way too smart to believe this lie again? Right?

Gee. Who could have imagined such a turn of events?

Yes, indeed. *Who?*

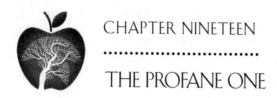

CHAPTER NINETEEN

••••••••••••••••••••••••••

THE PROFANE ONE

I will cast thee as profane out of the mountain
of God.

~Ezekiel 28:16, KJV

Back in Ezekiel 28, we get another potential clue concerning the
nature of the Garden shame. These are represented as the words of
Elohim Himself, and they are harsh:

Thou hast sinned: therefore I will cast thee *as profane* out of the
mountain of God: and I will destroy thee. (Ezekiel 28:16, KJV,
emphasis added)

The use of the word "profane" as the term describing Satan's sin is
found in the following Bible versions: KJV, ESV, NASB, ISV, NHEB,
the JPS Tanakh 1917, NAS 1977, King James 2000 Bible, ASV, Darby
Bible, ERV, Webster's Bible, and the Word English Bible translation.
Several other scholarly translations render the meaning in a similar manner by using the words "defiled" or "cast out in disgrace."[144]

CHALAL

There is a very good reason why the words "profane," "defiled," or even "disgrace" are used in so many Bible translations of this passage. The Hebrew word is *chalal*. That ancient expression, Strong's OT #2490, sometimes carries with it, in context, the idea of sexual defilement—or, at the very least, something obscenely wicked or utterly disgraceful.[145]

Vines Expository Dictionary of Old and New Testament Words says:

> The most frequent use of this Hebrew root is in the sense of "to pollute, defile." The word *is often used* to describe the *defilement which results from illicit sexual acts.*[146] (Emphasis added)

As an example of the accuracy of the *Vines* commentary, following are several Old Testament examples of *chalal* translated in this manner:

- "Do not profane [*chalal*] your daughter by making her a harlot, so that the land will not fall to harlotry and the land become full of lewdness" (Leviticus 19:29).
- "Also the daughter of any priest, if she profanes [*chalal*] herself by harlotry, she profanes [*chalal*] her father; she shall be burned with fire" (Leviticus 21:9).
- "The sons of Reuben the firstborn of Israel (he was the firstborn, but when he defiled [*chalal*] his father's marriage bed, his rights as firstborn were given to the sons of Joseph son of Israel" (1 Chronicles 5:1).
- "And a man and his father resort to the same girl in order to profane [*chalal*] My holy name" (Amos 2:7, NASB)
- To call Satan "profane" for what he did in the Garden of Eden is to use emphatically strong language. This Hebrew word, at the very least, carries with it the idea of polluting, befouling, or

defilement. At its worst, the word denotes unbridled corruption wrought through perverted sexual acts.

- The only thing left is to determine exactly what Yahweh meant when He used this specific term, *chalal*, in describing Satan's Garden activities. We can only surmise the intended message, but we do so with an abundance of additional and contextual biblical evidence, as you will soon see.

TREES. FRUIT. EATING.

Since we are certain the serpent of the Garden is a metaphor, it would logically follow that additional elements of the account are also symbolic. So, here we have to ask: *Are there other Scriptures that symbolically present "trees, fruit, and eating" that somehow might suggest something of a sensual nature?*

Following are several examples that answer this important question in the affirmative:

- "Like an apple tree among the trees of the forest is my beloved among the young men. I delight to sit in his shade, and his fruit is sweet to my taste" (Song of Solomon 2:3).
- "HE: You are a garden locked up, my sister, my bride; you are a spring enclosed, a sealed fountain.... SHE: Blow on my garden, that its fragrance may spread everywhere. Let my beloved come into his garden and taste its choice fruits" (Song of Solomon 4:12, 16).
- "This is the way of an adulterous woman: She eats and wipes her mouth and says, 'I've done nothing wrong'" (Proverbs 30:20).

Regarding the Song of Solomon 2:3 reference, *Jamieson-Fausset-Brown Bible Commentary* sees at least a connection to the Garden of Eden: "Man lost the tree of life (Ge[nesis] 3:22, 23). Jesus Christ regained it for him; he eats it partly now."[147]

The reference of the Song of Solomon 4:12 is also recognized by scholars as having similar connections. For example, *Pulpit Commentary* says:

> The idea *of a paradise* or garden is carried *from the beginning of Scripture* to the end, the symbol of *perfect blessedness*. The figure of the closed or shut-up garden represents the bridegroom's delight in the sense of absolute and sole possession—for himself *and no other*.[148] (Emphasis added)

No doubt these metaphors from the Song of Solomon and Proverbs are the same symbols employed in the biblical account of the Garden of Eden. However, this doesn't mean the examples are directly related to the Garden of Eden, nor do they tell us exactly what happened in the Garden. But the evidence does prove that the imagery of *trees, fruit,* and *eating* in sensually symbolic ways in Scripture is not a foreign concept.

Trees are personified throughout Scripture; so is the metaphorical phrase concerning the "fruit" they produce, or the "eating of their fruit." Jesus Himself uses this same imagery in His teaching about false prophets:

> Watch out for false prophets. They come to you in sheep's clothing, but inwardly they are ferocious wolves. By their fruit you will recognize them. Do people pick grapes from thornbushes, or figs from thistles? Likewise, every good tree bears good fruit, but a bad tree bears bad fruit. A good tree cannot bear bad fruit, and a bad tree cannot bear good fruit. Every tree that does not bear good fruit is cut down and thrown into the fire. Thus, by their fruit you will recognize them. (Matthew 7:15–20)

Consider the obvious: Didn't Satan stand in the Garden as the world's first "false prophet?" Of course he did. Don't all false prophets ultimately have their spiritual roots planted in the work of Satan? Of course they do.

Then, according to Jesus' teaching, Satan also metaphorically stood as a "tree" in the Garden of Eden, and he offered to Adam and Eve a bite of his "fruit." He was a rotten and perverted tree offering bad fruit. And he falsely prophesied: *You surely shall not die. God is a liar. You can be like the gods!*[149]

THE NEW TESTAMENT

The next question might be: Does the New Testament have anything to say about the potential interpretation of the nature of the Garden sin? After all, the New Testament is the most complete revelation of God's Word. *Right?* Of course it is. And the New Testament is the light in which we should seek to most accurately interpret the account of Genesis 3.

For thousands of years, the plain truth has been right before our eyes, in the words of four very important New Testament writers—the apostles John, Peter, James, and Paul.

If you are up for a few more huge surprises, turn the page...

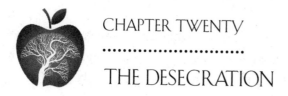

CHAPTER TWENTY

....

THE DESECRATION

Adam was not alone in the Garden of Eden,
however, and does not deserve all the credit;
much is due to Eve, the first woman, and
Satan, the first consultant.

~Mark Twain[150]

The church at Corinth was riddled with sexual defilement and shameless false teachers. Both these perversions were being used by Satan as instruments of ruin against the church.

The Apostle Paul made a shockingly direct comparison with the situation at Corinth to the Garden of Eden:

I am jealous for you with a godly jealousy. I promised you to one husband, to Christ, so that *I might present you as a pure virgin* to him. But I am afraid that *just as Eve was deceived by the serpent's cunning,* your minds may somehow be *led astray from your sincere and pure devotion* to Christ....

And no wonder, *for Satan himself masquerades as an angel of light.* (2 Corinthians 11:2–3, 14, emphasis added)

Once again, the *Bible Exposition Commentary (New Testament)* offers significant insight regarding the meaning of the 2 Corinthians passage:

The picture here is that of a loving father who has a daughter engaged to be married. He feels it is his privilege and duty *to keep her pure* [sexually], so that he can present her to her husband with *joy and not with sorrow.* Paul saw the local church as a bride, *engaged to be married to Jesus Christ* (see Ephesians 5:22ff and Romans 7:4).

Meanwhile, the church—and this means individual Christians—*must keep herself pure* [sexually and otherwise] *as she prepares to meet her Beloved.*

The peril, then, is that of unfaithfulness [sexual infidelity] to her fiancé. The engaged woman owes her love and allegiance to but one—her betrothed. If she shares herself [has sex] with any other man, she is *guilty of unfaithfulness* [sexual infidelity]. A divided heart leads to *a defiled life* [sexual defilement] *and a destroyed relationship.... The Person behind the peril is Satan, pictured here as the serpent.*[151] (Emphasis and bracketed words added)

Even in employing the euphemistic language of that day, the *Bible Exposition Commentary* doesn't leave much room for interpretation regarding its understanding of Paul's comparison of Eden's sin to the prevailing sins of the church at Corinth.

Ellicott's Commentary for English Readers addresses this passage in a similar fashion:

St. Paul either takes for granted that the disciples at Corinth will recognize the "serpent" as *the symbol* of the great Tempter, as in Revelation 12:9 or, without laying stress on that identification, simply compares the work of the rival teachers to that of the serpent.... The Greek for "corrupt" [implies] something which is *incompatible with the idea of purity*. The Apostle seeks, as it were, for *a chastity of mind as well as of body.*[152]

Then there is this striking assertion from the *Expositor's Greek Testament*:

It would appear that the belief of the synagogues was that the serpent literally "seduced" Eve [something sexual occurred]…

Carrying on the metaphor of 2 Corinthians 11:2, [Paul] expresses his anxiety lest the Corinthian Church, the Bride of Christ, should be *seduced by the devil* from her singleness of affection *and her purity*, and so should be *guilty of spiritual fornication.*[153] (Emphasis and bracketed words added)

RIGHT TO THE POINT

Look at Peter's statement concerning the foundational origin of the depravity that so thoroughly permeates our world:

Whereby are given unto us exceeding great and precious promises: that by these ye might be partakers of the divine nature, having escaped *the corruption that is in the world through lust*. (2 Peter 1:4, KJV, emphasis added)

Quite the shocking pronouncement, wouldn't you agree? Remember, Peter was one of the inner three of Jesus' disciples. I wouldn't be surprised to learn that Peter had gleaned his information from Jesus Himself.

Every process of corruption must have a point of beginning. Decay doesn't just burst into existence without warning. There has to be a moment in which the entire stinking, decaying mess begins. Something first must die.

Of course, we know the corruption of which Peter speaks. In this context, that corruption began in the Garden of Eden. That is where the stench of "original death" first wafted through the air. The Bible is inflexible regarding that point of fact (Romans 5:12–14; 1 Corinthians 15:22; Romans 5:12).

A number of the scholarly Bible versions use the word "lust" as the best translation of the Greek word that Peter employs in this text. A few of those translations are: NASB, KJV, New Heart English Bible, NAS 1977, Jubilee Bible 2000, King James 2000 Bible, AKJV, ASV, Darby Bible, ERV, Webster's Bible, and the Word English Bible.[154]

Most other translations use the words "evil desire" or something close. Either terminology, especially in this context, means the same thing.

EPITHUMIA

The Greek word for "lust" in this passage is *epithumia,* Strong's #1939. One of its most prolific translations is that of sensual lust—*the lust of the flesh.* As you will see in a moment, that appears to be the exact context of Peter's assertion here.[155]

In fact, *Meyer's New Testament Commentary* asserts that *epithumia* in *every case* in Scripture refers to sexual lust, except for three instances where the object of the emotion in question is clearly named otherwise:

> By [*epithumia*] is not denoted "innocent sensuousness," but it occurs here [James 1:14], *as everywhere* in the N. T. (except where its specific object is named, as in Luke 22:15; Ph[ilippians] 1:23; 1 Thessalonians 2:17).[156] (Brackets and emphasis added)

This truly is Peter's "big reveal" concerning the foundational understanding of the Garden sin. Consider a sampling of how the word *epithumia* is found in key New Testament passages:

- "Therefore God gave them up in the lusts [*epithumia*] of their hearts to impurity, to the dishonoring of their bodies among themselves" (Romans 1:24, ESV).
- "For you have spent enough time in the past doing what pagans choose to do—living in debauchery, lust [*epithumia*], drunkenness, orgies, carousing and detestable idolatry" (1 Peter 4:3).
- "And especially those who indulge in the lust [*epithumia*] of defiling passion and despise authority" (2 Peter 2:10, ESV).
- "Not in passionate lust [*epithumia*] like the pagans, who do not know God" (1 Thessalonians 4:5).
- "Put to death, therefore, whatever belongs to your earthly nature: sexual immorality, impurity, lust [*epithumia*], evil desires and greed which is idolatry" (Colossians 3:5).
- "Among whom also we all had our conversation in times past in the lusts of our flesh, fulfilling the desires of the flesh [*epithumia*] and of the mind; and were by nature the children of wrath, even as others" (Ephesians 2:3, KJV).
- "Let not sin therefore reign in your mortal body, that ye should obey it in the lusts [*epithumia*] thereof. Neither yield ye your members as instruments of unrighteousness unto sin" (Romans 6:12–13, KJV).
- "But each one is tempted when he is carried away and enticed by his own lust [*epithumia*]. Then when lust [*epithumia*] has conceived, it gives birth to sin; and when sin is accomplished, it brings forth death" (James 1:14–15, NASB).
- "Ye are of your father the devil, and the lusts [*epithumia*] of your father ye will do" (John 8:44, KJV).

The following half dozen commentaries also include declarations concerning Peter's use of the word *epithumia* in 2 Peter 1:4. Especially notice the emphasized words.

Adam Clarke's Commentary:

We have partaken of an **earthly, sensual, and devilish nature;** the design of God by Christ is to remove this, and to make us partakers of the Divine nature; and save us from all the corruption in principle and fact which is in the world; **the source of which is lust.... Lust,** or **irregular, impure desire, is the source** whence **all the corruption** which is **in the world springs.**[157] (Emphasis added)

John Gill's Exposition of the Whole Bible:

In the world through lust.... The corrupt manners of the world, or those corruptions and vices which, are prevalent in the world, and **under the power and dominion of which the world lies;** and **particularly the sins of uncleanness, adultery, incest, sodomy, and such like filthy** and **unnatural lusts,** which abounded in the world.[158] (Emphasis added)

Another *Gill's Exposition* assertion:

[From *Gill's* commentary on Genesis 3] Because **by those members** [their sexual organs] the **original corruption** of human nature has been **from the beginning,** and still is propagated from parents to children.[159] (Emphasis added)

The *Commentary Critical and Explanatory on the Whole Bible:*

"The corruption in the world" **has its seat,** not so much in the surrounding elements, as **in the "lust" or concupiscence** [impure sexual lust] of **men's hearts.**[160] (Emphasis added)

Greek Testament Critical Exegetical Commentary:

The corruption which is in the world in (consisting in, as its element and foundation) **lust.** Quoting John Calvin: [Translated from Latin] "These are not the elements that surround us, but **at the heart** of our vulgar brazenness."[161] (Emphasis added)

Matthew Poole's English Annotations on the Holy Bible:

All the pravity or wickedness of human nature, which is here said to be, i.e. to reign and prevail, in the world, or worldly men, **through lust, or habitual concupiscence** [impure sexual lust], which **is the spring and root** from which it proceeds.[162] (Emphasis added)

Whedon's Commentary on the Bible:

Fundamental to all, however, is the fleeing away from, the renunciation of, the **moral corruption that** so widely **befouls the world,** and that **has its source in base, wicked lust.** God's **call is to purity:** that of the false teachers is to corruption. 2 Peter 2:18.[163] (Emphasis added)

It would appear that Peter's meaning leaves little room for doubt. These comments could be summarized as "The process of global decay that continually defiles our existence has as its foundational seat, tracing back to Eden, the concupiscence of humanity's collective nature."

But Peter is not the only one to lay forth the blueprint of where all this mess began, and most importantly, *where it leads.* The two other *inner-circle* apostles, James and John, offer additional and startling insight into the matter as well.

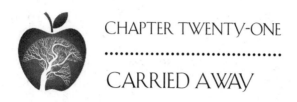

CHAPTER TWENTY-ONE

....

CARRIED AWAY

When lust has conceived, it gives birth to sin.

~James 1:15, NASB

While none of the New Testament writers appear to communicate that every human on the planet is necessarily a sexually licentious and slobbering Neanderthal, they most certainly identify that our entire sin nature was born, somehow, from the base of *epithumia*—and it dates back to the Garden of Eden. This fact is simply a foundational biblical truth.

To further punctuate the truth we are exploring, consider the following familiar passage of James 1:14–15. This passage also uses the word *epithumia* in laying forth its description of "how sin works":

But each one is tempted when he is carried away and enticed by his own lust [*epithumia*]. Then when lust [*epithumia*] has conceived, it gives birth to sin; and when sin is accomplished, it brings forth death. (James 1:14–15, NASB)

In context, James is, at least, describing the daily struggle with the sin nature that is common to all of humanity. But even more specifically, he is laying forth the "eternal pattern" of our common infection of fallenness. What is its end result? *Death*. What is its foundational origin? *Epithumia*.

Regarding this, the *Benson Commentary* on James 1:14—15 states:

> This is the *true genealogy* of sin and death. *Lust is the mother of sin*, and *sin the mother of death*; and the sinner the parent of both.[164] (Emphasis added)

Benson's reflection is in perfect alignment with Peter's assertion in 2 Peter 1:4—*the corruption that is in this world through lust.*

Sin was born in the Garden. Sin's "mother" was *epithumia*. And, in this context, the word denotes a lustfulness that was born in pure evil.

Jamieson-Fausset-Brown Bible Commentary offers this pointed observation regarding the claim of James 1:14 and its direct connection to the Garden of Eden:

> Lust, arising from his own temperament and habit. *Lust flows from the original birth-sin* in man, *inherited from Adam.*[165] (Emphasis added)

The context of James' illustration is obvious. Lust was born through the Garden sin—you know, the type of *epithumia* that, after committing a certain act, would make a man and woman want to quickly cover their genitals in horrid shame and then flee into the woods to hide. Now there's an interesting, and appropriate, point of context. Wouldn't you agree?

FOUNDATION OF DECAY

There simply is no way to soften the language we find in 2 Peter 1:4 or in James 1:14–15 and remain true to the contextual meaning of the Greek term these two apostles used.

Undoubtedly, Peter's original audience also understood the interpretation of these truths, especially when his declaration is read in the immediate context of the rest of his writings on the topic, all of which emphasize that brand of *epithumia*. Specifically, *epithumia* is rooted in perverted sensuality (See: 1 Peter 4:2–3; 2 Peter 2:4–10, 13–14, 18–19).

There is also very little doubt as to what version of *epithumia* James is addressing in James 1:14–15. The following commentaries assert:

Expositor's Greek Testament:

[James uses] a metaphorical use of alluring to sensual sin, and thus desire entices the man from his self-restraint as with the wiles of a harlot.[166]

Pulpit Commentary:

Here lust is personified, and represented as a seducing harlot, to whose embraces man yields, and the result is the birth of sin, which in its turn gives birth to death.[167]

Barnes' Notes on the Bible:

The whole passage, with the words and figures which are used, show that the idea in the apostle's mind was that of an enticing harlot.[168]

Gill's Exposition of the Scriptures:

The metaphor is taken…from a lascivious woman, who meeting with a young man, entices him, and draws him away after her to commit iniquity with her: by *"lust"* is meant the principle *of corrupt nature, which has its residence in the heart of man; is natural and hereditary to him.*[169] (Emphasis added)

Cambridge Bible for Schools and Colleges:

The imagery that follows here suggests the thought that St James had the picture of the harlot of Proverbs 7:6–23 present to his thoughts.[170]

Bengal's Gnomen:

Lust is, as it were, the harlot; human nature, the man.[171]

Jamieson-Fausset-Brown Bible Commentary:

"Lust" is here personified as the harlot that allures the man.[172]

And, according to an earlier quote we looked at from *Jamieson-Fausset-Brown*, the kind of *epithumia* of which James speaks was the "original birth-sin of man...inherited from Adam." The matter could not be made any plainer.

THE APOSTLE JOHN

John is yet another of the inner three of Jesus' disciples and the writer of the Gospel of John, 1–3 John, and Revelation. He also points us toward the Garden fall and the components of its "original sin." You've seen his words many times before; perhaps this time you will read them through a slightly different filter:

For everything in the world—the lust [*epithumia*] of the flesh, the lust [*epithumia*] of the eyes, and the pride of life—comes not from the Father but from the world. (1 John 2:16)

Based on all we have learned thus far, ask yourself this question: What if a person you have just met was described to you as having a particular problem with the "lust of the flesh" or the "lust of his eyes"? What would you assume was meant by that descriptive accusation? Would you think the person had a problem with lusting after apples, for example? Do you think his "wandering eyes" would refer to his lust towards ice cream cones? Of course not.

Interestingly, this passage from 1 John is also quoted by practically every foremost commentary as an interpretation of the defining pattern of what took place in the Garden of Eden.[173]

Now the matter becomes obvious: Each of these biblical writers acknowledged the source, but not the particular act, of the Garden defilement. And none mentions anywhere in their writings a walking, talking snake offering a literal piece of fruit.

A REVEALING ILLUSTRATION

In case you still have trouble wrapping your mind around all this, it might prove helpful to put what we have thus far discovered in a more modern context. What if a renowned pastor in your hometown was fired by his church, and the only statement released to the media was the following:

> Pastor _____ of _____ church was released from his ministry position due to his evil desires and the resulting profane actions issuing forth from those desires. The lust of his flesh, and the lust of his eyes, overcame him. He has eaten of a specific piece of forbidden fruit, and he has been disgraced—he has defiled himself, and his ministry. Therefore, we have cast him out of the pulpit. He will not be allowed to return.

Is that clear enough?

Tell the truth. Even though we don't know the specific act the pastor committed, we are at least fairly certain of which *category of sin* this information intends to convey. And that's using the same softer language currently used in a number of Bible translations and commentaries.

Think of it. Why would we believe this kind of language and context means one thing, but only when related to the example of our fired pastor, yet so many would believe it signifies something entirely different when interpreting the Garden narrative? *Tweaking?*

We now have heard from Paul (who wrote almost half the New Testament), as well as the *inner three* of Jesus' most intimate circle of disciples, Peter, James, and John.

They agree as to the foundational nature of the original Garden sin: it was *epithumia*. And they are all very clear as to the context in which they use this word. At the very least, the context refers to a particularly nasty brand of evil desire. At its worst, the context refers to something sexually perverted. And judging by the biblical description of our first parents' immediate reaction to their own Garden *epithumia*, the determination of the most likely answer doesn't appear to be rocket science.

Maybe it's finally time we own up to just how serious the matter of our fallen condition really is. It could be that it's time for the church to "eat meat" regarding this subject, rather than merely "drinking milk" (1 Corinthians 3:2; Hebrews 5:12).

What do you think?

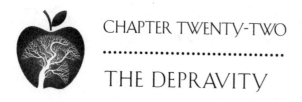

CHAPTER TWENTY-TWO

·······························

THE DEPRAVITY

It will be just like this on the day the Son of
Man is revealed.

~Luke 17:30

Obviously, we were not supposed to be privy to exactly what act transpired in the Garden of Eden. Was the deed a literal physical enactment of sexual perversion? Some think so, based upon the terms from the Hebrew (*chalal*) and Greek (*epithumia*).[174]

As already documented, though, even a number of the ancient Jewish scriptural authorities believed Satan actually had sex with Eve. Regardless of how repulsive that thought might be, it is impossible to deny that this interpretation was embedded within at least a certain segment of the early church. As a quick reminder of this fact, take another look at a few of those sources quoted in earlier chapters. Several additional sources are listed here as well. Remember that the vast majority of the earliest church was made up of Jewish believers in Yeshua as the Christ:

Expositor's Greek Testament:

It would appear that the belief of the synagogues was that the serpent literally "seduced" Eve.[175]

The Jewish Encyclopedia:

Satan was the seducer and the paramour [sexual lover] of Eve, and was hurled from heaven together with other angels because of his iniquity.[176]

The Jewish Encyclopedia:

Through the illicit intercourse of Eve with the serpent, however, the nature of her descendants was corrupted, Israel alone overcoming this fatal defect by accepting the Torah at Sinai.[177]

New World Encyclopedia

[Citing several early Christian and Jewish sources] Some early Christian sects and rabbinical sages, considered that the Fall was the result of sexual intercourse between Eve and the Serpent, usually understood to symbolize Satan.[178]

Bahar 199 (An ancient Kabbalistic commentary):

The serpent followed Eve, saying, "Her soul comes from the north, and I will therefore quickly seduce her." And how did he seduce her? He had intercourse with her.[179]

Studies in the Dead Sea Scrolls (A 2010 scholarly work):

One finds in rabbinic writings a number of exegetical traditions evolving around the serpent's passion for Adam's wife. In general, these traditions can be divided into the two main groups: those where the serpent's plot in Gen 3 is directed against Adam in order to get to his wife, and those where he (Satan) actually has sexual intercourse with Eve.

...There is a high probability that the basic motif of Eve having intercourse with the serpent goes back well into the Second Temple Period [roughly four hundred years before Christ].[180] (Brackets added)

BIO MANIPULATION?

Others have considered the possibility that the Garden deed might have involved some sort of technological manipulation (the *knowledge* of good and evil) akin to our own innovative genetic editing and stem-cell manipulation procedures.

The point is that if we mortals can imagine and invent new ways to influence the biological seeds of reproduction, and then ultimately the fabrication of a human embryo, do we really believe the fallen divine realm had no knowledge of these possibilities from the beginning? We lowly mortals have only begun to figure these things out, so that prospect seems highly unlikely.

This fact is especially important when we consider that the very thing Satan offered Adam and Eve was the "fruit" of the tree of the knowledge of good and evil. Surely that knowledge would have encompassed what we are now capable of doing regarding human reproduction and cloning and the like.

For example, in 2017, the headlines of mainstream media were filled with anticipation of potential breakthroughs in the recent IVG (in vitro gametogenesis) technology advancements. This technology, as reported by the *New York Times*, involves collecting adult skin cells and reprogramming them to become embryonic stem cells capable of growing into eggs or sperm. In this way, two men or two women could create their own child without the need for a member of the opposite gender. Some articles spoke of what an advancement this innovation would be to the global homosexual community.[181]

But that's not all. That same *NYT* article records other disturbing concerns coming from the scientific community:

> "It gives me an unsettled feeling because we don't know what this could lead to," said Paul Knoepfler, a stem cell researcher at the University of California, Davis. "You can imagine one man providing both the eggs and the sperm, almost like cloning himself. You can imagine that eggs becoming so easily available would lead to designer babies."
>
> Or a baby might have what one law professor called "multiplex" parents.
>
> "There are groups out there that want to reproduce among themselves," said Sonia Suter, a George Washington University law professor who began writing about I.V.G. even before it had been achieved in mice. "You could have two pairs who would each create an embryo, and then take an egg from one embryo and sperm from the other, and create a baby with four parents."[182]

BIOLOGICAL EDITING

Added to the nascent IVG technology is the field of the new biological genetic editing tool *Crispr-Cas9*. This technology mimics molecular scissors, letting scientists "snip" or repair selected components of DNA. Human and animal DNA can be mixed or even altered using the technology.

Experiments in both these realms are already taking place around the world. Even though altering human genetic material is not yet allowed in the United States, it is already taking place in China, as of January 2018.[183]

Of course, the implementation of genetically modifying the actual building blocks of life is loaded with ethical dilemmas. The use of *Crispr* might bring about unintended and/or irreversible changes in people that may not materialize for years.

Both these technologies, IVG and *Crispr*, have potential for wonderful "good" as well as for unthinkably horrendous evil. *Gee.* I wonder from what tree this knowledge could have emanated?

We learn from Scripture that by the time of Noah's Flood, all flesh had become "corrupted" (Genesis 6:12, KJV). We also know that Jesus said the very last days before His return would be characterized as being "just like the days of Noah" and "just like the days of Lot" (Luke 17:26–28). Numerous prophecy students believe we might be on the verge of those days.

DIVINE REALM TECHNOLOGY

Consider this scriptural truth. There exists an obvious biblical example concerning what we might call supernatural "technology," or bio manipulation, that emanated from the divine realm. The Virgin Mary conceived the Christ child through a mere command from God's throne, delivered through the announcement of an angelic being (Matthew 1). Obviously, Mary's conception involved no physical act, as Scripture clearly tells us she was a virgin.[184]

What happened with Mary was an example of Yahweh's divine power of speaking a thing into existence. Clearly, Satan does not possess that kind of authority. However, it could very well be that Satan and his company of fallen *elohim* do in fact already know how to "technologically" manipulate the human biological birth process. If humans have thought of a certain technology, surely the demonic realm already knew about it. How could they not? Are the fallen elohim learning technology from us? Hardly.

Some prophecy students believe the demonic realm may actually be guiding and/or manipulating our own knowledge of such things—especially in the particularly prophetic days in which we now live. The point is that the Garden deed might not have required an actual, physical, sexual union to have been a matter of defilement and profaneness.[185]

DEPRAVITY

The fact remains: We simply do not know exactly what happened in the Garden of Eden. The Bible is silent on that point of detail.

Whatever occurred there, God's Word says it was depraved, something far worse than eating a piece of literal fruit at the deceptive prompting of a walking, talking snake. With the Greek and Hebrew words used to give us hints as to the level of depravity, it appears the Garden defilement most likely involved something regarding human sexuality, both physical and literal, or through advanced biological manipulation.

Believe it or not, there is still more compelling scriptural evidence of the depraved depths of the Garden sin along these same lines of revelation.

A couple of specific New Testament churches give us additional insight.

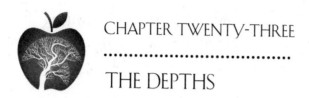

CHAPTER TWENTY-THREE

·······························

THE DEPTHS

He that becomes protector of [sin] shall surely become its prisoner.

~Augustine of Hippo, *City of God* [186]

Dr. Jeff Hood represents himself to be a Baptist minister in Texas. His doctorate, from Brite Divinity School, boasts a focus in "queer theology." Dr. Hood's story was told in an October 2017 *Patheos* article and posted at *Christiannews.net*. Following is an excerpt from that article:

[Hood says,] "Not only is polyamory [being sexually involved with more than one person at the same time, with consent of everyone involved] a positive thing, *I think it's a holy thing*. I think it *mimics the personhood of God…*

"The Holy Trinity is a polyamorous relationship…. You can't talk about the level of intimacy and ecstasy that these three beings are constantly experiencing without defining their relationship in such a way.

"Polyamorous folks are constantly oppressed and marginalized…. God is polyamorous, and if we want to get saved then we have to figure out a way to become connected to polyamory."

Hood acknowledged…that his views are rejected by many

Christians, who[m] he called "church [expletives] that have no knowledge of God."

"Do these people sound like they know anything about love? [Expletive] no. I ain't listening to a [expletive] word they say."[187] (Emphasis and bracketed words added)

Because of the unprecedented access to the instantaneous global communication and information technologies of our age, Dr. Hood's diabolical teachings possess the potential for boundless influence over millions of souls. Yet, the Bible warned us these days were on the way:

Now the Spirit speaketh expressly, that *in the latter times* some shall depart from the faith, giving heed to *seducing spirits*, and *doctrines of devils*; *Speaking lies* in hypocrisy; having their *conscience seared* with a hot iron. (1 Timothy 4:1–2, KJV, emphasis added)

THE CHURCH AT CORINTH

Although the variety of instruction that Dr. Hood espouses is still rather unthinkable, let us not forget, the same sexually profane apostasy was present in the early New Testament church. Therefore, this particular "modern" teaching is merely polishing up a very old satanic lie. Paul admonished the church at Corinth:

It is actually reported that there is sexual immorality among you, and of a kind that even pagans do not tolerate: A man is sleeping with his father's wife [a form of a polyamorous relationship]. *And you are proud!* Shouldn't you rather have gone into mourning and have put out of your fellowship the man who has been doing this?... Your boasting is not good. (1 Corinthians 5:1–2, 6, emphasis and bracketed words added)

Notice that along with the brand of perversion that "even pagans do not tolerate" (that's pretty bad, by the way) came a specific form of diabolical pride. Apparently, a majority of the church members actually approved of, and bragged about, the hideous sexual perversion in their midst. This was one of the primary reasons Paul directly compared the Corinthian church's debauchery to that of the Garden sin (2 Corinthians 11:2–3).

THE CHURCH AT THYATIRA

The church at Corinth was not the only congregation dealing with the infiltration of sexual defilement during the first century. These striking words are found in the book of Revelation, written to the church of Thyatira:

> Nevertheless, I have this against you: You tolerate that woman Jezebel, *who calls herself a prophet. By her teaching she misleads my servants into sexual immorality* and the eating of food sacrificed to idols [sexual immorality was often associated with rituals of food offerings to pagan idols].
> I have given her time to repent of her immorality, but she is unwilling. So I will cast her on a bed of suffering, and I will *make those who commit adultery with her* suffer intensely, unless they repent of her ways. I will strike her children dead. (Revelation 2:20–23; emphasis and bracketed words added)

This "teacher" apparently engaged in numerous adulterous affairs within the church family. Perhaps the activity was some kind of "spouse-swapping" arrangement? Regardless, the implication is that the perverse sexual liaisons were carried out not only in a consensual manner (polyamorous relationships), but also, most of the church had full knowledge of her teaching and her activities.

But hang on; we're not yet finished. The next few verses reveal a striking truth directly related to our study of sexual perversion's most likely candidate as the first teacher:

> Then all the churches will know that I [the Lord] am he who searches hearts and minds, and I will repay each of you according to your deeds. Now I say to the rest of you in Thyatira, to you who do not hold to her teaching *and have not learned Satan's so-called deep secrets.* (Revelation 2:23–24, emphasis and bracketed words added)

Wait a minute! Just whose "deep secrets" were the source of these profane acts of sexual immoralities at Thyatira? They were identified as none other than Satan's knowledge—his *deep secrets.* Jesus Himself makes this accusation.

The *Jamieson-Fausset-Brown Bible Commentary* states the following regarding the secrets of Satan found in Revelation 2:24 and its potential connection to the Garden of Eden:

> Hengstenberg [a renowned German scholar and biblical commentator] thinks the teachers themselves professed to fathom the *depths of Satan,* giving loose rein to *fleshly lusts,* without being hurt thereby. The *original sin of Adam* was a desire to know Evil as well as good, so in Hengstenberg's view, those who professed to know "the depths of Satan."[188] (Bracketed words and emphasis added)

There is also this assessment of Revelation 2:24 from *Vincent's Word Studies:*

> **The depths of Satan…** The *serpent,* therefore, *who tempted mankind to sin,* is no longer their destroyer but their benefactor. *He is the symbol* of intellect, *by whose means the first human pair*

were raised to the knowledge of the existence of higher beings [other] than their creator.

This conception, consistently carried out, would have resulted in *a direct inversion* of the *whole* teaching of scripture; in calling evil good and good evil; in *converting Satan into God and God into Satan.*[189] (Emphasis added)

Both *Jamieson-Fausset-Brown Bible Commentary* and *Vincent's Word Studies* point out obvious associations to the original Garden sin, especially regarding the "secrets of Satan." After all, wasn't this the very thing offered to Adam and Eve, by Satan? He offered them his "deep secrets" whereby they could have the "knowledge of the gods." And, he also had as his plan to set himself up as God, by replacing Yahweh's authority over the life of humanity.

SATAN'S DEATH SENTENCE

Many believers are also shocked to learn that Satan received the sentence of death for what he did. All the way back to the Garden itself, we hear Yahweh pronounce that impending punishment: "[The seed of the woman] will crush your head" (Genesis 3:15).

What Satan did in the Garden of Eden was no small thing in God's eyes. In effect, He told Satan: "I will utterly destroy you for this. You will be reduced to ashes (Ezekiel 28:17–19), then you will ultimately become the Lord of nothing. For this profanity, you will die!"

Now, we have come to another amazing element in our study of the Garden of Eden. This point connects the nature of the Garden sin directly to our own lives—and to yet another erroneous and potentially deadly teaching that has infiltrated modern churches.

Let me forewarn you, this will not be a particularly enjoyable truth to learn.

CHAPTER TWENTY-FOUR

....

THE EXCEPTION

Flee from sexual immorality. All other sins
a person commits are outside the body, but
whoever sins sexually, sins against their own
body.

~1 Corinthians 6:16

Think about this question: Is any one particular "sin" worse than another?

A claim often made within the Christian world goes something like this: "Sin is sin—there are no degrees of sin; there are no *special* sins as far as God is concerned."

How many times have you heard this "truth" proclaimed to a delighted chorus of "Amen" from the listeners? When this unbiblical teaching is presented, one can almost hear a collective "Phew!" from the congregation.

However, that teaching is not biblically accurate. We need only go back to the sexual sin-plagued Corinthian church to discover the truth.

Flee from sexual immorality. *All other sins* a person commits are outside the body, *but whoever sins sexually*, sins against their own body. Do you not know that *your bodies are temples of the Holy*

Spirit, who is in you, whom you have received from God? You are not your own; you were bought at a price. Therefore *honor God with your bodies.* (1 Corinthians 6:18–20, emphasis added)

WHAT DO THE SCHOLARS SAY?

Barnes' Notes on the Bible offers a remarkable commentary on the warning of 1 Corinthians 6:

> **Perhaps no single sin has done so much** to produce the most painful and dreadful diseases, to weaken the constitution, and **to shorten life** as this. Other vices, as gluttony and drunkenness, do this also, and all sin has some effect in destroying the body, **but it is true of this sin in an eminent degree.**[190] (Emphasis added)

Think of the implications of Barnes' declaration. Barnes proclaimed that no other sin has done so much harm to humanity than sexual sin. But wait! What about a bite of fruit offered by a really smart snake? Wouldn't that single sin be worse than a mere sexual sin? After all, the sin in the Garden was the utter downfall of everything! Isn't that correct? *Unless…*

The Expositor's Greek Testament also punctuates the seriousness of sexual sin as defined by 1 Corinthians 6:

> "Sins of the flesh"…engage and **debauch the whole person;** they "enter into the heart," for "they proceed out of the heart" and touch the springs of being; in the **highest degree** they "defile the man."[191] (Emphasis added)

Sexual sins are of the "highest degree?" *Really?* Again, what about the sins of a talking snake and a fruit-eating woman? Were those sins of a "lower degree?" Have our classic scholars completely forgotten the infamous Garden sin? Probably not. That may be the entire point of their commentary regarding this passage.

Have a look at a couple more profound observations about 1 Corinthians 6:

Cambridge Bible for Schools and Colleges:

For it is a violation of the **fundamental law** impressed upon man **from the beginning.**[192] (Emphasis added)

Ellicott's Commentary for English Readers:

Other sins may profane only the outer courts of the temple; **this sin** penetrates with its **deadly foulness** into the **very holy of holies.**[193] (Emphasis added)

Wow! Cambridge insists that the foundational understanding of sexual sin was within the heart of humanity from the very beginning. And Ellicott claims that the human soul itself has been fouled with death because of sexual perversion. So, just exactly *when* was the human soul first spoiled with the sentence of death, and *why*? The answer is obvious. How is it then that so many students, and even scholars of the Word of God, miss this biblical truth?

However, this is still not the final pronouncement upon the matter.

THE DEPRAVED MIND

The apostle Paul further describes a downward spiral emanating from a certain "class of sin" in which God finally allows the offenders to be given over to a reprobate mind. This truth ought to send chills up the spine of the modern church.

Have a look at the biblical declarations of the first chapter of Romans:

[18] The wrath of God is being revealed from heaven against all the godlessness and wickedness of people, who suppress the truth by their wickedness....

[24] Therefore God gave them over in the sinful desires of their hearts [*epithumia*] to sexual impurity for the degrading of their bodies with one another.

[25] They exchanged the truth of God for a lie, and worshiped and served created things rather than the Creator—who is forever praised. Amen.

[26] Because of this, God gave them over to shameful lusts. Even their women exchanged natural relations for unnatural ones.

[27] In the same way the men also abandoned natural relations with women and were inflamed with lust for one another. Men committed indecent acts with other men, and received in themselves the due penalty for their perversion.

[28] Furthermore, since they did not think it worthwhile to retain the knowledge of God, he gave them over to a depraved mind, to do what ought not to be done. (Romans 1:18, 24–28)

The words describing this passage in the following commentary entries are significant:

The *Expositor's Greek Testament*:

But conscience; when this is perverted, as in the people of whom Paul speaks ... [then] the last deep of evil has been reached.[194]

Vincent's Word Studies:

The tendency of this [class of sin] is ever downward toward that demoniac animalism which is incarnated in Lucifer at the apex of the infernal cone, and which is so powerfully depicted in this chapter.[195]

Matthew Poole's Commentary:

First, they were given up to their own hearts' lusts, Romans 1:24; then, to vile affections, Romans 1:26; and then, lastly, to a mind void of judgment; to such an evil habit, that they could do nothing but evil.[196]

Ellicott's Commentary for English Readers:

Their idolatry developed into shameless immorality and unnatural crimes. At last the extreme limit was reached.[197]

Benson Commentary:

As a punishment of this most unreasonable and scandalous idolatry, God withdrew his restraining grace from them as he did from the antediluvians; the consequence of which was, that their lusts excited them to commit every sort of uncleanness.[198]

THE EVIDENCE

Think of the cumulative message of the last several commentary references: "the last deep of evil has been reached;" "demoniac animalism which is incarnate in Lucifer;" "the apex of the infernal cone;" "a mind void of judgment;" "at last the extreme limit was reached;" and "most unreasonable and scandalous idolatry." Those are unmistakably condemning pronouncements.

Could this be the reason sexual perversion is the single most referenced sin in the Bible, and it's also one of the most pervasive connections to the worship of pagan idols?[199]

Might this account for the fact that one-third of the United States' population is now infected with a sexually transmitted disease? This means that at least 110 million people in America have a sexually transmitted disease at any given time. In addition, nearly twenty million cases of new STD infections are reported each year in the US.[200]

Could this "demonic animalism" also be why sexual assault and sexual exploitation are now officially recognized as "global scourges?"[201] Might this fact also have something to do with the worldwide blights of sex-slave trafficking and the various unimaginable forms of the global pedophilia blight?[202]

Could this biblically acknowledged moral plague also explain why the United Nations acknowledges that children make up one-third of all human trafficking victims worldwide, many of them used as sex slaves? The United Nations also asserts that women and girls comprise 71 percent of all human trafficking victims.[203]

In a 2017 report, even the FBI recognized what it called "The Scourge of Child Pornography." That report asserted: "Rarely a week goes by in the United States that a child pornographer is not charged or sentenced for federal crimes related to the sexual exploitation of children." And this is only the tip of the iceberg. Think of the numbers of child pornographers, pedophiles, and their decimated victims who are never discovered.[204]

Furthermore, all these horrendous stains upon human dignity are indisputably linked to the greatest digital plague ever to be leveled upon humanity: *ubiquitous online pornography*. This travesty places practically unlimited access to some of the vilest sexual perversions that the human mind can conceive right into the laps of our children and teens.

In America alone, pornography has grown into a $10 billion business. That amount is larger than the profits of the NFL, the NBA, and Major League Baseball combined. Some of the nation's best-known corporations like General Motors and AOL Time Warner, and major hotel chains such as Marriott, Hilton, and Weston, earn massive revenues by piping adult movies into America's homes and hotel rooms. In January 2018, former Surgeon General C. Everett Koop lamented, "The appetite for pornography seems to be insatiable."[205]

Despite the United States of America claiming to be the "largest Christian nation" on the planet, the fact is that an estimated 89 percent of all the world's porn is produced and exported from our country. This gives a whole new meaning to "Made in the USA," doesn't it?[206]

We are the first generation to experience such horrifying scenarios, both at home and around the globe. Experts tell us the true fallout will only become apparent over the next generations. And all of this filth is laid directly upon the altar of *epithumia*—the foundation of the Garden sin.

God help us.

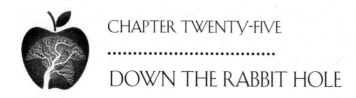

CHAPTER TWENTY-FIVE

·····························

DOWN THE RABBIT HOLE

And when sin is accomplished, it brings forth death.

~James 1:15

Award-winning journalist and bestselling author David Kupelian published a piece in January 2018 that offers a brilliant summary of the path upon which the plight of wanton *epithumia* has taken humanity. When the issue is summarized as Kupelian has done, the implications become much clearer:

> Since the 1960s, America has been engulfed in an unfolding sexual revolution as radical and life-changing as the most dramatic coup d'état.
>
> A million abortions per year (that's one dead child every 29 seconds), millions of out-of-wedlock births (40 percent of all U.S. births), a ubiquitous "hook-up" culture of casual sex, 110 million Americans with a sexually transmitted disease, and, of course, hard-core pornography pervading every nook and cranny of society all testify to the wholesale abandonment of the Judeo-Christian morality of previous generations. Not to mention the glorification of homosexuality (indeed, its elevation to the status of specially protected class), the redefinition of

marriage and the creation of dozens of bizarre new genders that never before existed in all of human history.

The predictable result of all this wild "sexual freedom"? Confusion, immorality, insecurity, pain, guilt, addiction, mental illness, infidelity, divorce, family breakdown, depression, self-destructive behavior and suicide.[207]

Also consider the following excerpts written by nationally syndicated radio host and bestselling author Dennis Prager, a man who was raised in the orthodox Jewish faith. His insight further illustrates how the issue of unbridled sexuality is so thoroughly ingrained in human history. In 1993, Prager authored an award-winning essay titled "Judaism's Sexual Revolution." The piece outlines several striking historical claims:

When Judaism demanded that all sexual activity be channeled into marriage, it changed the world....

Human sexuality, especially male sexuality is...utterly wild (far more so than animal sexuality). Men have had sex with women and with men; with little girls and young boys; with a single partner and in large groups; with total strangers and immediate family members; and with a variety of domesticated animals. There is little, animate or inanimate, that has not excited some men [sexually]....

Among the consequences of the unchanneled sex drive is the sexualization of everything—including religion. ...

Thus, the first thing Judaism did was to de-sexualize God— "In the beginning God created the heavens and the earth" by His will, not through any sexual behavior. This broke with all other religions, and it alone changed human history.

Judaism's restricting of sexual behavior was one of the essential elements that enabled society to progress. Along with ethical monotheism, the revolution begun by the Torah when it declared war on the sexual practices of the world wrought the most far-reaching changes in history.[208]

In that essay, Prager also lists the various *gods* that were revered in the ancient world, and then catalogs how virtually all those pagan deities were represented as engaging in wildly perverse sexuality.

Prager asserts, "Given the sexual activity of *the gods*, it is not surprising that the religions themselves were replete with all forms of sexual activity."[209]

Give that some thought. Why would it be that *the gods*, which we now know to be nothing less than demonic entities under the headship of *Nachash*, are so infatuated with the spread of perverted and unrestrained human sexuality? By now there should be little doubt as to the biblical answer to that question.

THE UNITED NATIONS OF EPITHUMIA

In February of 2018, *Christianity Today* carried a shocking headline that seemed to lay forth a macabre symbolism of the reality of the global pandemic of sexual perversion. The article's title proclaimed, "UN Aid Workers Carried Out 60,000 Rapes in a Decade." As devastating as the title sounded, the facts of the report were even more dreadful. Following are the gruesome details:

UN staff have carried out thousands of rapes all around the world.... Andrew MacLeod, who was chief of operations at the UN's Emergency Co-ordination Centre, warned that "predatory" abusers used aid jobs to prey on vulnerable girls.

He estimated 60,000 rapes had been carried out by UN staff in the past decade, with 3,300 paedophiles working in the organisation and its agencies. He added there is an "endemic" of cover-ups....

[MacLeod said] "There are tens of thousands of aid workers around the world with paedophile tendencies, but if you wear a Unicef T-shirt nobody will ask what you're up to. You have the impunity to do whatever you want. It is endemic across the aid industry across the world."[210]

Just one year earlier, the United Kingdom's *Independent* ran this headline: "The United Nations Is Turning a Blind Eye to Child Rape Within Its Own Ranks." The article began with this stunning first sentence, "The United Nations is raping children."

The *Independent* article continued:

Earlier this month, UN Secretary General António Guterres in releasing the 2016 UN annual review said that there were 145 cases of sexual exploitation and abuse involving troops and civilians across all UN peace missions in 2016 alone. The United Nations Secretary General is talking about his own organisation.

These 145 cases involved 311 victims and even the UN recognises that this is the tip of the iceberg. Many of the victims, by the UN's own admission, are children.

UN Peacekeepers and staff raping children is not a right-wing conspiracy or fake news, it is admitted by the UN itself.[211]

These articles are painfully difficult to read. And this news is from the same global institution that has charged itself with being the world's "trusted" advocate for the safety of abused and exploited women and children throughout the world. It seems the abject hypocrisy and the cavernous depths of evil associated with the Garden's foundational sin of *epithumia* are without boundaries—and they are globally epidemic.

Had you reviewed those particular articles before reading this book, you might have been tempted to ask something along the lines of, "Dear

Lord, where and when did this unthinkable worldwide evil implant itself in the heart of humanity?"

But now you don't have to ask that question, because you know the answer. However, we can be assured the Word of God promises there is a day of divine reckoning on its way (Romans 1:18–32; 2 Peter 3:7).

A SPECIAL SIN

The bottom line is this: If there is really such a thing as a gateway drug, then *epithumia* is the gateway sin.

As it turns out then, there actually is a "special" sin that is responsible for more overall devastation upon humanity than any other depravity. The Word of God has been telling us this truth for eons. That special category of depravity is the sin of defiling *epithumia*. And, God's Word says this sin is particularly *chalal*. The Bible also proclaims that immersion in that particular iniquity eventually results in a depraved mind and a profusely deplorable culture. The historical facts and current statistics reinforce this truth. *Who knew?*

Consider again the question we asked near the beginning of this chapter. If sexual perversion is so closely aligned with the last depth of evil one can reach, then what about the Garden sin? If it is not somehow associated with this class of sin, then the New Testament declarations about the consequences of this depravity and the commentary agreements on the subject are incorrect.

I have a feeling, though, that neither the Scripture nor the scholars are mistaken in this matter. *What say you?*

At this point in our study, you might still have a few questions, or even some objections, concerning the ground we have covered thus far. Don't worry, so do others. So, let's take some time and address these concerns.

But be prepared. As we answer them, get ready for even more biblical bombshells of evidence to be unearthed regarding the cosmic crime of the ages.

PART THREE

THE OBJECTIONS

The first to present his case seems right,
till another comes forward and questions him.
~Proverbs 18:17, ESV

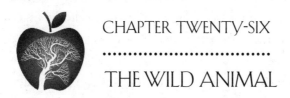

CHAPTER TWENTY-SIX

....

THE WILD ANIMAL

You were in Eden, the garden of God.

~Ezekiel 28:13

If you haven't studied the Garden sin in its fullest manner, as we're doing here, then what we have seen thus far can be pretty shocking. I warned you to expect the unexpected, didn't I? So, let's now get some answers to the most frequently asked questions.

THE CUNNING ANIMAL

We'll start with this one. How can the serpent of Genesis 3 be Satan himself, when the text plainly says it is an extremely cunning member of the animal kingdom—a mere wild animal?

> Now the serpent was more crafty than any of the wild animals the Lord God had made. (Genesis 3:1)

The word translated "wild animals" in this version is the focal point of the argument. The term, in the Hebrew language, is Strong's #2416, *chay*.

In addition to being translated in the way we find it in this passage, that Hebrew word can also denote any "living thing or creature." Indeed, the word can also mean a congregation, a multitude, or a troop. It can, as well, simply mean *life itself*—the life that is in any living thing, human or animal.[212]

In fact, the *Brown-Driver-Briggs* Hebrew lexicon lists numerous passages in the Old Testament where the word *chay* applies solely to humankind, not to animals at all, much less *wild animals*.[213]

Have a look at a few examples (with emphasis added) of how *chay* is used in very close proximity to the passage in Genesis 3:1.

> Then the LORD God formed man of dust from the ground, and breathed into his nostrils the breath of life; and man became a *living being* [*chay*]. (Genesis 2:7)

> In the middle of the garden were the tree of *life* [*chay*] and the tree of the knowledge of good and evil. (Genesis 2:9)

> Adam named his wife Eve, because she would become the mother of all the *living* [*chay*]. (Genesis 3:20)

> I am going to bring floodwaters on the earth to destroy *all life* [*chay*] under the heavens, *every creature that has the breath of life* [*chay*] in it. Everything [man and beast] on earth will perish. (Genesis 6:17)

> But while [Abraham] was still *living* [*chay*], he gave gifts to the sons of his concubines and sent them away from his son Isaac to the land of the east. (Genesis 25:6)

Since we know God declared that Satan was in the Garden as a guardian cherub (Ezekiel 28:14), we now understand that the metaphor of a serpent being called a "wild animal" is just that—*a mere metaphor*. The word *chay* is the perfect Hebrew word to use, because it applies to both the metaphorical serpent as well as the literal living and created being of Satan—the cherub. Satan certainly was a part of "all the *chay*" God had created.

Therefore, Genesis 3:1 could be translated, just as correctly, as something like: "Now *nachash* was the most intelligent, cunning, and astute of any of the *intelligent living beings* that God had ever made."

To illustrate the scholarly attestation of the unnecessary insistence upon a literal interpretation of Genesis 3:1, observe the commentary of *McLaren's Expositions*:

> *The temptation had a personal source.* There are *beings who desire to draw men away from God.* The *serpent*, by its poison and its loathly form, is the *natural symbol* of such an *enemy of man*. The insinuating slyness of the suggestions of evil *is like* the sinuous gliding of the snake, and *truly represents* the process by which temptation found its way into the hearts of the first pair, and of all their descendants.[214] (Emphasis added)

Though the authors of the *Jamieson-Fausset-Brown Bible Commentary (JFB)* fervently desire to make the serpent a literal beast that Satan somehow inhabited, the commentators do ultimately have to concede:

> Though Moses makes no mention of this wicked spirit [Satan]— giving only the history of the visible world—yet in the fuller discoveries of the Gospel, it is distinctly intimated that Satan [and not a literal animal] was the author of the plot (Joh[n] 8:44; 2 Co[rinthians] 11:3; 1 Jo[hn] 3:8; 1 Tim[othy] 2:14; Re[velation] 20:2).[215] (Brackets added)

The *fuller revelation* of the New Testament is clear. Satan himself was the author of the crime, rather than a mystical talking wild reptile. We simply must translate the Garden iniquity through the lens of the most complete revelation upon the matter.

By the way, Satan, the guardian cherub who was in the Garden, was indeed the smartest of all the *living things* (*chay*) God had ever created:

> You were the *seal of perfection, full of wisdom* and perfect in beauty. You were in Eden, the garden of God. (Ezekiel 28:12–13, emphasis added)

THE CURSE

Here's another good question directly connected to the *wild animal* problem. Why did God tell Satan he would crawl on his belly and "eat dust" all the days of his life?

> Cursed are you above all livestock and all wild animals! You will crawl on your belly and you will eat dust all the days of your life. (Genesis 3:14)

By now the answer should be apparent: The serpent metaphor simply continues. It's as plain as that. Satan is cursed above every living being and every living thing because he is utterly responsible for initiating the fall of humanity. He is an intelligent and accountable agent, not a mere wild beast.

The metaphorical phrases "eating dust" and "crawling on your belly" speak of Satan's horrific fall from his previously exalted position. He will be reduced to ashes. He will be destroyed. He will be cast down to the earth—into the dust of creation itself.

Scripture includes this same metaphorical imagery in other places. One example is found in the book of Micah, where the unbelieving nations are said to suffer the "curse" of licking the dust "like a serpent":

Nations will see and be ashamed, deprived of all their power.
They will put their hands over their mouths and their ears will
become deaf. They will lick dust like a snake, like creatures that
crawl on the ground. (Micah 7:16–17)

The Word of God bears out the dreadful sentence upon Satan,
as reflected in several other passages as well. For his Garden treachery,
Satan would be humbled, humiliated, and utterly defeated. See if you
detect shades of this symbolic "eating dust" and "crawling on your belly"
within these passages:

- "You have been cast down to the earth, you who once laid low
  the nations!" (Isaiah 14:12).
- "But you are brought down to the realm of the dead, to the
  depths of the pit" (Isaiah 14:15).
- "So I threw you to the earth; I made a spectacle of you before
  kings" (Ezekiel 28:17).
- "I reduced you to ashes on the ground in the sight of all who
  were watching" (Ezekiel 28:18).
- "Satan, who leads the whole world astray. He was hurled to the
  earth, and his angels with him" (Revelation 12:9).
- "For the accuser of our brothers and sisters, who accuses them
  before our God day and night, has been hurled down" (Revelation 12:10).
- "But woe to the earth and the sea, because the devil has gone
  down to you!" (Revelation 12:12).

The *Keil and Delitzsch Biblical Commentary on the Old Testament*
explains the colorful language of Genesis 3:14 like this:

The presumption of the tempter was punished with the deepest
degradation; and in like manner his sympathy with the woman

was to be turned into eternal hostility.... And its crawling in the dust is a sign [symbol or metaphor] that it will be defeated in its conflict with man.[216] (Bracketed words added)

Gill's Exposition of the Entire Bible also sheds light on the question:

As [crawling on the belly] respects the punishment of the devil, may signify, that he being cast down from the realms of bliss and glory, shall never be able to rise more, and regain his former place and dignity....

[That] this [eating dust] is applicable to Satan, designs the mean and abject condition in which he is, and the sordid *food he lives upon*; no more on angels' food and joys of heaven, but on the base, mean, earthly, and *impure lusts of men*; and this will be his case, condition, and circumstances, forever.[217] (Bracketed words and emphasis added)

Notice also that Gill equates Satan's state of being cast down to the earth and "eating dust" with that of *feeding upon* humanity's *epithumia*. In light of all we have discovered thus far, this is yet one more shocking affirmation of the connection of the Garden fall with Satan and the central element of *epithumia* (2 Peter 1:4).

So, here is the final analysis of the matter. Since the serpent is a mere symbol of the literal person of Satan, *everything* that follows in the text regarding a slithering, cunning, wild animal and the description of crawling on your belly and eating dust is also meant to be taken as symbolism.

However, there are still other objections we must address.

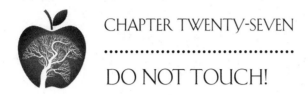

CHAPTER TWENTY-SEVEN

....

DO NOT TOUCH!

You must not eat fruit from the tree that is in
the middle of the garden, and you must not
touch it, or you will die.

~Genesis 3:3

The next objections are often thought to be among the strongest.
However, the exegetical answers reveal even more astounding revelations concerning the facts of the Garden crime scene.

The line of reasoning is usually stated like this:

If the Garden account is indeed a metaphor, then the trees of the Garden are, obviously, also metaphors. If that is so, then the tree of the knowledge of good and evil must have some connection to Satan himself. The metaphorical fruit of that knowledge would then have to be something directly related to the person of Satan.

If that is so, this would mean, most likely, that the other trees were living entities as well—perhaps other divine beings of the Heavenly Host of God.

The question is this: *If eating the fruit had something to do with a profane act, does that necessarily mean Adam and Eve would be permitted to commit profane acts with any other tree of the Garden—just not from the tree of Satan? That's ridiculous! That, in and of itself, sounds utterly vile!*[218]

Stated in that manner, admittedly, the analysis does sound rather sacrilegious. But there is something more here, much more. Read the determining passage again:

"Did God really say, 'You must not eat from any tree in the garden'?"

The woman said to the serpent, "We may eat fruit from the trees in the garden, but God did say, 'You must not eat fruit from the tree that is in the middle of the garden, and *you must not touch it*, or you will die.'"

"You will not certainly die," the serpent said to the woman. (Genesis 3:1–4, emphasis added)

YET AGAIN

Shockingly, the word "touch" in the original Hebrew has as one of its meanings: "A euphemism to 'lie with a woman' or to 'touch a woman' in a sexual manner." The Hebrew word is *naga* (naw-gaw).[219]

Following are a few examples of how *naga* is used in the Old Testament in connection with engaging in profane activity:

- "Can a man walk on hot coals without his feet being scorched? So is he who sleeps with another man's wife; no one who touches (*naga*) her will go unpunished" (Proverbs 6:28–29).
- "Watch the field where the men are harvesting, and follow along after the women. I have told the men not to lay a hand (*naga*) on you. And whenever you are thirsty, go and get a drink from the water jars the men have filled" (Ruth 2:9).

- "Then God said to him in the dream, 'Yes, I know you did this with a clear conscience, and so I have kept you from sinning against me. That is why I did not let you touch (*naga*) her'" (Genesis 20:6).

Even the New Testament employs the same euphemistic use of the word "touch." For example, the King James Version of 1 Corinthians 7:1 states:

Now concerning the things whereof ye wrote unto me: It is good for a man not to touch a woman.

Yet, most of the more recent translations render the verse in a more literal fashion:

Now for the matters you wrote about: "It is good for a man not to have sexual relations with a woman."

The Greek word for "touch" used in this passage is *haptomai*. It can mean literally "to touch," or it can also mean to "know carnally" or to "touch" in a sexual manner. *Thayer's Greek Lexicon* says the Greek word *haptomai* is the equivalent of the Hebrew word *naga*.[220]

What? Yet another word that might suggest some type of sensual profanity took place in the Garden? Yes—yet again. Is this continually appearing phenomenon a mere coincidence? Considering all we've uncovered to this point, it seems highly unlikely.

THE VERY FIRST SIN?

But, what do we make of what Eve told Satan in regard to *touching*?

But God did say, "You must not eat fruit from the tree that is in the middle of the garden, and *you must not touch it*, or you will die." (Genesis 3:3)

Most commentators will mark this statement up as Eve *adding to* God's Word. They will say something like, "Look! Even Eve misquoted God, or exaggerated God's original instruction."

An example of this position is found in the commentary of the *Keil and Delitzsch Biblical Commentary on the Old Testament*:

She was aware of the prohibition, therefore, and fully understood its meaning; but she added, "neither shall ye touch it," and proved by this very exaggeration that it appeared too stringent even to her, and therefore that her love and confidence towards God were already beginning to waver.[221]

However, considering what we have already learned about the Garden account, it doesn't appear this is what happened at all. Also consider that if Eve lied and/or purposely misrepresented God by dishonestly including this remark, then *that* would have technically been the first Garden sin, not eating the fruit. This is a hugely relative point of interpretation.[222]

Matthew Poole's Commentary agrees with the assessment that Eve did not lie, or add to God's command. For if she had done so, this would have been prima fascia evidence that her corruption had already taken place:

For it is not probable that the woman, being not yet corrupted, should knowingly add to God's word, or maliciously insinuate the harshness of the precept.[223]

Apparently, Eve spoke factually. She knew exactly what God had commanded them to do—and *not to do*. Satan never said, "Oh no, God *didn't* say that!" Instead, Satan simply called God a liar for having said it. As a matter of fact, Adam, who was with Eve at the time of this verbal exchange with Satan, did not correct Eve either (Genesis 3:6).

The more literal words of that conversation might have sounded something like: "God did say that we may eat (gain knowledge) from any 'tree' of the Garden we please. Just not from *this one*—in fact, we were especially commanded not to touch (*naga*) that tree! God said we would die if we did that!"

That's when Satan told the vile lie, "You surely shall *not* die."

It seems very likely, then, that eating the fruit of the *other trees* merely represented holy fellowship with the divine host of God's upper family in the "Garden of the gods" and gaining heavenly wisdom and knowledge from that fellowship.

Dr. Charles Haddon Spurgeon spoke of this metaphorical fact in regard to interpreting "eating" of the fruit of Jesus, the tree of life:

> We are right enough, then, in saying that Jesus Christ is a tree of life and we shall so speak of Him in the hope that some may come and pluck of the fruit and eat and live forever![224]

And don't forget our previous discovery that even Jesus used this type of symbolism of "fruit eating" as a way of gaining knowledge from another person—knowledge that is either good or bad. He used that symbolism to warn His followers about false prophets (represented as trees) and the false fruit (claims to divine knowledge) that they bore (Matthew 7:15–20).

So, with His initial instructions to Adam and Eve, in effect, Yahweh was telling them to beware of "that one," because he will tell you of knowledge that is "good," but he will also instruct you in the ways of evil. In fact, he will even call evil good and good evil. And then God added: And whatever you do, don't touch (*naga*) him. Telling Eve not to touch the "tree" would not necessarily mean *in a sexual manner* only—

but, the use of that specific Hebrew word indicates that it certainly could have included that idea as well.

WHY THE COVER-UP?

Here is another related question that many ask: Since a number of other places in the Bible are sexually explicit, why would Genesis 3 need to be couched in a metaphor? Why not just come out and describe what happened? Here is the apparent answer. We were never meant to know the specific act that occurred in the Garden, only that it was profane (*chalal*), it likely involved sensual touching (*naga*), and that the act was centered on some sort of perverted lust (*epithumia*).

Also, by couching the Garden scene within the husk of a metaphor, even children could be taught, without offending their sensibilities, something relevant about the Fall of humanity and why we have plunged into such unthinkable depths of depravity.

The *Expositor's Bible Commentary* addresses the matter like this:

> The very purpose of such representations as are here given [in the Garden of Eden account] is to suit all stages of mental and spiritual advancement. Let the child read it and he will learn what will live in his mind and influence him all his life. Let the devout man who has ranged through all science and history and philosophy come back to this narrative, and he feels that he has here the essential truth regarding the beginnings of man's tragical career upon earth. [225]

But there is yet another important question often asked about the Garden account: Was the tree of the knowledge of good and evil somehow directly connected with Satan himself; is Satan ever actually presented as a "tree" anywhere else in the Bible?

The answer might surprise you.

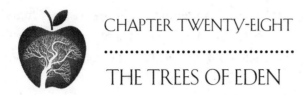

CHAPTER TWENTY-EIGHT

....

THE TREES OF EDEN

Which of the trees of Eden can be compared
with you in splendor and majesty?

~Ezekiel 31:18

Is Satan ever compared to a *tree* anywhere in Scripture? Yes, he is, in several places in both the Old and New Testaments, and even by Jesus Himself.

For our first example, let's scrutinize Ezekiel 31. There we find what appears to be yet another instance of a compound prophecy, similar to the ones found in Isaiah 14 and Ezekiel 28.[226]

In Ezekiel 31, Egypt's Pharaoh is compared to a tree standing in the midst of other trees. This *Pharaoh/tree* exalts itself in a most arrogant and prideful manner. The other trees are defined as nations and/or leaders. In other words, the "trees" of Ezekiel 31 are presented as *symbols* of literal living entities.

THE EDEN TREES

Probably the most shocking feature of Ezekiel 31 is that the entire story is placed in the Garden of Eden—by name. These are not just any trees;

they are said to be the *trees of Eden*. And they are described as being in the "garden of God."

Furthermore, just like the compound-prophecy passages found in Isaiah 14:12–15 and Ezekiel 28:13–17, portions of Ezekiel 31 set forth striking references that match the specific characteristics of Satan, as well as God's ultimate judgment upon that fallen one.

Additionally, when considered side by side, several portions of Isaiah 14, Ezekiel 28, and Ezekiel 31 are practically identical. In fact, in a few cases, the wording is *exactly* the same. Could this simply be an astounding coincidence—or, might it be a divine clue?

Let's begin with a quick review of Isaiah 14 and Ezekiel 28 references to Satan, and how these passages might be related to Ezekiel 31 as well.[227]

ISAIAH 14

The startling declarations of Isaiah 14 begin as a lament upon Babylon. However, the passage eventually portrays Satan's pride, and his ultimate fall and destruction. From *Delitzsch's Biblical Commentary on the Prophecies of Isaiah,* we read:

> A retrospective glance is now cast at the self-deification of the king of Babylon, in which he was the antitype of the devil and the type of Antichrist. The passage transcends anything that can be said of an earthly king and has been understood from earliest times to also refer to Satan's fall as described in Luke 10:18.[228]

EZEKIEL 28

The work of Robert Jamieson, A. R. Fausset, and David Brown, *Commentary Critical and Explanatory on the Whole Bible*, explains Ezekiel 28 and its designation as a compound prophecy, eventually moving from the king of Tyre to the person of Satan:

> The language, though primarily here applied to the king of Tyre, as similar language is to the king of Babylon (Isaiah 14:13, Isaiah 14:14), yet has an ulterior and fuller accomplishment in Satan and his embodiment in Antichrist (Daniel 7:25, Daniel 11:36, Daniel 11:37, 2 Thessalonians 2:4, Revelation 13:6).[229]

THE EZEKIEL 28 AND ISAIAH 14 CONNECTION

The *Benson Commentary* directly relates Ezekiel 28 and Isaiah 14 as possessing the same connection regarding the person of Satan. This will be an important point of consideration as we continue with a deeper study of Ezekiel 31, making those same comparisons.

The following *Benson Commentary* entry is specifically referencing Ezekiel 28:14–15:

> The words allude to the high advancement of Satan in heaven before his fall, where he was placed in one of the highest orders of angels, such as were nearest in attending upon the Divine Majesty."
>
> Whoever compares this place in Ezekiel with the parallel place in Isaiah 14:12, where the downfall of the king of Babylon is foretold in the same prophetic language, will soon perceive that they throw a reciprocal light upon each other, and that the fall of angels is alluded to in both.[230]

The Bible Exposition Commentary: Old Testament also assures us of the important relationship between Ezekiel 28 and Isaiah 14—and especially their connections to being, ultimately, prophecies about Satan:

The use of the word "cherub" (Ezek[iel] 28:4, 16) suggests that we're dealing here with an angelic creature, also the fact that he had been "upon the holy mountain of God" (v. 14). This sounds a great deal like the description in Isa[iah] 14:12 ff. Satan began as an obedient angel but rebelled against God and led a revolt to secure God's throne.[231]

THE EZEKIEL 31 LINK

As in Ezekiel 28 and Isaiah 14, Ezekiel 31 also begins as a warning against an earthly leader and kingdom, specifically Pharaoh of Egypt. The admonition of this passage winds up using descriptive language that closely matches the language of Isaiah 14 and Ezekiel 28.

The larger lesson of all three of these descriptive passages appears to be that Satan, at times, so influences certain kings of the earthly realm that God finally compares the kings to Satan himself, the prince of demons. The prominent message of each is that Satan is the one the kings are actually serving, whether they know it or not (Revelation 16:14).

There can be no doubt that the compound prophecy found in Ezekiel 31 is drawing its symbolism from the Garden of Eden, and its message is also directly related to that of Ezekiel 28 which, in turn, is related to Isaiah 14.

The *Jamieson-Fausset-Brown Bible Commentary* attests to this:

As in the case of Tyre (Ezekiel 28:13), the imagery that is applied to the Assyrian king [in Ezekiel 31], is taken from Eden.[232]

The *Pulpit Commentary* likewise compares Ezekiel 31 to the compound prophecy of Ezekiel 28, and emphasizes the Eden connection:

The cedars in the garden of God. As in Ezekiel 28:13, the thoughts of the prophet [in Ezekiel 31], dwell on the picture of Eden in Genesis 2:8.[233] (Brackets added)

Consider also this commentary from the *Encyclopedia Judaica: The Garden of Eden*:

While Genesis speaks only in general terms about the trees in the garden (2:9), Ezekiel describes them in detail (31:8–9, 18).[234]

There you have it. The *Encyclopedia Judaica* emphatically claims that the trees of Ezekiel 31 are indeed directly related to the "trees" of the Garden of Eden, and that Ezekiel 31 was clearly meant to be interpreted in that light.

I urge you to read the entire chapter of Ezekiel 31 on your own. It is too lengthy to reproduce here, but it should prove to be a real eye-opener, especially considering what we have learned thus far.

However, in the next chapter, we will undertake a verse-by-verse comparison of some of the key features of Ezekiel 31, particularly as they link to Isaiah 14 and Ezekiel 28.

In so doing, you can decide for yourself: Does Ezekiel 31 symbolically refer to Satan as that despicable and prideful "tree" that was in the Garden of Eden? You will probably be quite surprised by what you will discover.

CHAPTER TWENTY-NINE

....

THE DEVIL'S IN THE DETAILS

The very first radical known to man who
rebelled against the establishment and did
it so effectively that he at least won his own
kingdom—Lucifer.

~Saul D. Alinsky, *Rules for Radicals*[235]

Thus far, we have established that Ezekiel 28 and Isaiah 14 are distinctly related in their description of Satan.

We have also shown that Ezekiel 31 is directly connected to Ezekiel 28, specifically regarding the Garden of Eden link. Now, let's take a look at the remarkable similarities in the text of the three passages in question. I have highlighted in bold the key words throughout these comparisons. This exercise should prove to be a real eye-opener.

First, have a look at the following selected verses from Ezekiel 31:

Who can be compared with you in majesty? [The tree] was majestic in beauty, with its spreading boughs.... The cedars in the **garden of God** could not rival it, nor could the junipers equal its boughs...no tree in the **garden of God** could match its beauty. **I made it** beautiful with abundant branches, the envy of all the **trees of Eden** in the **garden of God**.... Which of the **trees of Eden** can be compared with you in **splendor and majesty?** (Ezekiel 31: 2, 7, 8, 9, 18)

Now compare the following words from Ezekiel 28, which we already know are about Satan:

You [Satan] were the seal of perfection, full of wisdom and **perfect in beauty. You were in Eden**, the **garden of God**.... every precious stone adorned you.... Your settings and mountings were made of gold; on the day **you were created** they were prepared.... You were blameless in your ways from **the day you were created**. (Ezekiel 28:12, 13, 15)

Pretty striking comparison, wouldn't you agree?

In both cases we are confronted with a living entity in the Garden of Eden, which is declared to be the very definition of perfect beauty and splendor. Likewise, in both cases, the entity is described as being "made" or "created" by God Himself. And, in Ezekiel 31, this living entity is also presented as a tree.

Let's have a look at another collection of verses from Ezekiel 31 as compared to Isaiah 14:

This is what the Sovereign Lord says: On the day it was **brought down to the realm of the dead** I covered the deep springs with mourning for it.... I made the nations tremble at the sound of its fall when I **brought it down to the realm of the dead to be with those who go down to the pit.** Then all the **trees of Eden,** the choicest and best of Lebanon, the well-watered trees, were consoled in the earth below.... Yet you, too, will be **brought down** with the **trees of Eden to the earth below.** (Ezekiel 31:15–16, 18)

But you [Satan] are brought down to the realm of the dead, to the depths of the pit. (Isaiah 14:15)

Those two passages are almost the same word for word, in regard to the judgment passed upon Satan in Isaiah 14. Concerning this observation, the *Benson Commentary* states: "Isaiah 14:8–16, a passage *exactly parallel* to this [in Ezekiel 31:16]" (brackets added).[236]

The following scholars are also among those who mention the distinctive parallels between Ezekiel 31:16 and Isaiah 14: *Ellicott's Commentary for English Readers, Cambridge Bible for Schools and Colleges, Pulpit Commentary, Jamieson-Fausset-Brown Bible Commentary, Matthew Poole's Commentary, Expositor's Bible Commentary,* and the *Lange Commentary on the Holy Scriptures.*[237]

Also consider the comparisons between several other verses in Ezekiel 31 and Isaiah 14, especially those that speak of the unholy loftiness of Satan's pride and arrogance, and the resulting judgment (emphasis added):

Therefore this is what the Sovereign Lord says: Because the great cedar towered over the thick foliage, and **because it was proud of its height.** (Ezekiel 31:10)

You [Satan] said in your heart, "**I will ascend to the heavens;** I will **raise my throne above the stars** of God; I will sit enthroned on the mount of assembly, **on the utmost heights** of Mount Zaphon. **I will ascend above the tops of the clouds;** I will make myself like the Most High." (Isaiah 14:13–14)

Now, read about Satan's ultimate demise:

Yet you, too, will be **brought down with the trees of Eden to the earth below;** you will lie among the uncircumcised, with those killed by the sword. (Ezekiel 31:18)

But you [Satan] are **brought down to the realm of the dead, to the depths of the pit.** Those who see you stare at you, they ponder your fate. (Isaiah 14:15–16)

There are also the following comparisons regarding Satan's final demise and the eventual loss of his earthly kingdom of the last days:

I cast it [the tree in question] aside, and the most ruthless of foreign nations cut it down and left it. Its boughs fell on the mountains and in all the valleys; its branches lay broken in all the ravines of the land. **All the nations** of the earth **came out** from under its shade **and left it.** (Ezekiel 31:11–12)

I reduced you [Satan] to ashes on the ground **in the sight of all** who were watching. **All the nations** who knew you are **appalled at you;** you have come to a horrible end and **will be no more.** (Ezekiel 28:18–19)

But you [Satan] are **brought down to the realm of the dead,** to the **depths of the pit.** Those who see you stare at you, they ponder your fate: "Is this the man who shook the earth and made kingdoms tremble, **the man who made the world [the nations] a wilderness,** who overthrew its cities and would not let his captives go home?" (Isaiah 14:15–17)

Let's face the facts: There are simply too many similarities between Isaiah 14, Ezekiel 28, and Ezekiel 31 to summarily dismiss Ezekiel 31 (as a number of commentaries do) as having nothing to do with a compound prophecy regarding Satan. All three passages follow a very similar pattern and use, in some cases, identical language. The parallels are undeniable and striking.

THIS IS PHARAOH

To clinch the intended compound message, Ezekiel 31 ends with these words: "This is Pharaoh and all his hordes, declares the Sovereign Lord" (Ezekiel 31:18).

Almost every scholarly commentary presents Pharaoh as *a type of Satan*—especially when commenting upon the Pharaoh of the Exodus event, or others who stood as unmitigated enemies of Israel. Dr. John W. Ritenbaugh, writing in the *Forerunner Commentary*, confirms this theological truth:

> We know that we are not completely free from Satan and this world.... We see this pictured in the children of Israel in the wilderness. They were physically free—that is, they had fled beyond the boundaries of Egypt—but they were still not free from Egypt's influence, which they carried right with them in their minds and displayed in their conduct and attitudes....
>
> Slavery in Egypt, where they faced certain, ignominious death, represents the world, and Pharaoh represents Satan.[238]

In keeping with this symbolic contrast, the phrase "all his hordes," as stated in Ezekiel 3:18, would most likely symbolize the demonic realm of the fallen angels who followed in Satan's blasphemous rebellion (Matthew 25:41; Revelation 12:7–9).

The *Jamieson-Fausset-Brown Bible Commentary* lays out the fact that the entire passage of Ezekiel 31 is ultimately presented in a parabolic sense, with deep and unavoidable connections to the Garden of Eden:

> The lesson on a gigantic scale of Eden-like privileges abused to pride and sin by the Assyrian, as in the case of the first man in Eden, ending in ruin, was to be repeated in Egypt's case.[239]

The Jewish Virtual Library confirms that Ezekiel 31 is indeed intended to give specific and further insight into the Garden narrative of Genesis 3, also connecting Ezekiel 31 with Ezekiel 28 in the comparison:

Ezekiel (28:11–19; 31:8–9, 16–18) in his description introduces new and variant details not present in the Genesis narrative of the Garden of Eden.… While Genesis speaks only in general terms about the trees in the garden (2:9), Ezekiel describes them in detail (31:8–9, 18).[240]

Obviously, this is yet another forthright clue designed to help us understand that Ezekiel 31 truly does morph into a compound prophecy. This revelation uncovers further connections to Eden—and even Satan himself—and especially the potentiality of Satan being represented as a tree.

So, at the very least, all three of these passages—Ezekiel 28, Ezekiel 31, and Isaiah 14—allude to Satan's pride and iniquity, humanity's Fall in Eden, and God's ultimate judgment pronounced upon the whole mess.

The passages examined together give us a transcendent glimpse back through the eons—straight into Eden.

THE SATAN TREE

Now that we have settled the issue of Satan being represented as a "tree" in the Garden of Eden, perhaps our earlier study of the context of Satan's conversation with Eve makes even more sense. Let's restate that conversation by inserting its most probable meaning. The conversation might have gone something like:

Eve replied, "God did say that we may eat (gain knowledge) from any of those divine beings in the Garden we please. Just not from you—

in fact, we were especially commanded not to even *touch* (naga) you! God said we would die if we did that!"

Satan then said, "Well—*God lied!* You will not die if you *naga* me, and He knows it!"

Does this bring the nature of the Garden sin into clearer focus?

But, there's still more.

What we have just finished examining is not the only biblical definition of Satan as a tree. Surprisingly, Jesus Himself also had something to say about that particular symbolism—and in more than one place.

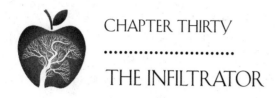

CHAPTER THIRTY

························

THE INFILTRATOR

As he was scattering the seed, some fell along
the path, and the birds came and ate it up.

~Matthew 13:4

It was now late in the afternoon. The gentle waves lapped the shores of Lake Galilee. A huge crowd had already gathered at the beach.

As Jesus looked at the throng of restless people, He reflected upon the events of the day thus far. This Sabbath had been a particularly tough one, beginning earlier that morning. The day's events involved one demonic attack after another.

It all started with Jesus being antagonized by a gaggle of scheming Pharisees. They had charged the disciples with flagrantly breaking the Sabbath laws as they gleaned their meager breakfast from the edges of a nearby grain field.

A little later in the morning, Jesus' group had also been involved in a synagogue service, one that had ultimately spilled out into the streets. In that service, Jesus had healed a man with a withered hand and then used the miraculous event to instruct the congregants about the true meaning of keeping the Sabbath.

Jesus and His entourage were later confronted by a demon-possessed man, whom Jesus delivered in the presence of an astonished crowd. In the meantime, the throngs continued to pour into Jesus' presence—anxious to touch Him, hear Him, and to be near Him.

The Pharisees had become enraged by all of these things, and eventually accused Jesus of working His miracles by the power of Satan himself. And based upon that imagined association, they plotted the demise of this teacher from Galilee.

Later in the afternoon, Jesus continued His ministry from inside a house that was situated at the edge of the lakeside town. Not to be ignored, however, the Pharisees showed up among the people again, hurling their challenges and accusations at Jesus while continually attempting to turn the crowds in their favor. But they lost every attack they leveled against the miracle-working Rabbi. Finally, they left in embarrassed exasperation. Their hearts were further engulfed by abject hatred. They agreed amongst themselves: *The teacher must die.*

So it was that Jesus eventually went out of the house late that afternoon and sat down by the lake. But the people had seen Him as He arrived at the beach, and news of His presence quickly spread. Such large crowds gathered around Him that He finally entered a boat and pushed it back from the shore in order to be able to teach the throngs gathered at the shore. Then Jesus began His message to them: "Behold! A farmer went out to sow his seed…"

After the events that had already transpired on this day, Jesus was determined to let His followers know what they were up against, especially if they were going to be a part of advancing the Kingdom of God, and more especially if they were going to sign up for the grueling task of directly challenging Satan's domain. Yes, Jesus' ministry was indeed advancing with power—but so was Satan's demonic horde. Jesus' disciples needed to be certain of their commitment. They needed to be prepared. This was war.

GROWTH OF THE CHURCH?

The Parable of the Sower, found in Matthew 13, is the first of seven back-to-back "kingdom parables" Jesus told from His boat-pulpit that afternoon.

The first four of these seven parables warn the listeners how God's Kingdom advancement can be infiltrated through the direct work of Satan and the fallen *elohim* that do his bidding. The last three parables focus on the value of the coming Kingdom of Christ on earth, and why the efforts we invest for its sake are worth any price that must be paid.

MORE ADJUSTMENTS

Surprisingly, a number of commentaries claim the first four of these parables are about the growth of the church. While that element certainly is present, the more complete meaning goes much deeper than that. When the Bible is allowed to contextually comment upon itself, that fact becomes abundantly clear. And even more so, now that you understand the dramatic backdrop in which these teachings took place that day. In fact, you will soon see that one of those story-like teachings will directly identify Satan and his kingdom as a "tree" planted in a "garden."

THE SOWER

In the first few verses of the Parable of the Sower, we are given an important contextual clue to help us interpret the focus of study among these parables:

Then [Jesus] told them many things in parables, saying: "A farmer went out to sow his seed. As he was scattering the seed, some fell along the path, *and the birds came* and ate it up. (Matthew 13:3–4, emphasis added)

Notice the words: "and the birds came." Who, or what, did the birds represent in this parable? Well, we don't need a modern-day scholar to illuminate the answer for us. Jesus Himself tells us the meaning, just a few verses later:

> Listen then to what the parable of the sower means: When anyone hears the message about the kingdom and does not understand it, *the evil one comes* [the birds] and snatches away what was sown in their heart. This is the seed sown along the path. (Matthew 13:18–19, emphasis added)

Jesus is clear: The birds represent the work of the evil one. There is no way to adjust His words or their meaning. And, since the word "birds" is plural, we also understand that Jesus is speaking of Satan's demonic horde who serves at his behest.

THE WEEDS

The second story Jesus told that day also has as its theme the work of the enemy. It is the Parable of the Weeds. The first verses state:

> Jesus told them another parable: "The kingdom of heaven is like a man who sowed good seed in his field. But while everyone was sleeping, *his enemy came* and sowed weeds among the wheat, and went away." (Matthew 13:24–25, emphasis added)

Again, Jesus interprets this parable just as He did the first one. Here is what He had to say about the enemy character of the story:

He answered, "The one who sowed the good seed is the Son of Man. The field is the world, and the good seed stands for the people of the kingdom. The weeds are the people of the evil one, and *the enemy who sows them is the devil.* The harvest is the end of the age, and the harvesters are angels." (Matthew 13:37–39, emphasis added)

Jesus could not have been any clearer in the interpretation of His meaning thus far. His teaching that day was going to be specifically about Satan's infiltration into God's Kingdom work. And Jesus was going to tell them yet another parable.

This next parable would also be about Satan—as *the tree.*

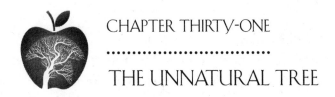

CHAPTER THIRTY-ONE

....

THE UNNATURAL TREE

The birds come and perch in its branches.

~Matthew 13:32

Now comes the third parable.

Since you have seen the context of the events of that day and the parables that came before this one, the following revelation should prove to be obvious.

This parable concerns an unnatural tree and *the birds* that perch in its branches. Remember what Jesus just said about birds in the first parable only a few verses back. Also remember the major theme of His parables thus far is how Satan relentlessly inserts himself into God's heavenly plan to try to thwart it. This was Jesus' main message, because He and His disciples had just lived the truth of it all day long, as witnessed by the crowds.

Just a few breaths after the second parable, Jesus relates the Parable of the Mustard Seed, in which He uses shocking symbolism:

> The kingdom of heaven is like a mustard seed, which a man took and planted in his field. Though it is the smallest of all seeds, yet when it grows, it is the *largest of garden plants* and

becomes a tree, so that *the birds come and perch* in its branches. (Matthew 13:31–32, emphasis added)

Only a handful of verses back, Jesus had defined "the birds" as the *work of Satan*, or Satan's demonic hordes. This time however, instead of picking seeds along the path, the birds are perching within the "branches" of an "unnatural" tree—one that is growing in a "garden." The direct context of the phrase "the birds" is still the same.

Surprisingly, a number of commentaries seem to miss these points entirely, insisting on identifying the parable as being about the amazing growth of the "church," with little or no reference at all to Satan's attempt to thwart the Kingdom work.

However, not all biblical scholars have missed the contextually obvious. The *Wiersbe Bible Commentary* wholeheartedly agrees with our exegetical assessment, connecting this passage directly to Matthew 13:19 as the proper context for interpretation:

> The Jews knew their scriptures and recognized the images that Jesus used. A mustard tree produces a shrub, not a great tree. The Kingdom would be infected with false teaching. And the small seed would grow into an organization [a tree] that would be a home for Satan. The birds represent the evil one (Matthew 13:19).[241]

The *Forerunner Commentary* entry on Matthew 13, written by Dr. Martin G. Collins, also confirms this truth:

> Matthew identifies the birds of the air as "the wicked one" (Matthew 13:4, 19). Mark connects them with "Satan" (Mark 4:4, 15), and Luke links them to "the devil" (Luke 8:5, 12)….
>
> In the parable, Jesus predicts the birds of the air would lodge in the branches. These "birds," demons led by "the prince of

the power of the air" (Ephesians 2:2), have continually tried to infiltrate the church. Upon the unsuspecting early church, Satan moved quickly to implant his agents in it to teach false doctrine while appearing to be true Christians.[242]

Jesus' meaning, in context, is evident. Matthew 13:31–32 declares that the "birds" (demons) perch themselves in the branches of an unnatural "tree" (Satan's growing empire within the realm of the church). Jesus drives home this point: *That particular "Satan tree" began its growth in a "garden."*

The "branches" of the unnatural tree represent all the tentacles of earthly powers and demonic thrones (Ephesians 6:10ff) by which Satan manipulates the kings of the earth (Revelation 16:14). It is in those branches of earthly governments and religious institutions of power that the demonic multitudes will settle. Those branches will come against God's Kingdom work.

THE LEAVEN

The next parable is called the Parable of the Leaven, or the Parable of the Yeast. It is almost as though, with this single sentence, Jesus intended to further clarify the meaning of the mustard seed mystery, as well as the parables that came before it:

He told them still another parable:

The kingdom of heaven is like yeast that a woman took and mixed into about sixty pounds of flour until it worked all through the dough. (Matthew 13:33)

To interpret this passage, we begin by affirming that *every other* place in Scripture where leaven (or yeast) is used symbolically, it always represents evil—specifically, the work of Satan. This is true of the ancient rabbinical writings as well; there simply are no biblical exceptions.

Even in the celebration of the orthodox Passover Feast, we find the tradition of every house purging every scrap of evil leaven. And the bread that was eaten during that feast was prescribed to be unleavened (1 Corinthians 5:8). Jesus Christ is also acknowledged as our "unleavened bread," "the bread of life"—without sin.

The Apostle Paul settles this issue about leaven, sin, Passover, and its connection to Jesus Christ:

> Do you not know that a little leaven leavens the whole lump? Therefore purge out the old leaven, that you may be a new lump, since you truly are unleavened. For indeed Christ, our Passover, was sacrificed for us. Therefore let us keep the feast, not with old leaven, nor with the leaven of malice and wickedness; but with the unleavened bread of sincerity and truth. (1 Corinthians 5:6–8)

The *Cambridge Bible for Schools and Colleges* serves as an example of numerous similar commentaries eager to interpret this parable as being about the supernatural growth of the church, yet finally admitting the indisputable biblical truth we have just illustrated:

> *Except in this one parable*, leaven is used of the working of evil; cp. "A little leaven leaveneth the whole lump," Galatians 5:9; 1 Corinthians 5:6; and "purge out therefore the old leaven," 1 Corinthians 5:7. So, too, in the Rabbinical writings.[243]

How can certain commentaries ignore the fact that every single Scripture verse regarding the subject of leaven depicts the substance as representing evil and sin? How can the same scholars make the gigantic leap that this sentence in Matthew must somehow mean the opposite or be some sort of exception to every other biblical and historical disclosure in the matter? By now, you know the answer—*tweaking*.

THE QUESTION

There is little room for doubt: Both Ezekiel 31 and Jesus (as recorded in Matthew 13:31–32) speak of Satan by symbolically linking him and his diabolical exploits with *a garden* and *a tree*.

However, there are still other very important connections of Satan to a tree. Again, these descriptions also involve what Jesus Himself declared.

CHAPTER THIRTY-TWO

....

A TALE OF THREE TREES

[Jesus said] even so every good tree bringeth
forth good fruit; but a corrupt tree bringeth
forth evil fruit.

~Matthew 7:17, KJV

Chief Crazy Horse was a Native American war leader of the Oglala Lakota tribe during the late 19th century. Crazy Horse joined several famous battles of the American Indian Wars on the northern Great Plains, including serving as one of the war chiefs in the Battle of the Little Bighorn in 1876.

Crazy Horse was also known as a man who often spoke of his many visions of the "other side." As he smoked the Sacred Pipe for the last time at Paha Sapa with Sitting Bull, just four days before he was slain, he announced, "I see a time of Seven Generations when all the colors of mankind will gather under the Sacred Tree of Life and the whole earth will become One Circle again."[244]

Please understand: I certainly am not suggesting that a quote from Crazy Horse should be considered equal revelation to the Word of God. However, biblical truth is biblical truth, regardless of whom the Lord might choose as revelator.

TREE OF LIFE

Of course, the focal point of our study here is the *tree of life*. The teaching of the Scripture is that this special tree is the centerpiece of the restored glory to come at the end of the age. It is this tree, in the midst of the restored garden paradise, that also guarantees the restoration of our divine nature, a promise assured to us through both the Old and New Testaments (Genesis 3:22; 2 Peter 1:4).

The term "tree of life" is found in the New Testament only in the book of Revelation (2:7; 22:2, 14, 19). And, it is found in only one other book of the Old Testament besides Genesis, in Proverbs. In that book, the tree of life represents wisdom and truth—the opposite of the diabolical tree of the "knowledge of good *and* evil" (Proverbs 3:18; 11:30; 13:12; 15:4).

The very first time we hear the term *tree of life* is in the second chapter of Genesis, in the narrative concerning the Garden of Eden.

> And the Lord God made all kinds of trees grow out of the ground—trees that were pleasing to the eye and good for food. In the middle of the garden were *the tree of life* and the *tree of the knowledge of good and evil.* (Genesis 2:9, emphasis added)

In the last chapter of Revelation, the tree of life is presented as a prominent feature in what many scholars describe as the restored Garden of Eden:

> Then the angel showed me the river of the water of life, as clear as crystal, flowing from the throne of God and of the Lamb down the middle of the great street of the city. On each side of the river stood *the tree of life*, bearing twelve crops of fruit, yielding its fruit every month. And the leaves of the tree are for

the healing of the nations. No longer will there be any curse. (Revelation 22:1–3, emphasis added)

Of course, the *curse* spoken of in this passage takes us all the way back to the Garden of Eden. The tree of life was there, but the curse was brought upon humanity because our first parents chose not to eat of that tree—instead, they chose to eat from another tree, the tree of the knowledge of good and evil. Thus the eternal scourge of our fallen sin nature was set into motion.

THE JESUS TREE

The point I wish to make next is a natural one. The ultimate *tree of life* represents Jesus Himself, particularly the cross of Calvary. How could it not?

Compare the following passages and note how they are linked in this matter:

To the one who is victorious, I [Jesus] will give the right to eat from the tree of life, which is in the paradise of God. (Revelation 2:7, bracket added)

This means only Jesus Himself is able to impart the gift of eternal life. Therefore, salvation is directly equated with the tree of life. But there is also this text, bringing the matter even closer to Jesus' personal sacrifice:

Blessed are those *who wash their robes*, that they may have the right to *the tree of life* and may go through the gates into the city. (Revelation 22:14, emphasis added)

This verse asserts that eternal life, through the tree of life, comes only by wearing a "washed robe." How are those robes washed? Revelation 7:14 gives us the answer. Eternal life is only available through the blood of the Lamb, Jesus—who, symbolically, is the "tree of life":

They have *washed their robes* and made them white in the blood of the Lamb. (Revelation 7:14, emphasis added)

The *Adam Clarke Commentary* proclaims that the tree of life symbolism in Revelation 22 is undeniably linked directly to the person and work of Jesus Christ: "This tree, in all its sacramental effects, is secured and restored to man by the incarnation, death, and resurrection of Christ."[245]

It is also well documented that, in the writings and teachings of the early church, the tree of life was pervasively identified with the cross of Jesus Christ.[246] In keeping with this historical truth, the commentary entry on the tree of life at the *Bible Study Tools* website identifies that tree of life with the cross:

Between the Fall in the Garden of Eden and the creation of the new heavens and earth, the cross of Jesus Christ is the tree of life for all who trust in His redeeming work (Acts 5:30; Galatians 3:13; 1 Peter 2:24).[247]

However, *Gill's Exposition of the Entire Bible* is even more direct, proclaiming the tree of life to be none other than Jesus Christ Himself (Revelation 22):

By the tree of life *is meant not* the Gospel, nor godliness, nor eternal life, *nor any other* of the divine Persons, *but Christ*, who is the author of life, natural, spiritual, and eternal.[248] (Emphasis added)

In *Gill's Exposition* of Genesis 2:9, where the Bible's first mention of the tree of life is found, we find this commentary:

[The tree of life] seems to have a further respect, even to eternal life; by Christ; for though it might not be a symbol of that life to Adam in his state of innocence, yet it became so after his fall: hence Christ is sometimes signified by the tree of life, who is not only the author of natural and spiritual life, but the giver of eternal life; the promise of it is in him.[249]

Dr. Charles Haddon Spurgeon agrees:

We believe our Lord Jesus Christ to be none other than that tree of life…. We are right enough, then, in saying that Jesus Christ is a tree of life and we shall so speak of Him in the hope that some may come and pluck of the fruit and eat and live forever![250]

SATAN'S TREE

If the tree of life is a symbol of Jesus and all He has done to affect our salvation, then who, or what, does the tree of the knowledge of good and evil, the exact counterpart to *the tree of life,* represent? Of course, the most exegetically correct answer is that it represents Satan, or at least his diabolical kingdom work. How could it not?

Both "trees" were present in the Garden. The first human couple ultimately chose Satan, the serpent and his deceit-filled promises, over Elohim. It was Elohim who created everything and who walked with Adam and Eve in the Garden—in the literal image and person of Yeshua/Jesus (Colossians 1:16; Hebrews 1:2; John 1:1–3). Again, both *trees* were symbolically represented as being in the Garden. On that point there can be little argument.

So, as it turns out, not only is Satan represented in Scripture as a "tree" growing in a "garden," but we have also discovered that the entirety of God's Word is actually a tale of three trees: the tree of the knowledge of good and evil; the tree of life; and, because of the Garden Fall, the resulting *tree* of the cross of Calvary:

> Christ hath redeemed us from the curse of the law, being made a curse for us: for it is written, Cursed is every one that hangeth on a tree. (Galatians 3:13, KJV)

Because humanity's first parents chose the tree of death, it became necessary for the Creator to place Himself upon the tree of Calvary. In this way, Jesus truly is "the Lamb who was slain from the creation of the world" (Revelation 13:8).

IMPORTANT LINKS

We've come a long way in our overall study thus far.

In the next section, we'll explore a few examples of how, with the contextual knowledge of the Garden of Eden you now possess, other biblical truths begin to explode with revelation before the eyes of your soul.

It is my prayer that you will, on your own, begin to see these kinds of contextual links throughout the rest of your life's study of God's Word.

On occasion, once you see them, you will literally have to pause, take a breath, *and worship.*

PART FOUR

THE CONNECTIONS

For my thoughts are not your thoughts,
nor are your ways, says the Lord.
For as the heavens are higher than the earth,
so are my ways and my thoughts than your thoughts.
~Isaiah 55:8

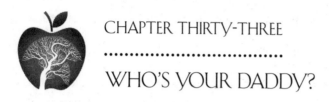

CHAPTER THIRTY-THREE

······································

WHO'S YOUR DADDY?

Listen, child—if you're at a party with a
hundred people and one of them is the devil,
he'll be the last one you'd suspect.

~Dean Koontz, *Deeply Odd*[251]

The following is a bitter truth to admit.

Have you ever considered that the pervasiveness of humanity's sin nature is *100 percent* present throughout every single generation and every single life since the Garden? There simply are no exceptions to the rule. Each of us falls short of the glory of God from birth (Romans 3:23).

The late Ian Fleming, author and former British Navy intelligence officer, is best known for his James Bond spy novels. Through one of his more popular novels, *Casino Royale*, Fleming opines upon the universality of our fallen nature with this astute observation:

There's a Good Book about goodness and how to be good and so forth, but there's no Evil Book about how to be evil and how to be bad. The Devil had no prophets to write his Ten Commandments, and no team of authors to write his biography. His case has gone completely by default.... He has no book from which we can learn the nature of evil in all its forms, with parables about evil people, proverbs about evil people, folklore about evil people. All we have is the living example of people.[252]

What's wrong with us?

As Mr. Fleming noted, we don't have to teach anyone *how to sin.* As a matter of fact, we don't even have to teach seemingly innocent little children the ways of evil. No one has to instruct them in matters of disobedience, dishonesty, selfishness, or possessiveness. Rather, we spend most of their young lives attempting to teach them how to be respectful, honest, dependable, and sharing, and how *not* to take what does not belong to them. Even with our best efforts, our instruction often falls short as they battle, for the rest of their lives, with their own sin nature.

Think of it. There are more than seven billion people on the planet, and not one of us can consistently keep ten little rules given by our Creator. Even if we don't violate them literally and physically, we continually break them mentally and spiritually (Matthew 5:17–48). What are the statistical chances that not one in seven billion people can live without breaking one of those rules? Suffice it to say, something is terribly wrong with us, *all of us.*

But, how can this be?

OUT OF THE DARKNESS

Exactly what "nature" did we inherit through the iniquity of that horrible day in the Garden? We inherited the very nature of Satan himself. In fact, all of humanity is in the same boat—unless, of course, one has "come over" from the dark side to the side of *the Light* (John 8:12).

Yeshua Himself made this fact clear through a striking passage of scriptural revelation:

Jesus said to them, "If God were your Father, you would love me, for I have come here from God. I have not come on my own; God sent me. Why is my language not clear to you? Because you are unable to hear what I say. You belong to your father, the devil, and you want to carry out your father's desires [*epithumia*].

He was a murderer from the beginning, not holding to the truth, for there is no truth in him. When he lies, he speaks his native language, for he is a liar and the father of lies. Yet because I tell the truth, you do not believe me! Can any of you prove me guilty of sin? If I am telling the truth, why don't you believe me? Whoever belongs to God hears what God says. The reason you do not hear is that you do not belong to God. (John 8:42–47)

Jesus was speaking of the *sin nature* we inherited from the Garden Fall. That nature is spiritual, it is universal, and it is thoroughly corruptive.

We have all sinned and fallen short of the glory of God (Romans 3:23). And the wages of that sin, apart from salvation in Jesus, is death— *for us all* (Romans 6:23). This truth is central to the premise of the Gospel message.

Commenting on God's pronouncement of judgment upon Satan in the Garden of Eden, the *Benson Commentary* says of Genesis 3:15:

All carnal and wicked men, who, in reference to this text, are called the children and seed of Satan.... But also, secondly, all the members of Christ, all believers and holy men, are here intended, who are the seed of Christ and the implacable enemies of the devil and his works, and who overcome him by Christ's merit and power.[253]

Way back in the Garden, Yahweh asserted that we are all under the moral "fathership" of Satan, the one who is the father of death.

John 8 is not the only place Jesus is recorded as asserting this universal truth:

> The field is the world; the good seed are the children of the kingdom; but the tares are the children of the wicked one. (Matthew 13:38, KJV)

Jesus' words are clear: you are either a child of the Kingdom, through Jesus Christ alone, or a child of Satan and this fallen world system. These are the only types of humans on this planet, it's as simple as that.

> Woe to you, teachers of the law and Pharisees, you hypocrites! You travel over land and sea to win a single convert, and when you have succeeded, you make them twice as much a child of hell as you are. (Matthew 23:15)

In Matthew 23, Jesus' immediate audience was the Pharisees. However, they characterize the lost condition of humanity in general. They fancied themselves to be "saved" by their own righteousness, but in reality they were still infested with humanity's fallen sin nature. They refused to submit their lives to Jesus Christ as Lord; therefore, Yeshua told them they were still Satan's children.

JOHN'S CONCURRENCE

The apostle John further clarified the matter for us, as if to make certain there would be no mistaking Jesus' plain meaning of this great doctrinal truth:

> The one who does what is sinful is of the devil, because the devil has been sinning from the beginning. The reason the Son of

God appeared was to destroy the devil's work. This is how we know who the children of God are and who the children of the devil are: Anyone who does not do what is right is not God's child, nor is anyone who does not love their brother and sister. (1 John 3:8–10)

The classical scholars offer supporting commentary concerning the passage in John 8. Take a look at a few examples.

Bengel's Gnomen:

Thus here the devil is said to be both a liar himself and father of every liar. For the opposition is clear between God and the devil, and between the sons of God and the sons of the devil. The man who is a liar, is a son of the devil.[254]

The Pulpit Commentary:

Our Lord repudiated [the Pharisee's claim of God's fatherhood in their lives] in this terrible language.... I tell you plainly that you are from, you are manifesting the very essence and substance of, the father who is the prime enemy of God and man.[255]

Meyer's New Testament Commentary:

The conscious will of the child of the devil is to accomplish that after which its father, whose organ it is, lusts. This is rooted in the similarity of their moral nature.[256]

Jamieson-Fausset-Brown Bible Commentary:

It is quite impossible to suppose an accommodation to Jewish views, or a metaphorical form of speech, in so solemn an assertion as this.... The lusts of your father—his impure, malignant, ungodly propensities, inclinations, desires—Ye will do—are willing to do; not of any blind necessity of nature, but of pure natural inclination.[257]

PAUL'S AGREEMENT

The Apostle Paul also emphasizes the great truth we are examining: either God is our Father, or Satan is our father; there is no middle ground. Also note, once again, the use of the word *epithumia* in Paul's attestation of this important spiritual fact:

> And you hath he quickened, who were dead in trespasses and sins; Wherein in time past ye walked according to the course of this world, according to the prince of the power of the air, the spirit that now worketh in the children of disobedience: Among whom also we all had our conversation in times past in *the lusts of our flesh, fulfilling the desires of the flesh* [*epithumia*] and of the mind; and were by nature the children of wrath, even as others. (Ephesians 2:1–3, KJV, emphasis and brackets added)

The *Benson Commentary* on Ephesians 2:3 stresses that we come into this world with Satan as our "father"—because we possess his nature, even at birth:

> And were by nature—That is, in our natural state, or by reason of our natural inclination to all sorts of evil, and this even from our birth; children of wrath—having the wrath of God abiding on us. This expression, *by nature*, occurs also in Galatians 4:8; Romans 2:14; and thrice in [Romans] chap[ter] 11.[258]

Since these great doctrinal truths appear to be so obvious, then what can we do about it? What options do we have?

That's a great question! Turn the page...

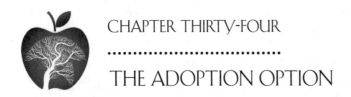

CHAPTER THIRTY-FOUR

....

THE ADOPTION OPTION

The Spirit you received brought about your
adoption to sonship.

~Romans 8:15

The Bible is clear: We possess Satan's fallen nature within us from the moment we arrive to this life. It's in our DNA, either physically or spiritually—or both. That corrupt condition is under eternal judgment, unless we are born again through Jesus Christ, and are thus adopted into the true family of God.

- "Jesus answered, 'Truly, truly, I say to you, unless one is born of water and the Spirit he cannot enter into the kingdom of God'" (John 3:5, ESV).
- "Therefore if anyone is in Christ, he is a new creature; the old things passed away; behold, new things have come" (2 Corinthians 5:17, ESV).
- "For you are all sons of God through faith in Christ Jesus" (Galatians 3:26).
- "That which is born of the flesh is flesh, and that which is born of the Spirit is spirit" (John 3:6, ESV).

- "God decided in advance to adopt us into his own family by bringing us to himself through Jesus Christ. This is what he wanted to do, and it gave him great pleasure" (Ephesians 1:5, NLT).
- "The Spirit you received brought about your adoption to sonship. And by him we cry, 'Abba, Father.' The Spirit himself testifies with our spirit that we are God's children" (Romans 8:15–16, ESV).

Regarding the understanding of being "adopted" as children of God, as stated in Romans 8:15, *Meyer's New Testament Commentary* states:

[Adoption to sonship] does not represent believers as children of God by birth, but as those who by God's grace (Ephesians 1:5–8) have been assumed into the place of children.[259]

Gill's Exposition of the Scriptures further clarifies the point:

Men in a state of nature are under a spirit of bondage to the lusts of the flesh; by these they are captivated and enslaved, and the consequence of it is a fearful apprehension, when convicted, of death, judgment, and wrath to come. They are in slavery to the god of this world, who leads them captive, and by injecting into them fears of death, are subject to bondage…adoption makes men the children of God.[260]

The matter is settled. Only through Christ do we have access to the eternal Kingdom of God (John 14:6; Acts 4:12; John 3:16). The Garden choice belonged to Adam and Eve. The choice for God's offer of divine deliverance through Jesus Christ is ours alone.

PERSPECTIVE

Also, consider the fact that those famous Ten Commandments (Exodus 20:1–17)—which no one on the planet seems to be able to keep—are entirely reasonable considerations. So why do we still have such difficulty with them?

Think about it. They are as simple as this: 1) Don't worship other *elohim*; 2) Don't build idols to any of the fallen *elohim* in an attempt to summon their presence and power; 3) Do not misuse the LORD's name; 4) Do not neglect to worship Him (thank and honor Him) for all that He has done; in other words—honor the Sabbath rest; He has established it for your sake (Mark 2:23–27; Hebrews 4).

Those are the first four commandments. The vast majority of the planet, refusing to come to Jesus Christ as Lord, breaks all four…every day.

The last six of the commandments speak directly to our day-to-day, personal relationships: 5) Do not dishonor your parents. In so doing, one is also dishonoring the God-ordained institutions of marriage and family; 6) Do not murder; 7) Do not be unfaithful to your spouse; 8) Do not steal; 9) Do not participate in slander and false witness; 10) Do not enviously desire something that someone else possesses.

The religious elite of Jesus' day, in an attempt to trap Him, inquired about God's commandments and which of them was the greatest. You probably remember Jesus' answer:

> Jesus replied: "Love the Lord your God with all your heart and with all your soul and with all your mind." This is the first and greatest commandment. And the second is like it: "Love your neighbor as yourself." **All the Law and the Prophets hang on these two commandments.** (Matthew 22:37–40, emphasis added)

Gee. Just how difficult could it be to simply remain faithful, truthful, trustworthy, and honoring to our Creator—and to be good and decent to our family, as well as to our fellow human beings? Apparently, *it's impossible.*

Not one of us has ever done it throughout the entirety of human history.

So, what does this fact have to do with the Garden of Eden?

Get ready for yet another shocking discovery.

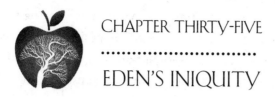

CHAPTER THIRTY-FIVE

....

EDEN'S INIQUITY

They are no longer to slaughter their sacrifices
to the goat demons, with whom they have
been committing prostitution. This will be
a perpetual statute for you throughout your
generations.

~Leviticus 17:7, ISV

In October 2015, under an order from the Oklahoma Supreme Court, a large crane was used during the night to remove a massive monument of the Bible's Ten Commandments from the grounds of the Oklahoma State Capitol. The Satanist-friendly website *Jezebel* lamented, "Tragically, this also means that the Satanic Temple probably won't be able to place their own competing monument beside it."[261]

What was the *competing monument* the Satanists had planned for the capitol grounds? None other than a statue of Baphomet, the horned goat-man idol image (Leviticus 17:7, ESV) known globally as the most recognized symbol of satanic worship.[262]

The Baphomet monument, sculpted in anticipation of its display, was comprised of a *stripped-to-the-waist goat-man god figure* sitting upon his throne, flanked by a little girl on one side and a little boy on the other, gazing adoringly upon Baphomet's half-naked figure.

However, by June 2017, the bordering state of Arkansas passed a law permitting a six-foot-tall Ten Commandments monument to be installed outside the Arkansas Capitol. In reaction to that news, the Satanic Temple immediately promoted the installation of a statue of the goat-headed deity Baphomet as well—right next to the Ten Commandments. That effort was ultimately upset when Arkansas passed a law requiring legislative sanction before the state commission would consider another monument proposal.[263]

Here's the question of point regarding the preceding examples. What is Satan's infatuation with having a symbol of his graven image erected beside monuments of the Ten Commandments? Trust me, it's a much deeper matter than you might imagine.

THE CRUX OF EDEN'S INIQUITY

Humanity simply cannot be 100 percent obedient to those ten seemingly common-sense instructions. Yet, they somehow appear to be the very definition of our inherent sin nature. Why would this fact be so true—and so universal?

Consider that each of the Ten Commandments was violated by Satan on that fateful day in Eden's Garden. *All ten*. This is where the ultimate iniquity began. This is where Satan became humanity's "father":

1. Satan demanded that Adam and Eve revere him—*not God.*
2. Satan insisted *he* would be their "leader, instructor, deliverer, and savior"—*their idol.* He desired to be the adored focus of their attention from that day forward.
3. Satan took God's name in vain: *Did God really say? God knew that in the day you ate of it, you would be like the gods!* Satan flippantly tossed the name of God around as though somehow he was equal to Yahweh.

4. Satan profaned God's creation and His eternal plan for it. We are to honor the Sabbath because this is the day upon which Yahweh declared that creation was "very good." God called this day *holy*. Satan's rebellion declared, "This is not a *special* thing at all."[264]

5. Considering what we have learned about the Garden sin, we understand how the honor of marriage, home, family, childhood, motherhood, and fatherhood were all violated that day. They are still Satan's direct targets of assault.

6. Satan "murdered" all of humanity. He ensured that Adam and Eve would die, and that the curse of death would follow all of us. The actual act of murder among humans was soon to follow, through Cain's murder of Abel. Satan was a murderer from the very beginning, just as Jesus said.

7. At the very least, Satan committed *spiritual adultery* in the Garden, and perhaps some sort of physical adultery as well. So did Adam and Eve, regardless of what "act" took place that day.

This truth was Paul's point in 2 Corinthians 11:1–3, when he made the connection between Eden's sin and Corinth's sin.

The *Expositor's Greek Testament* confirms our assertion:

Carrying on the metaphor of 2 Corinthians 11:2, [Paul] expresses his anxiety lest the Corinthian Church, the Bride of Christ, should be seduced by the devil from her singleness of affection and her purity, and so should be guilty of spiritual fornication.[265]

8. Satan robbed paradise from us. He stole our immediate fellowship away from Yahweh. He robbed us of our "divine nature."

9. Satan called God a liar when he declared: *You surely shall not die*. He defamed God's character by bearing false witness against

the Creator. He also bore false witness against the first couple, claiming they had not clearly understood God's intentions. Everything Satan did in the Garden was predicated upon deceit and false witness. He was a liar from the very beginning, just as Jesus claimed.

10. And, of course, the entire quagmire of filth associated with the breaking of the first nine commandments was brought about because of one thing: *Satan coveted what was not his.* He was prideful, arrogant, and jealous. He determined in his heart that he, and he alone, would have the creation of "Eden" for himself.

There you have it. All ten commandments were profaned on that day. Everything Satan did was *chalal.* And, every bit of it was rooted in *epithumia.*

This is exactly what God told us in Ezekiel 28, and it is exactly what John, Peter, and Paul told us in their New Testament attestations about Eden's iniquity.

Even though the Ten Commandments had not yet been given to the people of Israel, Satan already knew them, and so did Adam and Eve:

Indeed, when Gentiles, who do not have the law, do by nature things required by the law, they are a law for themselves, even though they do not have the law. They show that the requirements of the law are written on their hearts, their consciences also bearing witness, and their thoughts sometimes accusing them and at other times even defending them. (Romans 2:14–15)

The *Benson Commentary* expresses the universal truth of Romans 2:14–15. Especially note the highlighted portions:

The law in this context signifies divine revelation…which is also in part discovered by men's natural reason and conscience, influenced by the light and grace of God; on which account it is said to be *written on their hearts....* It is a revelation from God *written originally* on the heart or mind of man.[266]

The knowledge of God's heart had already been written upon the souls of Adam and Eve. The law was a part of their original nature from the very beginning. And the law was previously known by Satan as well. After all, he had come straight from heaven's throne.

Thus the knowledge of right and wrong was held out to humanity's first couple by Satan—through the forbidden fruit. In so doing, he knew that a perverted obedience to him would mark utter disobedience to the Creator.

Today's worldwide evil is rooted in the desecration of the sanctity God originally established in Eden. Satan, like a warlock standing over a black kettle, brewed that original paradise into a bubbling cauldron of profanity and lust. That vile filth continues to burst forth before our eyes every day.

This contextual view of the iniquity of Eden's collapse is a much different picture than that of the more popular children's storybook version of the Garden of Eden, is it not?

Never doubt, Satan hates the monumental and public declaration of the Ten Commandments precisely because they stand as a testimonial of his ultimate and coming judgment.

The Ten Commandments are Satan's indictment papers—and they were written in stone.

Heaven's Holy Court has spoken. Satan's time is short...and he knows it.

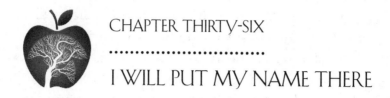

CHAPTER THIRTY-SIX

....

I WILL PUT MY NAME THERE

> But you shall seek the LORD at the place which
> the LORD your God will choose from all your
> tribes, to establish His name there for His
> dwelling, and there you shall come.
>
> ~Deuteronomy 12:5

In the late 1990s, my wife and I stood on the Mount of Olives gazing upon the Holy City of God. What happened next changed an Israeli-born tour guide's life forever.

Pam and I were part of a large international tour group. We were at the spot of the Jerusalem overlook known in Israel as Mitzpe Gandhi. Our tour guide and a former IDF officer held up a map of the Old City of Jerusalem for all to see. He carefully pointed out some of the locations we would visit within the city's walls.

At an appropriate moment in his presentation, I asked if I could show him something amazing. We had already become very good friends, and he graciously obliged.

I took my index finger and slowly began to trace the three significant valleys that were an integral part of the Jerusalem landscape. One of them, the Kidron Valley, flanks the eastern side of the Old City. It was the valley through which Jesus and His disciples crossed, having traversed the Brook Kidron in order to get to the Garden of Gethsemane.

I continued moving my finger down the Kidron Valley until it came just south of the city, and then eventually connected to the Hinnom Valley. That valley traverses the far western side of the city and was the ancient garbage dump area in Jesus' time. The connection of those two valleys form a rough *U* shape that surrounds the greater part of the Old City.

From there, I slowly moved my finger back down the Hinnom Valley until it reached the bottom of the *U*. From that point, I took my finger and began to slowly move it up the Tyropoeon Valley. This valley travels almost due north, beginning at the bottom of the *U*, with a slight "crook" to the left, as it nears the top of its route. As a result of my finger movements, I had traced out what looked similar to the letter *W* in the English language.

I noticed that as I began to trace the path of the Tyropoeon Valley, The guide's face broke into a broad grin. The revelation was bursting forth in front of him.

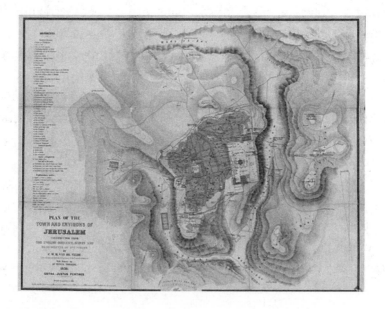

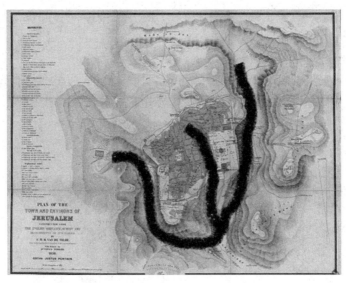

Jerusalem Valleys

"What do you see?" I asked him.

"Oh my!" he exclaimed. "The valleys outline the shape of a *shin*! It is the Hebrew letter that stands for the Name of God! The *Name of God* is on our city! It is literally there!"

"Yes," I said. "And it has always been there, at least from the very first days after Noah's Flood. Perhaps it had been there even from the days of the Garden of Eden itself."

"One thing is certain," I continued, "this city surely is the place where God has put His Name—and in many different ways."

"I have never seen this before," he admitted. "From now on, I will show this to everyone!"

THE SHIN

The letter *shin* (pronounced *sheen*)[267] is the twenty-first letter of the Hebrew alphabet. And, it truly does look similar to the English letter *W*.

The *shin* is the first letter of the Hebrew word *Shaddai* (The Almighty). This is the reason the *shin* came to be used by the ancient Hebrew people as a *one-letter-representation* for the Name of God. That letter designation particularly signifies that God alone is Elohim, *the Almighty.*[268]

Shin: 21st letter of the Hebrew alphabet

THE MEZUZAH

To this day, one will see the *shin* found in many significant places within the orthodox Jewish life, the most significant of which is the Hebrew Scripture box known as the *mezuzah*. The word *mezuzah* means "door-post." This Scripture box is found on the door frames, both inside and outside, of almost every orthodox Jewish home and business. Today, it is found on the doorposts of many Christian homes as well.

Within the *mezuzah* is a scroll of parchment with a certain biblical text written on it. The enclosed text is known in Hebrew as the *Shema Israel*, Hear O Israel! The Scripture portion is largely from Deuteronomy 6:4–9, which first called the ancient Israelites to love their God with all their heart, soul, and strength:

Hear, O Israel: The Lord our God, the Lord is one. Love the Lord your God with all your heart and with all your soul and with all your strength. These commandments that I give you today are to be on your hearts. Impress them on your children. Talk about them when you sit at home and when you walk along the road, when you lie down and when you get up. Tie them as symbols on your hands and bind them on your foreheads. Write them on the doorframes of your houses and on your gates. (Deuteronomy 6:4–9)

Upon the face of almost every mezuzah is the letter *shin,* signifying the home to be separated unto Yahweh, the Almighty.

And the presence of the letter *shin,* carved out by the valleys of Jerusalem, indicates the same designation upon this one special place, out of any other place on the planet.

But, believe it or not, this is just the beginning of this astounding revelation.

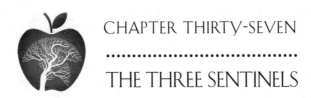

CHAPTER THIRTY-SEVEN

....

THE THREE SENTINELS

Then God said, "Take your son, your only
son, Isaac, whom you love, and go to the
region of Moriah."

~Genesis 22:2

The valleys of Jerusalem are not the only way we see God's name upon the city. Shockingly, the mountains themselves also tell a story pointing to His Name.

Jerusalem, also called the City of David, contains three prominent mountainhead locations. Those mountains are called:

- Mount Zion (*The Western Hill*—sometimes used symbolically in a wider sense for the city of Jerusalem itself, or even the entire land of Israel)
- Mount Moriah (*Upper Eastern Hill*—the location of the Temple Mount)
- Mount Ophel (*Lower Eastern Hill*—the old City of David. Probably where the Wilderness Tabernacle was restored by David before Solomon built the temple on Moriah)[269]

OPHEL

In a messianic prophecy found in the fourth chapter of Micah, we find these words:

> As for you, watchtower of the flock, **stronghold** of Daughter Zion, the former dominion will be restored to you; kingship will come to Daughter Jerusalem. (Micah 4:8, emphasis added)

The word in bold, "stronghold," is an interpretation of the Hebrew word *Ophel*. That Hebrew term means "the hill of: stronghold, fortress, or the tower of strength."[270]

Throughout the Old Testament we find affirmation that Elohim Himself is known as our rock, our fortress, our high tower, and our place of strength. The Person of Yahweh, our Heavenly Father, is represented by the underlying concept of the word *Ophel*.

> Jotham rebuilt the Upper Gate of the temple of the Lord and did extensive work on the wall at the hill of Ophel. (2 Chronicles 27:3; This passage is one of five times that Ophel is mentioned by name in the Scriptures.)

ZION

The term *Zion* is found dozens of times in the Bible, from 2 Samuel to the book of Revelation. Its meaning is deeply spiritual and is used with several different nuances of significance. *Zion* can mean anything from the specific hilltop found in Jerusalem to the city of Jerusalem or, in its fullest spiritual sense, Heaven itself.

The root-verb of Zion (*sawa*) means *to command or charge*. The masculine noun (*siyun*), means the *signpost or monument*. While the feminine noun (*miswa*), means *commandment*. When the feminine form of the noun is preceded by the article *the*—Zion then means *the full code of the law.*[271]

MORIAH

As powerfully as this name's significance relates to the entire biblical message, *Moriah* is found only twice in Scripture. *Moriah* was where Abraham offered up his only son, Isaac, to the Lord:

> Then God said, "Take your son, your only son, Isaac, whom you love, and go to the region of Moriah. Sacrifice him there as a burnt offering on one of the mountains I will tell you about." (Genesis 22:2)

> *Moriah* was also where Solomon was led of the Lord to build the Temple:

> Then Solomon began to build the temple of the Lord in Jerusalem on Mount Moriah, where the Lord had appeared to his father David. (2 Chronicles 3:1)

Not only is the word *Moriah* used as the proper noun for the location of a specific mountaintop, it also comes from the root of two Hebrew words that together mean "to be seen of Yahweh."[272]

The root-verb of Moriah means *to see* or *to look at*. It can also mean to "to intently consider." Additionally, the many scriptural references of the Lord, or an angel, *appearing* upon the earth use this same verb. In this context, the verb form of Moriah is used in the sense of "becoming visible or understandable."[273]

In other words, *Moriah* often means "God sees" or "to see God."

THE MOUNTAINS DECLARE

The implications of what we have learned thus far are astounding. As the tracing of the valleys that surround and bisect the city of Jerusalem literally declare the Name of God, so do the mountaintops of the city.

Mt. Ophel can represent the biblical characterization of God the Father; God is our strong tower, He is our fortress, and He is our strength (Psalm 18:2; Psalm 46:7, 11).

Mt. Zion can easily characterize the Holy Spirit of God, who is the *mark* or the *monument* signifying that we belong to the Lord (Ephesians 1:13). And the Holy Spirit is the one that Yahweh uses to write the *commands* of God's law and word upon our hearts (Hebrews 8:10; 10:16; 2 Corinthians 3:3; Romans 2:15).

Mt. Moriah is obviously the very place where Abraham "saw God," and was, at the same time, "seen of God." Abraham proclaimed that "God will provide himself a lamb" (Genesis 22:14, KJV). And "In the mount of the LORD it shall be seen" (Genesis 22:14, KJV).

Moriah is also where the Temple was finally erected by King Solomon. There the people of God "met" with Him—they "saw Him," and He "saw them."

But most importantly, it was on Moriah, just outside the gates of Jerusalem, within a stone's throw of the Temple, where Jesus was crucified. On Calvary's cross, through the eyes of Jesus, we were "seen of God." And, it was on that cross, in the Person of Jesus, that the world "saw God" (Zechariah 12:10).

Think of it! One mountain comprising three different "hills" or "heads"—Ophel, Zion, and Moriah. One place that is actually three places. *The three that are the one.* All three speak something significant about the totality of the Name of God. And all three places make up the city of Jerusalem.

Surely the ancient Hebrews would never have dreamed of giving even a veiled reference to what we now know as the concept of the Trinity by using those names. That thought is not even a human possibility. Yet, apparently, the Holy Spirit put it upon the hearts of men to give the mountain heads, upon which the City of God was built, those particularly significant names, the very names by which they are known to this day.

Thus, though these amazing connections could not have been planned in the minds of mortal men, they obviously *were* planned at the throne of God.

SILENCE THEM!

On the first day of the last week of Jesus' life, He rode into Jerusalem upon the back of a donkey's colt, thus fulfilling yet another prophecy concerning the coming of the true Messiah (Zechariah 9:9; Matthew 21:5).

Before that week was over, in the place where Elohim had put His name, Jesus would fulfill many more messianic prophecies. The people lined the streets by the thousands. They shouted words of praise and worship. They declared Jesus to be the "King" who was finally among them, the One who would come "in the name of the Lord"—a distinctly messianic identification. They waved palm branches and laid their cloaks on the road in the path of the donkey. In other words, they gave Him the reception of an arriving sovereign.

Among the throngs of the common people were also the religious elite scattered throughout the crowd like leaven in a batch of dough.

They had self-righteous jealousy and murder in their hearts. Soon, Satan would oblige their dark thoughts, for he was still their father.

The branches of the diabolical tree of Satan were filled with the *birds of the air*. The father of death, the murderer from the beginning, would soon pull the strings of his willing little bird-puppets, and they would scatter about to do his bidding.

As [Jesus] went along, people spread their cloaks on the road. When he came near the place where the road goes down the Mount of Olives, the whole crowd of disciples began joyfully to praise God in loud voices for all the miracles they had seen:

"Blessed is the king who comes in the name of the Lord!"

"Peace in heaven and glory in the highest!"

Some of the Pharisees in the crowd said to Jesus, "Teacher, rebuke your disciples!"

"I tell you," he replied, "If they keep quiet, the stones will cry out." (Luke 19:36–40)

In years past, I gave serious contemplation as to how and why Jesus used what seemed to be such apparent hyperbole in His response to the Pharisees. I wondered: *How could the stones actually cry out?*

Now we know it wasn't hyperbole. Because the stones had been crying out for thousands upon thousands of years, carved in the valleys and mountains, and in the rocks that form them. Yahweh told His people, over a thousand years before Jesus arrived there on the back of a donkey: *This is where I have put my Name.*

His Name is there to this day. It's literally carved in stone.

And for a very important reason…

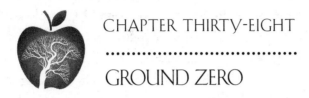

CHAPTER THIRTY-EIGHT

....

GROUND ZERO

Why do the nations conspire and the peoples
plot in vain? The kings of the earth rise up and
the rulers band together against the Lord and
against his anointed.

~Psalm 2:1–2

D r. Jim Sibley is the director of the Pasche Institute of Jewish Studies. He is also a faculty member and editor of *Mishkan*, an international journal dealing with the Gospel and the Jewish people. He has
taught courses related to Judaism and Jewish evangelism as a guest professor at seminaries and Bible colleges across North America. His articles
have been published in Israel, England, and the United States.[274]

Consider the theological opinion of Dr. Sibley:

Scripture equates Satan's presence in the Garden with his presence in Jerusalem." In Ezekiel 28:12–15, Ezekiel describes Lucifer as the power behind the king of Tyre and the description
is given to Satan that he was "in Eden, the garden of God" (v.
13). In verse fourteen God seems to equate Eden with "the holy
mountain of God," which is identified in Scripture as Mount
Moriah, the Temple Mount in Jerusalem.

If Jerusalem is the site of the Garden of Eden, then where Abraham was told to offer Isaac (Gen[esis] 22), [and where] Solomon was told to build the house of the Lord (2 Chron[icles] 3:1), [and] where oceans of blood were spilled in the centuries of sacrifice," is where Jesus, the second Adam—the faithful one—died on the cross. And it's where Jesus will reign as the King of kings and Lord of lords when he comes back to establish his Kingdom.[275]

Following are a couple of other passages also identifying the "holy mountain of the God" as the site of Jerusalem's temple:

In the last days the mountain of the LORD's temple will be established as the highest of the mountains; it will be exalted above the hills, and all nations will stream to it. (Isaiah 2:2)

This is what the LORD says: "I will return to Zion and dwell in Jerusalem. Then Jerusalem will be called the Faithful City, and the mountain of the LORD Almighty will be called the Holy Mountain." (Zechariah 8:3)

In the graduate research project of Dr. Eric Baker titled "The Eschatological Role of the Jerusalem Temple: An Examination of Jewish Writings Dating from 586 BCE to 70 CE," we find the following observation:

The Garden of Eden, the tabernacle, the first Jerusalem temple, the second Jerusalem temple, and Ezekiel's temple vision (Ezek[iel] 40–48) are depicted as places for God to dwell. The Garden of Eden is the garden of God and the place where human and divine first coexisted (at least for a time). This original coexistence has been interpreted as the original dwelling of God.

The first Jerusalem temple and the temple vision of Ezek[iel] 40–48 contain many symbols of creation. The capitals on the pillars at the temple are symbolic of the Garden of Eden, as well as the date palms engraved on the paneling (Ezek[iel] 41:18). The cherubim in the Holy of Holies connect the most holy place to Eden…. In biblical texts, the Jerusalem temple is depicted as a dwelling place of God equivalent to Eden.[276]

Dr. Margaret Barker, author of seventeen books, has developed an approach to biblical studies known as "Temple Theology." Relative to the possibility of the Garden of Eden being in Jerusalem, she writes:

But the temple was also built in accordance with a heavenly plan to represent on earth the garden of God…. The Garden of Eden was the first dry land created in the midst of the primeval waters and so the temple was the centre of the created order.

[It] has often been observed that the Garden of Eden in Israel's tradition replaced the temple of other creation myths, and this is certainly true of the Old Testament in its present form. There is, however, a great deal which suggests that the Garden of Eden and the temple had at one time been one and the same.[277]

PROPHETIC LINKS

In the year 2017–2018, Israel marked its seventieth anniversary since the nation's rebirth. That national resurrection was the fulfillment of a nearly 2,500-year-old prophecy.

However, that same "seventieth year," also happened to be the "fiftieth year" since Israel had reclaimed Jerusalem as a part of its territorial jurisdiction after the Six-Day War of 1967. Most students of biblical prophecy understand the importance of the symbolism of the numbers seventy and fifty as they relate to prophetic interpretation.[278]

Additionally, both 1967 and 2017 happened to be years of Jubilee. The Year of Jubilee was the fiftieth year after a designated seven cycles of seven-year periods known as the *Shemitah* cycle.[279]

It was the Year of Jubilee that God declared to be, among other things, the year in which all property was to revert back to its original owner (Leviticus 25:10–17).

In 1967, the prophetically revenant nation of Israel reclaimed Jerusalem. In 2017, fifty years later, on another Year of Jubilee, the United States of America, under the leadership of President Donald J. Trump, officially declared Jerusalem as home for the US Embassy and the legally recognized capital of Israel.[280] Thus, the last two successive Jubilee years have each resulted in Jerusalem being reattached to Israel as the "rightful owner."

On Wednesday, December 7, President Trump announced from the Diplomatic Reception Room of the White House:

> Today we finally acknowledge the obvious: that Jerusalem is Israel's capital. This is nothing more or less than a recognition of reality. It is also the right thing to do. It's something that has to be done.[281]

With those words, global history was made. Yet once again, the eyes of the world were focused squarely upon Israel—specifically, the city of Jerusalem. An unprecedented prophetic unfurling had just occurred, and we were the heaven-privileged generation to live in the midst of its fulfillment.

GLOBAL PANIC

Of course *the gods behind the thrones* of the earth's ecclesiastical and geo-political powers went absolutely maniacal.

By December 21, 2017, four days before Christmas, the United Nations voted 128-9, with thirty-five countries abstaining, to ignore President Trump's legal recognition of Jerusalem as Israel's capital. The vote signified, at least symbolically, that essentially the entire world stood against the United States and Israel regarding this historical move.[282]

Think of the implications. Jerusalem is the only city on the planet that is the global focal point of the most deeply seeded contention concerning "property rights" among nearly all the nations. It has been so, to one degree or another, for thousands of years.

It appears Jerusalem truly is the spiritual Ground Zero for the coming war of the ages, just as the Bible declares it to be. And if it is, indeed, the original location of the Garden of Eden as well as the heaven-declared location of Yahweh's soon to be restored Eden/Paradise, then why should we be surprised by the demonic outpouring that accompanied Jerusalem's legal declaration as Israel's capital?

As prophecy continues to unfold, the Bible predicts that most of the unveiling will center upon the land of Israel, and particularly the city of Jerusalem, the place where God placed His Name from the beginning and, the place where, more than likely, the original Garden of Eden stood.

Is today's world making a little more sense to you now?

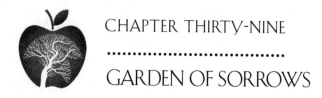

CHAPTER THIRTY-NINE

....

GARDEN OF SORROWS

And being in agony he prayed more earnestly;
and his sweat became like great drops of blood
falling down to the ground.

~Luke 22:44, ESV

In light of all we have discovered thus far, consider this. *What if* the Garden of Gethsemane was the exact location where the original Garden sin took place?

And *what if* Calvary's garden location, as well as the garden tomb of Jesus' resurrection, are all trying to indicate to us the bigger picture of what took place in that holy locale?[283]

Do you find it to be a little more than mere coincidence that Scripture pointedly describes the places of Jesus' crucifixion and burial as being in a "garden," especially in light of the fact that He had just been praying and arrested in yet another area called a garden?[284]

Now in the place where He was crucified there was a garden, and in the garden a new tomb in which no one had yet been laid. (John 19:41)

The *Pulpit Commentary* makes the connection of the Garden of Gethsemane to the Garden of Eden, and the potential direct link of one to the other:

> [John] clearly saw the significance of the resemblance to the "garden" where Christ agonized unto death, and was betrayed with a kiss, and also to the garden where the first Adam fell from the high estate of posse non peccare [*original innocence*].[285] (Brackets added)

FOLLOW THE BREADCRUMBS

Consider the evidence thus far. We have established that Jerusalem, the place where God has always "had His Name," is more than likely the site of the original Garden of Eden. If that is so, then how far of a stretch would it be to consider that an ancient garden orchard known as Gethsemane, just outside the walls of the Temple Mount, on God's Holy Mount of Eden, might not also be the precise location where Satan's original *chalal* and *epithumia* took place?

Wouldn't Gethsemane then be the obvious place where Jesus would chose to do yet another battle with Nachash in heaven's grand design to right every wrong, for the purpose of bringing about the restitution of all things? It certainly seems to be a distinct biblical possibility.

It was in the Garden of Gethsemane where Jesus would kneel, while sweating great drops of blood, and cry out, *"Nevertheless, not my will, but thine!"* This was the opposite declaration of Satan's heart in the original Garden. It was also the opposite attitude displayed by Adam and Eve. Jesus was reversing the curse—in a very specific location of His choosing—and in a very particular garden.

Satan and Eve, along with Adam, declared their mutiny in the Garden of Eden with the words, *"My will!"* Jesus knelt, perhaps in or near the very spot of that rebellion and declared *"Not my will. Your will! Let it be done!"*

What the diabolical cohort of rebels had refused to do in the first Garden, Jesus willingly did in Gethsemane: He obeyed. What the first Adam had lost, the last *Adam* would take back (1 Corinthians 15:45, 47–49). The victory of Jesus' resolve would be our portal of entry into the dimension of the new and restored Garden of Eden. Jesus is the door through which we can enter the renewed Paradise.

> I am the door. If anyone enters by me, he will be saved and will go in and out and find pasture. (John 10:9, ESV)

GETHSEMANE

The word *Gethsemane* means "olive press." It was in Gethsemane where Jesus had the weight of the world's original Garden *chalal* and *epithumia* pressed down upon Him. The punishment that would bring our salvation was laid upon Him—*and only Him.* He was crushed for our iniquities (Isaiah 53:5). That weight crushed Jesus so thoroughly that His sweat literally became mingled with His blood (Luke 22:44).[286]

Think of it. Olive oil was used for anointing. Jesus is called the Christ, *the Anointed One.* Also, the olive tree provides the imagery of Isaiah 11:1, "A shoot will come up from the stump of Jesse; from His roots a Branch will bear fruit." Jesus was the "olive branch" of Isaiah's prophecy.

Furthermore, Paul tells us in Romans 11 that we are "grafted into" Jesus (the olive tree) by faith, to become a part of the church, which is the Body of Christ. And now we find the "olive branch" of God, on His last day of earthly ministry, in the garden of the *Olive Press.* How much clearer could the imagery be?

Without the "first" Adam's sin in the Garden of Eden, there would have been no reason for Jesus to have agonized in the Garden of Gethsemane. And without Eden and Gethsemane, there would be no need for the crucifixion in the garden of Calvary's cross. And without the garden cross, there would have been no need for a resurrection of the "last Adam" from the garden tomb.

The connections are undeniable. And they are astounding.

However, the distinctive link to Jesus' battle in the Garden of Gethsemane to what happened next is almost unthinkable.

Yet, even that event was also a specific requirement of heaven's divine plan—decreed from the throne of God...*from the very beginning.*

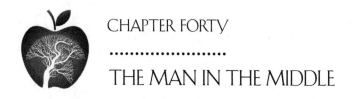

CHAPTER FORTY

....

THE MAN IN THE MIDDLE

14th day of Nissan AD 30
Passover Week
Just outside the gates of Jerusalem—
at *Golgotha*
55°–63° F. 9 am–3 pm.
Cloudy, but growing darker.
~Roman Emperor: Tiberius Caesar—
Dīvī Augustī Fīlius[287]

The crowd scurried through the narrow streets of Jerusalem. They were headed just outside the city gates. There was to be another execution, and they didn't want to miss it.

Three men would suffer animal-like deaths before the eyes of the jeering hordes. The spectacle would take place during Passover week, just when the city increased by several hundred thousand people—Jewish pilgrims fulfilling their religious laws and customs.

One man, just one of the burgeoning throng of nondescript pilgrims, was inexplicably drawn into the heart of the commotion. He didn't know it at the time, but later, he would come to understand that he had witnessed the unfolding of the most significant piece of divine history the planet had ever seen—a prophesied decree from the throne of heaven given before the foundation of the world.

The following is that pilgrim's story…

EYEWITNESS

This is how it happened.

I will never forget that day. Every time I tell the story, it is as if I am back there again—right there in the crowd. I can still see his eyes; those deeply penetrating eyes that pierced through to the depths of my soul…

It seemed the Romans were always executing someone, even during the holy days. So when I heard the commotion, I went along—with the crowd. To be a part of the throng. Just to see. That's all.

Chink – *clinkkkk!* Chink – *clinkkkk!* Chink – *clinkkkk!* I heard the unmistakable reverberations of huge hammers crashing down upon iron spikes.

I had heard those sounds before.

As I approached, it was obvious that the brutal skewers found their targets, ripping through flesh, muscles, sinew, and bone…. Horrific screams pierced the air.

The *patibulum*, horizontal cross-bars, were lifted and fitted into place by Rome's crucifixion squads. Each piece of timber boastfully exhibited their trophies of writhing victims.

Horrid groans continued to emanate from the sufferers as the overwhelming dread of what they were just beginning to face seemed to descend upon them like a tidal wave.

Crucifixion shrieks transmit a very distinct intonation—high-pitched, whimpering squeals, more like the sound of a panicked, wounded animal than a human being. There's no sound on earth like it. A normal person is usually sickened by it. Apparently, the Romans delight in the sound.

It was now the third hour—9 a.m.[288]

The man in the middle had six hours to live.

Now it begins... *Dear God in heaven—have mercy...*

I watched as the three impaled creatures battled for each breath they were able to pilfer into their fiery, throbbing lungs. With their hands spiked to the wings of the crucifix and their feet firmly impaled, one on top of the other, their bodies collapsed under the agonizing pain.

But then their lungs would buckle as well, as the weight of their sagging bodies cut off their ability to breathe. So, they pushed themselves up with their legs—to clear the lungs for another breath. But that gruesome chore was done under the torture of the spike piercing through the top of the feet. It was an impossible situation. But they *had to breathe.* So they pushed. And they writhed. And they pushed... And—*we watched.*

Desperately, they worked for each agonizing gasp. *Up and down. Up and down...* For hours...upon hours...*upon hours...* the spectacle continued.

Panicked gasps. Raspy gurgling. Whimpering. Gagging. Cursing. Crying. Pitiful, pathetic ...mournful pleading. Uncontrollable bodily functions. Completely humiliating. Entirely demoralizing. Less than human. *Gut-wrenching.* Some people laughed, others mocked. I stared in horror—speechless.

The moaning—*the wretched and maddening moaning.* Why does it take so dreadfully long to die? What demented mind invented such a cruel demise?

Please God, let it stop soon...

But it wasn't even close to being finished. Not yet.

Not yet.

Hours to go before the sweet relief of death. *Still many hours.*

The blood thickened as it dribbled down the legs, puddling onto the ground just under the poles. The stench of the hours-ago whipped and mangled human flesh, along with the tang of putrefying blood and other bodily fluids, punctuated the air—violently assaulting my nostrils. The Roman scourging had dutifully done its vile deed. It always does.[289]

And then came the flies. Thousands of demon flies.

With hands pinned to the beams, not even those maddening flying ogres could be shooed away by the pitiful ones on the crosses. The marauding insects descended upon them—invading their nostrils, eyes, ears—looking for a meal.

The birds of the air circled overhead, waiting patiently for their dinner. *Everybody has to eat*—the Roman soldiers were fond of joking at the sight of the flies and vultures. *The circle of life.*

"Father forgive them…they know not what they do."

What? He speaks!

The man in the middle utters a declaration? And he *prays*? The crowd huddled closer to listen…to hear every single word.

The words were uttered through tortured agony, but everyone could hear them. Even the soldiers who had slammed the spikes into his mangled body—they heard them, too.

More cursing. More wailing.

The truth of the matter was that the only cursing and wailing came from the two men on the outside stakes. The man in the middle said very little at all. He never cursed, he did not scream…he only prayed for the forgiveness of his executioners, *and he moaned*—hideous moans—of anguish.

The *horror*. The growing, thick, suffocating, abject horror. Why would anyone look upon such a thing? But we watched anyway. In fact, we gawked. We could not, *would not,* avert our eyes. How could we?

Was this not why we came? *To see? To hear?* Even to ogle?

No one moved.

I didn't move. I was frozen in place, halted in time. What strange force of nature held me there? It was as though I was buried in the earth, up to my waist, yet still in a standing position.

Soldiers dropped to their knees under the crosses. Laughing. Cursing. Scuffling with each other over *something*. What is that?

They threw dice to see who would get the expensive seamless tunic. That particular article of clothing had previously belonged to the man in the middle.[290]

This is odd, I remember thinking. I've read something about this very thing—somewhere. Maybe in the Scriptures?

"They gamble for my clothing…" *Where was that?*[291]

I determined to ask someone about this…later.

The self-important religious rulers, in their gaudy flowing robes, *mocked him.*

"You saved others; save yourself!" They held up their clenched fists as they screamed their taunts. "If you are the Christ, come down off that cross! Surely you can save yourself!" They spat on the ground as they continued their shrieking taunts.

Why was there so much focus on *that one? Why so much scorn?* Why so much dark hatred? Did they say he claimed to be *The Christ?*

It was then the sixth hour, very close to noon.

It had been three long hours since the first spike had been driven.

Up and down. Up and down, they still pumped for each life-sustaining breath. They had no choice. There would be no mercy, no relief. Only a wickedly disrespectful death.

The day faded from deep hues of gloomy gray to an eerie, thickening darkness—ultimately congealing into a dull blackness. What was *this?* Where was the sun? Why did it refuse to shine? *A miracle?* Maybe an omen?

A group attempted to huddle below the one in the middle—but they were forced back by the Roman soldiers. A few women and a couple of men stood at the feet of *that one.* Friends? Family? They sobbed with such anguish. Heartbreaking anguish. With the back of my dusty hand, I quickly pushed the tears from my eyes.

Another word came from the man in the middle.

"Woman—behold your son."

More weeping from the women. They were inconsolable.

One woman—his mother, I was told—was allowed only a brief moment at the foot of the man's cross. She reached up and caressed his feet, as one might comfort an infant, then collapsed into the dust. She was retrieved by her entourage and brought back to the edges of the throng.

Some claimed this man they called Yeshua[292] had actually predicted— even longed for—this day. *Ridiculous.* How could anyone desire such a death? A madman? Surely! What purpose would a "predicted" death serve anyway? Especially *this* kind of death.

Others claimed he had entered the city only a few days earlier in a boisterous procession. The crowds had lined the streets that day shouting that he was their Messiah—the divine Son of God...the son of David.

The divine *Son of God?* A few said so. Silly believers.

Fanatics? Yes. Probably simpletons. Someone was *always* looking for a messiah. But their messiahs never came. They never would. The Romans would simply eliminate the so-called messiahs, one by one.

"Come down now, if you can—*if you dare*—if you really are the Messiah!"

The Messiah? Surely not.

Save himself? Truly doubtful.

I'd never heard of anyone coming down off a Roman cross before. It wasn't going to happen. I was certain of it. Not that day. *Not ever.*

Two thieves and an infamous religious personality. That's who was hanging on the crosses before us. But...why such a crowd...for *these* three pitiful ones? Or, were the multitudes actually gathered just for *the one?*

Apparently, that pious one had come very close to bringing the wrath of Rome down upon all our heads—at least, that's what our rulers told us. What a horror that consequence would have been! If the threat had come to pass, then that could have been *me,* or members of my family, up there on that cross!

I had seen the unspeakable horridness of such a thing on full display lining the Roman roads by the thousands…men, women, children— entire families. Roman cruelty knew no boundaries for those who challenged Tiberius Caesar, *the Divine Son of God.*[293]

Oh well, maybe our rabbis had been right.

Better that one should die instead of the many.[294]

At least that's the way the religious elite had finally convinced most of the crowd to view the necessary execution of the trouble-making teacher, *the man in the middle.* They told us that if he didn't die, then *we* probably would.

What was this now? An argument among the dying? Two thieves slinging accusations, something about how the teacher was perhaps a fraud; those were the words from one of the thieves. But, the other one defended the teacher!

"This man has done no wrong. We deserve what we are getting. This man is innocent! Leave him alone!"

Well—would you look at this! Out of the mouth of a thief! A declaration of innocence on behalf of *someone else.* That's probably a first… especially coming from a Roman crucifix victim.

The repentant thief turned to the man in the middle and mournfully admitted his fate. Yet, he also asked for a favor: "Lord, remember me when you come into your kingdom."

The man in the middle slowly turned his head, looked directly into the eyes of that terrified, dying thief, and smiled. He smiled! *He smiled?*

"I tell you the truth, today you will be with me in paradise," he said. "Today, we will be in the Garden together…just like it was in the beginning." When Jesus used the word "paradise," we Jews knew exactly what He meant. That was merely another expression for the divinely hidden Garden of Eden! [295]

Yeshua looked down again. His eyes scanned the crowd. *He looked at me!* Did he really faintly smile—*at me?*

It was as though he was saying to each of us —and this offer is for you as well—"if you would only believe."

Was I going mad? Imagining things? Imagining that he saw *me?* Imagining that he spoke of paradise, and that on this exact day they would somehow be there...in Eden? How could *he* offer *anyone* paradise? How could he offer us the Garden of Eden?

Some in the crowd were speaking of a resurrection. They claimed Yeshua had promised he would rise from the grave after his crucifixion. *Impossible!* How could such an incredulous feat be accomplished—and by a Galilean carpenter-turned-preacher? Yet...he *had* managed to get himself crucified...just like he said...

Oh well. Getting crucified in this day was not such an impossible feat. But, rising again, from the dead? That miracle just wasn't going to happen. How could it?

Yeshua rasped for another breath, pushing his ever-slumping body upwards to make possible another filling of his lungs.

Maybe one more wonder from the acclaimed miracle worker? Just maybe? Before it's all over? Let us see *just one.*

Surely, after all, if he really could save *others*...

The day was nearing the ninth hour, 3 p.m.

Six. Long. Grueling. Hours. But, the man in the middle only had moments to live.

Between the excruciating, seemingly eternal moments of trying to breathe, the thief, who had been promised paradise, wept uncontrollably.

Yeshua's voice suddenly boomed into the air...startling the crowd.

"Eloi, Eloi, lama sabacthani?"

Listen! *Shhh!* Everyone be quiet!

Did this man just call for Elijah? *Really?*

We watched! We looked to the heavens! Was *this* the spectacle for which the others had gathered? Were some of them really expecting Elijah to split those suffocating clouds? Was this the wonder we had hoped for?

The entire affair had become an odd sight, and was growing more peculiar by the moment.

"I thirst!"

A rag on a stick, offered by Roman soldiers, was sloppily shoved up to the mouth of the one in the middle. A quick sip offered. *Refused.*

Why? Didn't he know they had slipped a bit of painkiller in the wine? Did he *want* to suffer?

Who *was* this man?

Now, when he *did* speak, the crowd came to an immediate hush. It was as though a drum major stood high above us all, directing the rhythmic upsurge followed by the falling of our collective voices.

Things were beginning to make sense to me. The thieves were not the cosmic focus. *He* was. We were there because of *him*—yet his followers were claiming that he was there—on that cross—because of *us!*

Madness! I had not been among those who had passionately cried out for his crucifixion, though some standing right here beside me had done so.

I turned to leave. I had seen enough. I had heard enough. I was not responsible. My conscience began to torture me, convicting me that somehow I had played a part in this mess. *Ridiculous!*

Crack!

The ground rolled under my feet!

I stumbled to my knees, as did almost everyone. It was as though the earth had reached up and grabbed me, pulling me down and shouting the command in my face: *No! Stay right here! I demand it!*

I was going nowhere. The earth had spoken.

Earthquake! Earthquake!

Screaming. Panic. Shrieks. The earth still rolled. Buildings and crucifixes swayed like trees in a tempest. Dogs howled. Animals scampered about.

Then, finally, stillness.

It had passed. An earthquake—yes. Not unusual in Jerusalem. But, why *at that very moment?* How incredibly odd. A sign?

No one uttered a sound. Not the crowd. Not the soldiers. Only the unclean birds circling overhead cried out for their meal… *Hurry! Hurry!*

Soon, rumors ripped through the crowd. Reports emanated from the Temple and spilled into the streets. Announcements were proclaimed that the curtain to the Holy Place had been ripped from top to bottom as a result of the earthquake. Was this true? A sign from heaven? Had Yahweh reached down and ripped it open Himself? Some said so.

What *was it* about this day? An earthquake. The sun refused to shine. Black sky. Shouts of pandemonium coming from the Temple. The Holy Place exposed. The holy day of Passover. Temple sacrifices. A thief promised paradise. A crucified one, refusing to revile his tormentors…refusing to take medicated relief. Crying out to Elijah? Claims of fulfilled prophecies.

Who *was* this man? I had never seen anyone like him. I had never seen a crucifixion—or anything—like this!

Did heaven find this Yeshua to be particularly special? Or did the gods find him to be despicably cursed and rejected?

It had now been a little over six hours since the first spike had been driven, since the first screams had pierced the air.

The time had come for the priests in the temple to slaughter the official Passover lambs. Just then, the temple shofar blasted its startling explosion of haunting reverberations, signifying the beginning of the Passover sacrifices. The trumpet's voice rolled on and on—through the city, over the walls, and across the surrounding hills.[296, 297]

And that's when it happened.

Just then, at that exact moment, from the cross of Yeshua, *another shout!* Louder than all the others. A shout of agony? No. It was more like a shout of victory...

The man in the middle looked up into the black clouds, which seemed to be parting upon his signal. Suddenly a brilliant shaft of light burst through, bathing his face in an ethereal glow.

"Father, into your hands, I commend my spirit!"

"It. Is. Now. Finished!"

At that very moment, he simply stopped breathing.

Just like that, Yeshua dropped his head to his chest and was gone. It was over. It was finished.

But...how could that be? How could he know? How could he order the exact second of his own death? How could he measure the moment of his last breath, his last heartbeat? How could he make it all correspond with the blast of the Passover shofar? Impossible! Utterly impossible!

Unless...could it be? Could it actually be?

But he *did* command his own last breath. I saw it. *We all saw it.* The Romans saw it. Something unnatural was happening there. The air had grown thick with the feel of it.

I had a sense of panic, deep within my chest. Had we done something terribly wrong? *Oh God...would you ever forgive us if we had?* I felt so...*unclean.*

The centurion in charge of that day's execution had been standing guard close to the crosses. He had, in obedience to his orders, witnessed the entire grueling ordeal, having heard everything uttered upon each one of those crucifixion beams. He saw it, too. And he was dumbfounded. Never before had he seen anything like this.

Upon Yeshua's last breath, the centurion removed his helmet.

No one in the crowd or among the soldiers uttered a word.

The dying thief, who had been promised paradise, *wept.*

My eyes welled with tears. I was ashamed.

The centurion slipped to his knees right there under the cross. He reverently looked up at the body of Yeshua and announced eight insightful words destined to be recorded in the deepest annals of history:

Surely this man was the Son of God.[298]

That was when *I knew*.

It had only just begun. The world would never be the same.[299]

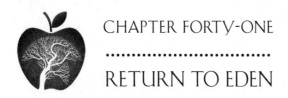

CHAPTER FORTY-ONE

....

RETURN TO EDEN

Do not hold on to me, for I have not yet
ascended to the Father.

-John 20:17

Not long after Jesus exclaimed His last words from the cross, His
body was sealed away in a borrowed tomb.

With permission from Pontius Pilate, Jesus' tortured, mangled
corpse was collected from the crucifixion beam by Nicodemus and
Joseph of Arimathea and interred in Joseph's private garden tomb, not
far from Golgotha. Ironically, Joseph and Nicodemus were powerful,
wealthy, and respected members of the Sanhedrin Council—the same
religious body that had appealed to Rome for Jesus' death.[300]

Also, upon the orders of Pontius Pilate, Roman guards were placed
at the site of the borrowed crypt. The Sanhedrin officials had lobbied
this particular safeguard because of Jesus' well-known claims that He
would "rise from the dead" on the third day.

In spite of the enormous efforts of Rome and the Jewish rulers to
prevent such a spectacle, on precisely the third day following crucifixion,
Jesus' tomb was indeed empty. The body of the "man in the middle" had
vanished, apparently into thin air; no one seemed to have a clue where
it might be.

The worst nightmare of the Sanhedrin Council and Rome burst to life before their eyes. *How could this be? What else could go wrong? Could this fiasco grow any worse?*

If they had only known…

NOT YET ASCENDED TO THE FATHER

According to John's biblical account, the resurrected Jesus uttered an amazing assertion to Mary Magdalene on that morning that has puzzled many students of the Word ever since:

> Jesus said, "Do not hold on to me, for I have not yet ascended to the Father. Go instead to my brothers and tell them, 'I am ascending to my Father.'" (John 20:17)

What did Jesus mean when He said, "I have not yet ascended to the Father"? Of course, we now understand that He did, in fact, ascend into heaven some forty days later. But if He truly had not yet ascended into the Father's presence in any way whatsoever at the time he spoke to Mary, then where *did* Jesus go during those three days?

You already know the answer to that question.

The Scriptures tell us where He went. He spoke the beautiful words of promise to the dying thief who had placed his trust in Yeshua on that fateful, barbarically miserable afternoon. Jesus was clear: "*Today, we're going 'back to the Garden!'*"

They were headed to another dimension of reality. They were bound for the unseen realm, a place that can only be entered with the explicit permission of Jesus Christ. He is the only door, the only portal. Yeshua had called the place "*paradise.*"

But, we still have to ask, "*Wouldn't 'going to paradise' be the same as going into the presence of the Father?"* The answer to that lies in the following biblical truths. Let's connect the dots, starting at the beginning.

THE ISLAND OF PARADISE

Following is a conceptualization that might help make this mystery a bit clearer. Think of Eden as an island of paradise that exists in another dimension, yet in the realm of true physical reality. In the middle of that glorious island is an indescribably beautiful mountain.

On top of the island's mountain is a lush garden. A life-giving river of crystal clear water flows from the base of the mountain. Also, on top of the mountain is a place of glorious holiness: the temple of Yahweh. But human admittance to the inner sanctum of the temple is not yet available.

For fallen humanity to come into the Holy Presence within the temple, even a redeemed human who is now on the island of paradise through faith must come through the blood of the Son of sacrifice. Before Jesus' offering on Calvary's cross, that access was denied.

When Jesus accompanied the crucified thief to the "island of paradise," He, at that particular time, did not go up the Holy Mount and enter the temple of Yahweh. The opening of the temple to the residents of paradise would not happen until Jesus' ascension day. On that glorious day, He would finally present His blood in heaven's temple, thus opening the way to the throne of the Father (Hebrews 9–10).

This is exactly what thousands of years of the Jerusalem temple and the wilderness tabernacle rituals of sacrifice had symbolized. Jesus would eventually fulfill the role of the ultimate Great High Priest. However, He had no need to offer a blood sacrifice for His own sin, because He is the sinless Son of God, our Great High Priest (Hebrews 9:11–15) who also gave Himself as the offering (Genesis 22:8).

Now, let's review the biblical "timeline" concerning all we have laid out thus far:

IN THE BEGINNING OF JESUS' MINISTRY

Jesus said, "No one has gone into heaven, except the one who has come down from heaven" (John 3:13). He said this to Nicodemus the Pharisee, who had come to Jesus at night to seek further clarification about the Rabbi's teachings.

Jesus had spoken the absolute truth to Nicodemus—only Jesus had come from God's throne room. No mortal had set foot in that place since the Garden Fall—*not yet*. But, in a little over three years from that night's meeting with Nicodemus, Jesus would change all of that.

It is true that Daniel had experienced a *vision* of the Holy Presence (Daniel 7). Even Isaiah "saw the glory of it" through a vision (Isaiah 6). Moses had come near His Holy Presence in the burning-bush experience (Exodus 3:1–17). And Abraham had spoken to Yahweh in human form (Genesis 18). But no one had ever gone into Paradise and then ascended the Holy Mountain of God to enter the literal and physical presence of the Great I Am—to see Him and know Him as He is. *No one* (Exodus 33:20; John 1:18).

IN THE MIDDLE OF JESUS' MINISTRY

As an illustration of the dimensional divisions beyond the earthly realm, Jesus told about the rich man who had died outside of faith in Yahweh. He had gone through life in total self-absorption, ignoring God's sovereignty over his life (Luke 16:19–31).

As a result of his faithless life, the rich man went to hell (prison) when he died. Yet, while in hell, he was totally aware of himself, and he was in physical torment. He was also aware of what he had missed by not being in paradise.

The rich man recognized someone he knew quite well from his days upon the earth. His name was Lazarus, and he was living in a state of *paradise blessing* because he had been faithful to the ways of God. But the rich man had mistreated, even looked down upon, Lazarus all his life.

Abraham informed the rich man that a great and unscalable chasm existed between paradise and hell's prison, and Lazarus was in Abraham's bosom because he had been a man of great faith. The Jews understood "Abraham's bosom" to mean *paradise*— or more importantly, the spiritual Garden of Eden.

Ellicott's Commentary for English Readers:

In the figurative language in which the current Jewish belief clothed its thoughts of the unseen world, the Garden of Eden took its place side by side with "Abraham's bosom," as a synonym for the eternal blessedness of the righteous.[301]

Vincent's Word Studies:

In the Septuagint, Genesis 2:8, of the Garden of Eden. In the Jewish theology, the department of Hades where the blessed souls await the resurrection; and therefore equivalent to Abraham's bosom (Luke 16:22, Luke 16:23).[302]

Pulpit Commentary:

The place whither the blest Lazarus went is termed "Abraham's bosom." This term was used by the Jews indifferently, with "the garden of Eden."[303]

In relating the account of the Rich Man and Lazarus, Jesus clearly established the fact of a literal paradise, as well as the reality of a literal hell—the prison/waiting place for the coming judgment. Jesus also acknowledged that after our physical/earthly departure (death), there was no "second chance" (Hebrews 9:27). Sadly, the rich man knew that full well. But, it was far too late.

NEAR THE END OF JESUS' EARTHLY MINISTRY

Jesus fulfilled every messianic prophecy of the Old Testament concerning His first coming, ultimately delivering himself to Calvary's cross (Psalm 22; Isaiah 53; Zechariah 12; John 10:18). He spilled His own blood as divine payment for fallen humanity's sin nature—the penalty required by the Garden Fall. At His last earthly breath, Jesus entered paradise, where Lazarus, Abraham, and all the saints of old were waiting. The thief would follow soon, on the promise of Jesus' word from the cross.

In that moment of earthly departure, even as Nicodemus and Joseph were situating His body in the borrowed tomb, Jesus had entered the myriad dimensions of the unseen realm. He could do this because He was the sovereign Creator of those realms. All things, and all dimensions, were "created by Him and for Him, and nothing that was made was made without Him—and in Him all things hold together" (John 1:1–12; Colossians 1:15–20; Hebrews 1:1–3).

As Jesus entered those dimensions, He presented Himself to the realm of hell itself (i.e., the rich man's waiting cell) as a testimony of His glory and His ultimate victory over Satan.

He was put to death in the body but made alive in the Spirit. After being made alive, he went and made proclamation to the imprisoned spirits. (1 Peter 3:18–19)

He also presented himself to the "island of paradise"—in the presence of all who had previously left this world in faith, those who were looking forward to the eventual coming of Messiah's redemption. This was the day for which paradise had been waiting.

AFTER THE RESURRECTION

It was now three days later. Jesus still had forty days of earthly ministry left before His mission would be complete. He must return to the earthly dimension and present himself in the presence of many hundreds of His followers (1 Corinthians 15:6). He would also perform other divine miracles to verify to the earthly, as well as the demonic, realms of authority that Christ had indeed risen, and had forfeited none of His divine power and glory (John 21:6).

Jesus also demonstrated to the demonic realm and the principalities of the earth that He is the undisputed victor, and that the Genesis 3:15 prophecy was being completed. The divine Seed had finally come to crush the head of the serpent (Ephesians 4:8–10; 1 Corinthians 2:7–8; Colossians 2:15).

During those forty days, Jesus thumbed His nose at Satan, making a spectacle of Nachash, saying to the entire demonic realm and their fallen prince: "*You lost. And soon...you will be gods of nothing.*"

> Having canceled the charge of our legal indebtedness, which stood against us and condemned us; he has taken it away, nailing it to the cross. And having disarmed the powers and authorities, he made a public spectacle of them, triumphing over them by the cross. (Colossians 2:14–15)

AFTER THE ASCENSION

On the Mount of Olives, Jesus returned to the right hand of the Father, from whence He had originally come. This is the event of which He was speaking when He told Mary that He had not yet ascended to the Father. Now, however, even this last important detail would be completed.

Upon His ascension, Jesus returned to paradise and entered the Holy of Holies in the temple in heaven—the *real* temple (Hebrews 9–10). It is there where Jesus would present His blood (Hebrews 1:3–4). He had fulfilled the role of the real Great High Priest (Hebrews 4:14–16). The Holy Place had been opened, and we can now approach the throne of our Creator in boldness, through the blood of Jesus (Hebrews 8–10).

PAUL IN PARADISE

The Apostle Paul died in AD 67, but sometime before his death, he was physically caught up to paradise. It was not a vision, a dream, or an angelic visitation; Paul was *there* in the temple of paradise. He informed his readers that he was caught up to the "third heaven," into the presence of Yahweh Himself (2 Corinthians 12:2–4). Paul was in heaven's temple. He was in the literal presence of the Creator of the Universe.

The *Benson Commentary* gives elucidation upon Paul's visit to the third heaven:

The third heaven is the seat of God, and of the holy angels, into which Christ ascended after his resurrection.[304]

Barnes' Notes on the Bible offers a similar assessment:

It was this upper heaven, the dwelling-place of God, to which Paul was taken, and whose wonders he was permitted to behold—this region where God dwelt; where Christ was seated at the right hand of the Father.[305]

In the third heaven, at the throne of God, Paul was given the end-time revelations of the Rapture, the Antichrist, the last-days apostasy, the sounding of the last trumpet, the coming great deception, the return of Jesus Christ, the demonic outpouring of the last days, and more. Paul revealed those truths in his letters to the various churches of that day. He assured them they could not even begin to comprehend what lay ahead for those who are under the blood of Jesus Christ. He had seen it, and it was utterly indescribable.

However, as it is written: "What no eye has seen, what no ear has heard, and what no human mind has conceived"—the things God has prepared for those who love him. (1 Corinthians 2:9)

From that point forward, Paul preferred to be absent from the earthly dimension of reality, and to be "present with the Lord," living in paradise (2 Corinthians 5:8).

JOHN IN PARADISE

Sometime in the AD 90s, about three decades after Paul's experience, the Apostle John was also caught up to paradise (Revelation 4:1). He was given the fullest revelation of end-time events that had ever been passed down to mortal man.

As in the case of Paul, John also physically entered the heavenly temple of God. He gazed upon the Holy Creator. John saw the Lamb in the middle of the throne. And he saw the *Divine Council*: the holy cherubim, the thrones around the thrones, and the ten thousand times ten thousand angels of the heavenly host (Revelation 4–5).

The Expositor's Greek New Testament affirms:

[John] is no longer in the island but up at the gates of heaven.... A heavenly voice comes after he has seen...a door set open (ready, opened) in the vault of the mysterious upper world which formed God's house.[306] (Parenthesis appears in the original quote.)

The reason John and Paul could be allowed physical access into the Holy Presence of the Ancient of Days was because the divine portal had finally been opened by the blood of Jesus Christ. They had literally stood in the *Garden of God*—and were, thankfully, allowed to come back and testify of its reality.

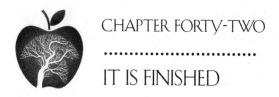

> There was a handwriting of ordinances
> against us, but Christ has taken it away, He
> has nailed it to His Cross. 'It is finished,'
> finished forever.
>
> ~Charles Spurgeon[307]

Yeshua, the true Tree of Life, faithfully, willingly, and lovingly laid down His life *on a tree*. In so doing, he destroyed the power of the tree of death, that diabolical and primeval tree of the knowledge of good and evil.

The entire corrupted mess in which humanity continues to wallow is among us because of what happened in the Garden of Eden. We, through our ancient ancestors, chose the perverted and profane father of lies as our master. Thus, apart from Christ, we are lost and without hope, every last one of us. Each of us carries around within our spiritual makeup the nature of that *father of lies and filth*. But Yahweh already had a plan of redemption, even before He formed the first human being (Revelation 13:8).

When judgment was pronounced upon Nachash in the Garden of Eden (Genesis 3:15), Yahweh told Satan about the eventual arrival of his future judgment and destruction. But, Satan had not been told exactly who would bring the judgment or precisely when it would occur.

Because of this lack of crucial information, Nachash became obsessed with finding and destroying the "seed" that would one day crush his head. Satan deployed his demonic horde to lead the thrones of men down through the ages into effecting the destruction of that one who would be known as the Seed.

- "Then Pharaoh gave this order to all his people: 'Every Hebrew boy that is born you must throw into the Nile, but let every girl live'" (Exodus 1:22).
- "When Herod realized that he had been outwitted by the Magi, he was furious, and he gave orders to kill all the boys in Bethlehem and its vicinity who were two years old and under, in accordance with the time he had learned from the Magi" (Matthew 2:16).
- "The dragon stood in front of the woman who was about to give birth, so that it might devour her child the moment he was born. She gave birth to a son, a male child, who 'will rule all the nations with an iron scepter.' And her child was snatched up to God and to his throne" (Revelation 12:4–5).

But heaven's plan outsmarted Satan, as well as the human pawns he controlled and manipulated:

No, we declare God's wisdom, a mystery that has been hidden and that God destined for our glory before time began. None of the rulers of this age understood it, for if they had, they would not have crucified the Lord of glory. (1 Corinthians 2:7–8)

It was decreed that Yeshua would become *the curse* for us, in our place, so that heaven's eternal penalty could be paid in full. He took the Law that was blasphemed in the Garden and nailed it to the cross (Colossians 2:14). Our debt has been paid in full—for all who believe (Romans 10:9).

EDEN/PARADISE

Throughout this book, you have discovered that the biblical use of the word "paradise" signifies the spiritual Garden of Eden. You also learned there are only three places in the New Testament where the word "paradise" is used.

With this in mind, have a look at the three passages—and in place of "paradise," let's insert "the Garden of Eden." This is what the Hebrew mind would have heard and understood. When you see it in this way, perhaps an entire new world of understanding will be opened.

- "Jesus answered [the thief], 'I tell you the truth, today you will be with me in [*the Garden of Eden*]'" (Luke 23:43).
- "I know that this man…was caught up to [*the Garden of Eden*]. He heard inexpressible things, things that man is not permitted to tell" (2 Corinthians 12:4–5).

And my personal favorite:

- "He who has an ear, let him hear what the Spirit says to the churches. To him who overcomes, I will give the right to eat from the tree of life, which is in [*the Garden of Eden*]" (Revelation 2:7).

REVERSING THE CURSE—EDEN RESTORED

And now, just like the thief on the cross, who spiritually represents us all, there awaits a completely restored paradise for anyone who will repent and surrender his or her life to Jesus Christ as Lord. This is heaven's promise, witnessed by the ten thousand times ten thousand angelic beings of the Divine Council that surround God's throne.

On each side of the river stood the tree of life, bearing twelve crops of fruit, yielding its fruit every month. And the leaves of the tree are for the healing of the nations. No longer will there be any curse. The throne of God and of the Lamb will be in the city, and his servants will serve him. (Revelation 22:2–3)

Even so, come Lord Jesus!

I can almost hear angels singing. How about you?

Thank you for taking this journey with me. I pray the Holy Spirit of Yahweh has revealed marvelous biblical treasures to you along the way.

May the Lord Jesus Christ, the Elohim of *elohim*, bless you and keep you until the veil is forever pulled back and we finally arrive on the other side, in the Garden of God—Yahweh's ultimate glory.

I will look for you there—somewhere around the Tree of Life.

ABOUT THE AUTHOR

Carl Gallups has been the senior pastor of Hickory Hammock Baptist Church in Milton, Florida, since 1987. He is the founder of the internationally viral online PNN News and Ministry Network (www.ppsimmons.com).

Carl is a graduate of the Florida Police Academy, Florida State University (BS, Criminology) and New Orleans Baptist Theological Seminary (MDiv), and serves on the Board of Regents at the University of Mobile in Mobile, Alabama.

Carl is a former decorated Florida law enforcement officer, having served under three sheriffs with two different sheriff's offices. He was also appointed as a special deputy, in January 2016, under former Sheriff Joe Arpaio, Maricopa County, Arizona.

Pastor Gallups is a critically acclaimed Amazon Top-60 bestselling author of multiple books, a talk-radio host since 2002, and a regular guest pundit on numerous television and radio programs as well as various print media sources. He is also a frequent guest preacher at national prophecy and Bible conferences.

Carl has been featured on *Fox News Business Report* as an "influential evangelical leader," publicly endorsing then candidate Donald Trump for the office of president. Carl was asked by the Donald Trump campaign to open the internationally broadcast *Trump for President Rally* in Pensacola, Florida, in January 2016. More than twelve thousand people were in attendance at that rally.

Pastor Gallups lives in Milton, Florida, with his wife, Pam.

You can find more information about pastor Gallups at www.carl-gallups.com.

NOTES

1. Mitchell, David. "Ghostwritten," Vintage Press, 12-18-2007:202.
2. Clarence Darrow, "Quotes," Good Reads, https://www.goodreads.com/quotes/1039129-do-you-good-people-believe-that-adam-and-eve-were.
3. GoodReads, "Quotes about Other Side," (C. S. Lewis) accessed October 13, 2017, https://www.goodreads.com/quotes/tag/other-side.
4. Ralph Waldo Emerson (1803–1882). The Complete Works. 1904. Vol. VIII. Letters and Social Aims, XI. Immortality, accessed on December 7, 2017 http://www.bartleby.com/90/0811.html.
5. Psalm 82:1, "Parallel Comparisons," Biblehub.com, http://biblehub.com/psalms/82-1.htm.
6. For additional scholarly study of the concept of the Divine Council in the Old and New Testaments, please see the following resources:
   a) Gallups, Carl. *Gods and Thrones: Nachash, Forgotten Prophecy, and the Return of the Elohim,* (Defender Publishing, 2017):37–67.
   b) Dr. Heiser, Michael. *The Unseen Realm: Recovering the Supernatural Worldview of the Bible,* (Lexham Press, 2015):23–61.
   c) Summer, Paul B. "The Divine Council in the Hebrew Bible," (April 1991–corrected Feb. 2013), http://www.hebrew-streams.org/works/hebrew/divinecouncil-ch2.pdf.
7. This topic is covered extensively in my previous book, *Gods and Thrones: Nachash, Forgotten Prophecy, and the Return of the Elohim.*
8. Tolstoy, Leo. "The Kingdom of God Is Within You Quotes," Goodreads.com, accessed December 8, 2017, https://www.goodreads.com/work/quotes/3137652.
9. This topic is covered extensively in my previous book, *Gods and Thrones.*

10. Elohim—OT #430, "Concordances," Biblehub.com, http://biblehub.com/hebrew/430.htm.

11. For additional scholarly study of the concept of the Divine Council in the Old and New Testaments, please see the following resources:

a) Gallups, Carl. *Gods and Thrones: Nachash, Forgotten Prophecy, and the Return of the Elohim*, (Defender Publishing, 2017):37–67.

b) Dr. Heiser, Michael. *The Unseen Realm: Recovering the Supernatural Worldview of the Bible*, (Lexham Press, 2015):23–61.

c) Summer, Paul B. "The Divine Council in the Hebrew Bible," (April 1991–corrected Feb. 2013), http://www.hebrew-streams.org/works/hebrew/divinecouncil-ch2.pdf.

12. Colossians 2:18, *John Eadie's Commentary on Galatians, Ephesians, Colossians and Philippians*, Studylight.org, https://www.studylight.org/commentary/colossians/2-18.html.

13. Deuteronomy 32:17, *Gill's Exposition of the Entire Bible*, Biblehub.com, http://biblehub.com/commentaries/deuteronomy/32-17.htm.

14. Deuteronomy 32:17, *Adam Clarke's Commentary*, Biblehub.com, http://biblehub.com/commentaries/clarke/deuteronomy/32.htm.

15. Ritenbaugh, John W. "Colossians 2:18–22," Bibletools.org, https://www.bibletools.org/index.cfm/fuseaction/Bible.show/sVerseID/29513/eVerseID/29513.

16. Colossians 2:18, *Calvin's Commentary on the Bible*, Studylight.org, https://www.studylight.org/commentary/colossians/2-18.html.

17. Caution against angel-worship, Colossians 2:18–19. *Whedon's Commentary on the Bible*, Studylight.org, https://www.studylight.org/commentary/colossians/2-18.html.

18. Milton, John, "Paradise Lost Quotes," Good Reads, accessed Dec. 12, 2017, https://www.goodreads.com/work/quotes/1031493-paradise-lost.

19. Blake, John. "When Exorcists Need Help, They Call Him," CNN, August 4, 2017, http://www.cnn.com/2017/08/04/health/exorcism-doctor/index.html.

20. Ibid.

21. Armstrong, Patti. "US Exorcists: Demonic Activity on the Rise: A Look at the Growing Need to Battle the Devil," National

Catholic Register, 3-11-17, http://www.ncregister.com/daily-news/
us-exorcists-demonic-activity-on-the-rise.

22. For scholarly considerations supporting this thesis, SEE:

   a) *Forerunner Commentary*, "Bible verses about Lucifer's Rebellion," accessed
      December 14, 2007, https://www.bibletools.org/index.cfm/fuseaction/
      Topical.show/RTD/cgg/ID/486/Lucifers-Rebellion.htm.

   b) Hovind, Eric. "When Did Satan Fall from Heaven?" 5-6-10, http://
      creationtoday.org/when-did-satan-fall-from-heaven.

23. Eden, *Strong's Concordance,* Biblehub.com, http://biblehub.com/strongs/
    hebrew/5730.htm.

    See: *Thayer's Greek Lexicon,* http://biblehub.com/greek/3857.htm.

    See: *Gill's Exposition of the Entire Bible*, http://biblehub.com/
       commentaries/2_corinthians/12-4.htm.

    See: *Keil and Delitzsch Biblical Commentary on the Old Testament,* http://
       www.sacred-texts.com/bib/cmt/kad/gen002.htm.

    Thayer's Greek Lexicon says this word (NT: 3857 *paradeisos*) means:
    "Universally, a garden, pleasure-ground; grove, park…that delightful region,
    'the garden of Eden,' in which our first parents dwelt before the fall." *Keil
    and Delitzsch Biblical Commentary on the Old Testament* (Genesis 2) says,
    "[The garden of Eden] is generally called Paradise from the Septuagint
    version." See Endnote #19.

24. Eden, "International Standard Bible Encyclopedia Online," accessed
    December 4, 2017, http://www.internationalstandardbible.com/E/eden.
    html.

25. Ibid.

26. Dr. Krell, Keith. "Party in Paradise (Genesis 2:4–25),"
    Bible.org, accessed December 7, 2017, https://bible.org/
    seriespage/5-party-paradise-genesis-24-25#P36_11331.

27. Berkowitz, Adam Eliyahu. "Has the Location of the Garden
    of Eden Been Found?" *Breaking Israel News*, September
    21, 2016, https://www.breakingisraelnews.com/76029/
    prophetic-rebirth-dead-sea-reveal-garden-eden/#63wcA3e9kqg0prA3.99.

28. Genesis 2:8, *Benson Commentary*, Biblehub.com, http://biblehub.com/
    commentaries/genesis/2-8.htm.

29. Hosea 6:7, *Pulpit Commentary*, Biblehub.com, http://biblehub.com/commentaries/hosea/6-7.htm.

30. For additional examples of this assertion, SEE:

    a) Mercedescoleen. "News Flash—Scripture Shows That Jerusalem Is the Garden Of Eden," (Introduction to "Jerusalem is the Garden of Eden") accessed December 5, 2017, https://pppministries.wordpress.com/2013/06/22/news-flash-scripture-shows-that-jerusalem-is-the-garden-of-eden/.

    b) "Israel and the Land of Eden: The Mysterious Israel-Eden Connection," accessed December 5, 2017, http://www.factsaboutisrael.uk/israel-eden-garden-of-eden.

    c) Wellman, Jared. "WELLMAN: Where on Earth was the Garden of Eden?" OA Online, 1-3-15, http://www.oaoa.com/people/religion/article_7d948064-935d-11e4-90c2-4b09cc36f260.html.

    d) Baker, Eric W. "The Eschatological Role of the Jerusalem Temple: An Examination of Jewish Writings Dating from 586 BCE to 70 CE," (Andrews University-Digital Commons, 2014): 33-36, https://digitalcommons.andrews.edu/cgi/viewcontent.cgi?article=1012&context=dissertations.

    e) Barker, Margaret. "The Gate of Heaven: The History and Symbolism of the Temple in Jerusalem," (London: SPCK, 1991): 57, 63–64.

31. Keidar, Doron. "Jewish History on the Temple Mount: Did the Jews Abandon It?" Cry for Zion, 3-30-2015, http://cryforzion.com/jewish-history-on-the-temple-mount-did-jews-abandon-it/#_ftn7.

32. Dolphin, Lambert. "Early History of the Temple Mount," accessed December 12, 2017, http://www.templemount.org/earlytm.html.

33. See my previous books *Gods and Thrones* and *When the Lion Roars* for additional discussion on this topic.

34. The Israel Bible, "Gan Eden," accessed December 8, 2018, https://theisraelbible.com/glossary/gan-eden/#7QIdZLlMJxLCuFrf.99.

35. Peter J. Gentry, Stephen J. Wellum. *Kingdom through Covenant: A Biblical-Theological Understanding of the Covenants,* (Crossway, Jun 30, 2012):212.

36. Ibid.

37. Several additional scholarly works are cited in chapter 38 of this book

(Ground Zero). Those sources further insist that the original Garden of Eden was in and around the vicinity of Jerusalem.

38. Polythress, Vern. "The Shadow of Christ in the Law of Moses, (Brentwood, TN: Wolgemuth & Hyatt, Publishers, 1991), p. 19.

39. Revelation 22, "Eden Restored," Biblehub.com, http://biblehub.com/niv/revelation/22.htm.

40. David, Ariel. "400,000-year-old 'School of Rock' Found in Prehistoric Cave in Israel," 11-22-27, https://www.haaretz.com/archaeology/1.824356.

41. Eisenbud, Daniel K. "Israeli Scientists Discover Earliest Modern Human Fossils Outside Africa," Jan. 25, 2018, *Jerusalem Post*, http://www.jpost.com/HEALTH-SCIENCE/Israeli-scientists-discover-earliest-modern-human-fossils-outside-Africa-539864.

42. Ezekiel 28:11–19, *The Bible Exposition Commentary: Old Testament*, Biblesoft PC Study Bible—copyright from 1988–2008 *The Bible Exposition Commentary: Old Testament* © 2001–2004 by Warren W. Wiersbe. All rights reserved. Accessed on December 14, 2017.

43. Ezekiel 28:14, *Cambridge Bible for Schools and Colleges*, Biblehub.com, http://biblehub.com/commentaries/ezekiel/28-14.htm.

44. Ezekiel 28 14, *Pulpit Commentary*, Biblehub.com, http://biblehub.com/commentaries/ezekiel/28-14.htm.

45. Dr. Heiser, Michael. "The Divine Council," accessed December 12, 2017, http://www.thedivinecouncil.com/HeiserIVPDC.pdf.

46. Dr. Heiser, Michael. *The Unseen Realm: Recovering the Supernatural Worldview of the Bible*, (Lexham Press, 2015):67.

47. Ibid. Ezekiel 28:11–19, *The Bible Exposition Commentary: Old Testament*. Biblesoft PC Study Bible.

48. Jewish Virtual Library, "Encyclopedia Judaica: The Garden of Eden," accessed December 3, 2017, http://www.jewishvirtuallibrary.org/garden-of-eden.

49. Ibid.

50. Ezekiel 28, *Expositor's Bible Commentary*, Biblehub.com, http://biblehub.com/commentaries/expositors/ezekiel/28.htm.

51. Ezekiel 28, *Pulpit Commentary*, Biblehub.com, http://biblehub.com/commentaries/pulpit/ezekiel/28.htm.

52. The biblical and historical equating of Eden with paradise/heaven is developed much more extensively as we continue in the pages ahead.

53. Monogenés, NT 3439. "Greek Concordances," Biblehub.com, http://biblehub.com/greek/3439.htm.
For an excellent, updated word study of *monogenés* also see: Dr. Heiser, Michael. *The Unseen Realm: Recovering the Supernatural Worldview of the Bible,* (Lexham Press, 2015):36–37.

54. In my previous book, *Gods and Thrones,* the argument that the words "let us" and "our" simply refers to a "plural of majesty," or to "the trinity," is refuted through a study of verified contextual Hebrew grammatical concerns.

55. Dr. Heiser, Michael. "ET Gods in the Garden of Eden?" (Posted by Dr. Heiser in the comments section) May 6, 2008, http://drmsh.com/et-gods-in-the-garden-of-eden.

56. Ibid.

57. Genesis 1:26, *Cambridge Bible for Schools and Colleges,* Biblehub.com, http://biblehub.com/commentaries/genesis/1-26.htm.

58. Gods ('*elohim; theoi*), "Super Human Beings: Gods and Angels," International Standard Bible Encyclopedia Online, accessed November 19, 2017, http://www.internationalstandardbible.com/G/gods.html.

59. Genesis 1:26, *Cambridge Bible for Schools and Colleges,* Biblehub.com, http://biblehub.com/commentaries/genesis/1-26.htm.

60. Ibid.

61. Job 38:7, *Barnes' Notes on the Bible,* Biblehub.com, http://biblehub.com/commentaries/job/38-7.htm.

62. Job 38:7, *Matthew Pooles' Commentary,* Biblehub.com, http://biblehub.com/commentaries/job/38-7.htm.

63. Schoenheit, John W. "God's Divine Council," Issue: 4th quarter 2015, accessed Jan. 2, 2018, http://thesowermagazine.com/gods-divine-council/#_ftnref5.

64. Hovind, Eric. "When did Satan Fall from Heaven? 5-6-10, http://creationtoday.org/when-did-satan-fall-from-heaven.
See also: Hodge, Bodie, "What about Satan and the Origin of Evil?" 7-29-10, https://answersingenesis.org/angels-and-demons/satan/

what-about-satan-and-the-origin-of-evil/.

Got Questions? "How, Why, and When Did Satan Fall from Heaven?" accessed January 8, 2018, https://www.gotquestions.org/Satan-fall.html.

65. Genesis 3, *Expository Notes of Dr. Thomas Constable*, (Bible Commentaries—Verses 6–8 – Note: Thomas p. 46), accessed 1-12-2018, https://www.studylight.org/commentaries/dcc/genesis-3.html.

66. Mitchell, David. "Ghostwritten," Vintage Press, 12-18-2007:202.

67. The nine NT writers are Matthew, Mark, Luke, John, Peter, Paul, James, Jude, and the author of Hebrews. As you will soon see, the "serpent" is mentioned a handful of times in the New Testament but only as a normal snake, or as a mere symbol of the literal person of Satan. Never is the serpent presented as a literal walking, talking snake.

68. The Old Testament will mention a "serpent" again several times, but never as a literal walking and talking creature. It is either represented as a normal snake, or in a clearly symbolic sense. A "serpent" is never again directly connected with the Garden of Eden in the Old Testament.

69. Laie, Benjamin T. "Garden of Eden," *Ancient History Encyclopedia*, January 12, 2018, https://www.ancient.eu/Garden_of_Eden.

70. Genesis 3, *Lange Commentary on the Holy Scriptures*, Biblehub.com, http://biblehub.com/commentaries/lange/genesis/3.htm.

71. Genesis 3, *Expositor's Bible Commentary*, Biblehub.com, http://biblehub.com/commentaries/expositors/genesis/3.htm.

72. Genesis 3, *Adam Clarke Commentary*, Biblehub.com, http://biblehub.com/commentaries/clarke/genesis/3.htm.

73. Genesis 3, (See the *Pulpit Commentary*, and *The Benson Commentary* as several examples of this assertion), Biblehub.com, http://biblehub.com/commentaries/genesis/3-1.htm.

74. Quotes About Snakes, "Aldous Huxley, Brave New World," accessed December 15, 2017, https://www.goodreads.com/quotes/tag/snakes.

75. Dr. Morris, Henry, *The Genesis Record*, (Baker Book House, 1976):107–109.

76. Genesis 3, *Matthew Henry's Commentary on the Whole Bible*, Biblehub.com, http://biblehub.com/commentaries/mhcw/genesis/3.htm6.

77. Genesis 3:14, *Adam Clarke*, Biblehub.com, http://biblehub.com/commentaries/clarke/genesis/3.htm.

78. Genesis 3:14, *Matthew Poole,* Biblehub.com, http://biblehub.com/commentaries/poole/genesis/3.htm.

79. Luther, Martin. *Luther's Works,* vol. 1, ed. Jaroslav Pelikan (St. Louis, MO: Concordia Publishing House, 1958): 186.

80. Hodge, Bodie, "Did the Serpent Originally Have Legs?" (Conclusion), 1-26-2010, https://answersingenesis.org/genesis/garden-of-eden/did-the-serpent-originally-have-legs.

81. Thomas, Brian, "Snakes with Legs?" Institute for Creation Research, updated Nov. 2, 2016, http://www.icr.org/article/snakes-with-legs.

82. Morgan, Mark. "Did the Serpent Walk before He Was Cursed in the Garden?" 2-21-10, BibleQ.net, http://bibleq.net/answer/2044.

83. Numbers 22:28, *Cambridge Bible for Schools and Colleges,* Biblehub.com, http://biblehub.com/commentaries/numbers/22-28.htm.

84. Genesis 3:1, *Cambridge Bible for Schools and Colleges,* Biblehub.com, http://biblehub.com/commentaries/genesis/3-1.htm.

85. Numbers 22:28, *Pulpit Commentary,* Biblehub.com, http://biblehub.com/commentaries/numbers/22-28.htm.

86. Numbers 22:28, *Keil and Delitzsch OT Commentary,* Biblehub.com, http://biblehub.com/commentaries/kad/numbers/22.htm.

87. See each of their commentaries on the "talking snake," as quoted in the remaining pages of this chapter.

88. Hodge, Bodie, "Shouldn't the Woman (Eve) Have Been Shocked that a Serpent Spoke? Satan, the Fall, and a Look at Good and Evil," 2-2-10, Answers in Genesis, https://answersingenesis.org/bible-characters/adam-and-eve/eve-shocked-a-serpent-spoke.

89. Note how that even though the admission is correctly made concerning the complete absence of biblical attestation of Satan's power to make animals talk, this commentator still insists that this is exactly what Satan did in the Garden.

90. "Why didn't Adam and Eve Find It Strange that a Serpent Was Talking to Them?"Gotquestions.org, accessed November 23, 2017, https://www.gotquestions.org/talking-snake.html.

91. Genesis 3:1, *Pulpit Commentary,* Biblehub.com, http://biblehub.com/commentaries/genesis/3-1.htm.

92. Genesis 3:1, *Cambridge Bible for Schools and Colleges*, Biblehub.com, http://biblehub.com/commentaries/genesis/3-1.htm.

93. Genesis 3:1, *Ellicott's Commentary for English Readers*, Biblehub.com, http://biblehub.com/commentaries/genesis/3-1.htm.

94. Genesis 3, *Keil and Delitzsch OT Commentary*, Biblehub.com, http://biblehub.com/commentaries/kad/numbers/22.htm.

95. Genesis 3:1, "Warren Wiersbe BE Bible Study Series: The Plan," (See: Study This: Commentaries), Biblegateway.com, https://www.biblegateway.com/passage/?search=Genesis+3%3A1&version=NIV.

96. "The Works of Robert G. Ingersoll, Vol. 3 (of 12) Dresden Edition-Lectures Quotes," Accessed October 4, 2017, https://www.goodreads.com/work/quotes/9843241-the-works-of-robert-g-ingersoll-vol-3-of-12-dresden-edition-lecture.

97. Dolansky, Shawna. "How the Serpent Became Satan: Adam, Eve and the serpent in the Garden of Eden," Bible History Daily, 10-13-17, https://www.biblicalarchaeology.org/daily/biblical-topics/bible-interpretation/how-the-serpent-became-satan/.

98. Ibid.

99. Job 1:6, *Ellicott's Commentary for English Readers*, Biblehub.com, http://biblehub.com/commentaries/job/1-6.htm.

100. Job 1:6, *Barnes' Notes on the Bible*, Biblehub.com, http://biblehub.com/commentaries/job/1-6.htm.

101. Job 1:6, *Barnes' Notes on the Bible*, Biblehub.com, http://biblehub.com/commentaries/job/1-6.htm.

102. Job 1:6, *Jamieson-Fausset-Brown Bible Commentary*, Biblehub.com, http://biblehub.com/commentaries/job/1-6.htm.

103. Revelation 12:9, *The IVP New Testament Commentary Series*, (See: Study This: Commentaries—The Dragon's Past and Present (12:7–9)), https://www.biblegateway.com/passage/?search=Revelation+12%3A9&version=NIV.

104. Revelation 12, *Expositor's Greet Testament*, (Revelation 12:9), Biblehub.com, http://biblehub.com/commentaries/egt/revelation/12.htm.

105. Sémeion, NT #4592, Biblehub.com, http://biblehub.com/greek/4592.htm.

106. NT 3789. Ophis, (Concordances and Lexicons), Biblehub.com, http://biblehub.com/greek/3789.htm.

107. Ibid.

108. Matthew 4:1, *Pulpit Commentary*, Biblehub.com, http://biblehub.com/commentaries/matthew/4-1.htm.

109. Matthew 4, *Clarke's Commentary*, Biblehub.com, http://biblehub.com/commentaries/clarke/matthew/4.htm.

110. Matthew 4, *Gill's Exposition*, Biblehub.com, http://biblehub.com/commentaries/gill/matthew/4.htm.

111. Revelation 12:9, *The IVP New Testament Commentary Series*, (See: Study This: Commentaries—The Dragon's Past and Present (12:7–9)), https://www.biblegateway.com/passage/?search=Revelation+12%3A9&version=NIV.

112. 2 Corinthians 11:1-6, *The Bible Exposition Commentary (New Testament)*. Copyright © 1989 by Chariot Victor Publishing, and imprint of Cook Communication Ministries. All rights reserved. Used by permission—through PC Study Bible Software, Copyright 1988–2008 Biblesoft, Inc.

113. Dr. Heiser, Michael S, PhD. "The Nachash and His Seed: Some Explanatory Notes on Why the "Serpent" in Genesis 3 Wasn't a Serpent," Dept. of Hebrew and Semitic Studies, UW-Madison, accessed November 2, 2017, http://www.pidradio.com/wp-content/uploads/2007/02/nachashnotes.pdf.

114. Ritenbaugh, John W. "Ezekiel 28:14-17," *Forerunner Commentary*, accessed Dec. 14, 2017, 2017, https://www.bibletools.org/index.cfm/fuseaction/Topical.show/RTD/cgg/ID/486/Lucifers-Rebellion.htm.

115. 2 Corinthians 11:3, *Expositor's Greek Commentary*, Biblehub.com, http://biblehub.com/commentaries/2_corinthians/11-3.htm.

116. Genesis 3:1, *McLaren's Exposition*, Biblehub.com, http://biblehub.com/commentaries/genesis/3-1.htm.

117. Singer, Isidore, PhD (projector and managing editor), *The Jewish Encyclopedia: A Descriptive Record of the History, Religion, Literature, and Customs of the Jewish People from the Earliest Times to the Present Day,* , Vol. XI (copyright 1905, pages 69–70), accessed Dec. 1, 2017, https://ia800409.us.archive.org/18/items/1901TheJewishEncyclopediaIAachApo

calypticLiterature_201605/The_jewish_encyclopedia_-_XI_-_Samson_-_Talmid_Hakam_text.pdf.

118. 2 Corinthians 11:3, *Benson Commentary*, Biblehub.com, http://biblehub.com/commentaries/2_corinthians/11-3.htm.

119. Nachash, Heb. #5175, *Strong's Exhaustive Concordance* (And other Hebrew lexicons found at this site, Biblehub.com, http://biblehub.com/hebrew/5175

    See Also: Nachash, Heb. #5172, *Strong's Exhaustive Concordance* (And other Hebrew lexicons found at this site, Biblehub.com, http://biblehub.com/hebrew/5172.

120. Nehushtan, *Easton's Bible Dictionary*, Bible Study Tools, accessed December 3, 2017, https://www.biblestudytools.com/dictionary/nehushtan.

121. 2 Corinthians 11:3, *Benson Commentary*, Biblehub.com, http://biblehub.com/commentaries/2_corinthians/11-3.htm.

122. Strauss, Dr. Lehman. "Bible Prophecy (The First Prophecy)," Bible.org, accessed November 4, 2017, https://bible.org/article/bible-prophecy.

123. Genesis 3:15, *Benson Commentary*, Biblehub.com, http://biblehub.com/commentaries/genesis/3-15.htm#.

124. Genesis 3:15, *Benson Commentary*, Biblehub.com, http://biblehub.com/commentaries/genesis/3-15.htm.

125. Strauss, Dr. Lehman. "Bible Prophecy (The First Prophecy)," Bible.org, accessed November 4, 2017, https://bible.org/article/bible-prophecy.

126. Dr. Deffinbaugh, Bob. "The Anticipation of Israel's Messiah," Bible.org, June 22, 2004, https://bible.org/article/anticipation-israels-messiah#P24_5301.

127. Dr. Stewart, Don. "What Does Genesis 3:15 Mean?" Blue Letter Bible— Commentary, accessed November 29, 2017, https://www.blueletterbible.org/faq/don_stewart/don_stewart_756.cfm.

128. Genesis 3:15, (See as examples: *Benson Commentary; Pulpit Commentary; Matthew Henry's Concise Commentary; Matthew Poole's Commentary; Gill's Exposition of the Entire Bible;* and *Jamieson-Fausset-Brown Bible Commentary*), Biblehub.com, http://biblehub.com/commentaries/genesis/3-15.htm.

129. Galatians 3:15–19, *The Bible Exposition Commentary*, © 1989 by Chariot Victor Publishing, and imprint of Cook Communication Ministries. All rights reserved. Used by permission—through PC Study Bible Software, Copyright 1988-2008 Biblesoft, Inc.

130. Romans 16:20, *Jamieson-Fausset-Brown Bible Commentary*, Biblehub.com, http://biblehub.com/commentaries/romans/16-20.htm.

131. Founders Online, "Abigail Adams to Elizabeth Smith Shaw, 20 March 1791," accessed December 17, 2017, https://founders.archives.gov/documents/Adams/04-09-02-0112.

132. Genesis 3:7, *Gill's Exposition of the Entire Bible*, Biblehub.com, http://biblehub.com/commentaries/genesis/3-7.htm.

133. Genesis 3:7, *Guzik Commentary*, (Man's Temptation and Fall), Blueletterbible.org, https://www.blueletterbible.org/Comm/guzik_david/StudyGuide_Gen/Gen_3.cfm.

134. Genesis 3:7, *Matthew Poole's Commentary*, Biblehub.com, http://biblehub.com/commentaries/genesis/3-7.htm

135. According to the online University of Pennsylvania Archives for *Ephraim Avigdor Speiser*: Dr. Speiser was professor of Semitics at the University of Pennsylvania. During World War II, he served as chief of the Office of Strategic Services' Near East Section of the Research and Analysis Branch in Washington. He translated and wrote extensive commentary for the volume on Genesis in the Anchor Bible Series and was one of the editors of the Torah in the New Jewish Publication Society of America Version of the Old Testament. Dr. Speiser served as University of Pennsylvania's Chairman of the Department of Oriental Studies from 1947 until his death in 1965.

136. Genesis 3, *Expository Notes of Dr. Thomas Constable*, Studylight.org, accessed January 2, 2018, https://www.studylight.org/commentaries/dcc/genesis-3.html.

137. Isaac M. Kikawada, PhD, taught Near Eastern Studies at the University of California at Berkeley. Arthur Quinn taught Rhetoric at the University of California at Berkeley and holds an MA and PhD from Princeton University.

138. Kikawada and Quinn. *Before Abraham Was: The Unity of Genesis 1-11*,

(Wipf and Stock, March 23, 2017):81, https://books.google.com/books
?id=2g8rDwAAQBAJ&pg=PA81&lpg=PA81&dq=E.+A.+Speiser+gene
sis+the+original+sin+was+sexual&source=bl&ots=9Sezu5wpbG&sig=y
nxbdljam8LkB-SNVbCaH-Exmtc&hl=en&sa=X&ved=0ahUKEwioqY
v4p97YAhVNeKwKHdbNAmAQ6AEIKTAA#v=onepage&q=E.%20
A.%20Speiser%20genesis%20the%20original%20sin%20was%20
sexual&f=false.

139. Genesis 3:6, *John Calvin's Bible Commentary*, (Genesis 3 Bible
    Commentary), Christianity.com, accessed January 16, 2018, https://www.
    christianity.com/bible/commentary.php?com=clvn&b=1&c=3.

140. Dr. Spooner, Henry G. (Editor). "The American Journal of Urology and
    Sexology," University of Michigan Library (November 5, 2009); 72–73,
    https://books.google.com/books?id=VD1YAAAAMAAJ&printsec=frontc
    over&source=gbs_ge_summary_r&cad=0#v=onepage&q&f=false.

141. *Cambridge Dictionary*, "Forbidden Fruit," accessed January 19, 2018,
    https://dictionary.cambridge.org/us/dictionary/english/forbidden-fruit.

142. Waugh, Rob. "The Church of Satan Believes that Sex Robots Could Save
    Our Society," Metro UK, Jan. 15, 2018, http://metro.co.uk/2018/01/15/
    church-satan-believes-sex-robots-save-society-7231168.

143. Wikipedia, "Church of Satan," accessed Jan. 2, 2018, https://
    en.wikipedia.org/wiki/Church_of_Satan.

144. Ezekiel 28:16, "Parallel Translations," Biblehub.com, http://biblehub.
    com/ezekiel/28-16.htm.

145. Chalal. OT. #2490, (See *Brown-Drivers-Brigg* and *Strong's*), Biblehub.com,
    http://biblehub.com/hebrew/2490.htm.

146. Chalal. *Strong's* Heb. #2490, *Vines Expository Dictionary of Old and New
    Testament Words*, Profane, by W. E. Vine, Merrill F. Unger, and William
    White, Jr.: 287, http://www.ultimatebiblereferencelibrary.com/Vines_
    Expositary_Dictionary.pdf.

147. Song of Solomon 2:3, *Jamieson-Fausset-Brown Bible Commentary*,
    Biblehub.com, http://biblehub.com/commentaries/songs/2-3.htm.

148. Song of Solomon 4:12, *Pulpit Commentary*, Biblehub.com, http://
    biblehub.com/commentaries/songs/4-12.htm.

149. There are three chapters in section 3 of this book that deal with the clear

presentation of "Satan as a tree," from several other contextual Scripture references.

150. Strathcarron, Ian. *Innocence and War: Mark Twain's Holy Land Revisited*, Dover Publications (November 21, 2012): 35.

151. 2 Corinthians 11:1–6, *The Bible Exposition Commentary (New Testament)*. © 1989 by Chariot Victor Publishing, and imprint of Cook Communication Ministries. All rights reserved. Used by permission— through PC Study Bible Software, Copyright 1988–2008 Biblesoft, Inc.

152. 2 Corinthians 11:3, *Ellicott's Commentary for English Readers*, Biblehub. com, http://biblehub.com/commentaries/2_corinthians/11-3.htm.

153. 2 Corinthians 11:3, *Expositor's Greek Testament*, Biblehub.com, http:// biblehub.com/commentaries/2_corinthians/11-3.htm.

154. 2 Peter 1:4, "Parallel Versions," Biblehub.com" http://biblehub.com/2_ peter/1-4.htm.

155. Epithumia. *Strong's* Heb. #1939, Biblehub.com, http://biblehub.com/ greek/1939.htm.

156. James 1:14, *Meyer's New Testament Commentary*, Biblehub.com, http:// biblehub.com/commentaries/james/1-14.htm.

157. 2 Peter 1:4, *Clarke's Commentary on 2 Peter 1:4*, Godvine.com, Accessed 5-12-17, http://www.godvine.com/bible/2-peter/1-4.

158. 2 Peter 1:4, (Verse by Verse Commentary) *John Gill's Exposition of the Whole Bible*, Studylight.org, accessed January 1, 2017, https://www. studylight.org/commentary/2-peter/1-4.html.

159. Genesis 3:7, *Gill's Exposition of the Entire Bible*, Biblehub.com, http:// biblehub.com/commentaries/genesis/3-7.htm.

160. 2 Peter 1:4, (Verse by Verse Commentary) *Commentary Critical and Explanatory on the Whole Bible*, Studylight.org, accessed January 1, 2017, https://www.studylight.org/commentary/2-peter/1-4.html.

161. 2 Peter 1:4, (Verse by Verse Commentary) *Greek Testament Critical Exegetical Commentary*, Studylight.org, accessed January 1, 2017, https:// www.studylight.org/commentary/2-peter/1-4.html.

162. 2 Peter 1:4, (Verse by Verse Commentary) *Matthew Poole's English Annotations on the Holy Bible*, Studylight.org, accessed January 1, 2017, https://www.studylight.org/commentary/2-peter/1-4.html.

163. 2 Peter 1:4, (Verse by Verse Commentary) *Whedon's Commentary on the Bible*, Studylight.org, accessed January 1, 2017, https://www.studylight.org/commentary/2-peter/1-4.html.

164. James 1:14, *Benson Commentary*, Biblehub.com, http://biblehub.com/commentaries/james/1-14.htm.

165. James 1:14, *Jamieson-Fausset-Brown Bible Commentary*, Biblehub.com, http://biblehub.com/commentaries/james/1-14.htm.

166. James 1:14, *Expositor's Greek Testament*, Biblehub.com, http://biblehub.com/commentaries/james/1-14.htm.

167. James 1:14, *Pulpit Commentary*, Biblehub.com, http://biblehub.com/commentaries/james/1-14.htm.

168. James 1:14, *Barnes' Notes on the Bible*, Biblehub.com, http://biblehub.com/commentaries/james/1-14.htm.

169. James 1:14, *Gill's Exposition of the Scriptures*, Biblehub.com, http://biblehub.com/commentaries/james/1-14.htm.

170. James 1:14, *Cambridge Bible for Schools and Colleges*, Biblehub.com, http://biblehub.com/commentaries/james/1-14.htm.

171. James 1:14, *Bengal's Gnomen*, Biblehub.com, http://biblehub.com/commentaries/james/1-14.htm.

172. James 1:14, *Jamieson-Fausset-Brown Bible Commentary*, Biblehub.com, http://biblehub.com/commentaries/james/1-14.htm.

173. (See the *Benson Commentary*, the *Pulpit Commentary*, and the *Jamieson-Fausset-Brown Bible Commentary* entries for this verse as a few examples of this assertion), Biblehub.com, http://biblehub.com/commentaries/genesis/3-6.htm.

174. The fairly popular "Serpent Seed" postulation holds to the belief that Satan actually had sex with Eve, and from that sexual union Cain was born. However, Genesis 4:1 clearly dispels the notion that Cain was the result of such a union. For this reason, and several other wayward elements of the teaching, I do not promote the Serpent Seed idea.

175. 2 Corinthians 11:3, *Expositor's Greek Testament*, Biblehub.com, http://biblehub.com/commentaries/2_corinthians/11-3.htm.

176. Singer, Isidore, PhD (Projector and Managing Editor), *The Jewish Encyclopedia: A Descriptive Record of the History, Religion, Literature, and*

Customs of the Jewish People from the Earliest Times to the Present Day,
Vol. XI (copyright 1905, page 69–70), accessed Dec. 1, 2017, https://
ia800409.us.archive.org/18/items/1901TheJewishEncyclopediaIAachApo
calypticLiterature_201605/The_jewish_encyclopedia_-_XI_-_Samson_-_
Talmid_Hakam_text.pdf.

177. Kaufmann Kohler and Emil G. Hirsch, "Fall of Man," *Jewish Encyclopedia:
The Unedited Full-Text of the 1906 Jewish Encyclopedia,* accessed March 11,
2017, http://www.jewishencyclopedia.com/ articles/5999-fall-of-man.

178. *New World Encyclopedia,* "Human Fall," (The Forbidden Fruit),
accessed March 11, 2017, http://www.newworldencyclopedia.org/entry/
Human_Fall.

179. Ibid.

180. Levison, John R. (General Editor), *With Letters of Light: Studies in
the Dead Sea Scrolls, Early Jewish Apocalypticism, Magic, and Mysticism
(Ekstasis: Religious Experience from Antiquity to the Middle Ages)* 1ˢᵗ Edition,
De Gruyter; (November 26, 2010): 95, http://www. michaelsheiser.
com/PaleoBabble/Minov%20Serpentine%20Eve%20 in%20Syriac%20
Christian%20Literature%20of%20Late%20Antiquity. pdf.

181. Dr. Ringler, Guy. "Get Ready for Embryos from Two Men or
Two Women," *Time,* 3-18-15, http://time.com/3748019/
same-sex-couples-biological-children.

182. Lewin, Tamar. "Babies from Skin Cells? Prospect Is Unsettling to
Some Experts," *New York Times,* 5-16-17, https://www.nytimes.
com/2017/05/16/health/ivg-reproductive-technology.html.

183. Preetika Rana, Amy Dockser Marcus, and Wenxin Fan. "China,
Unhampered by Rules, Races Ahead in Gene-Editing Trials," 1-21-18,
https://www.wsj.com/articles/china-unhampered-by-rules-races-ahead-in-
gene-editing-trials-1516562360.

184. This illustration is also used in *Gods and Thrones.* It is somewhat
abbreviated here.

185. I refer the reader to my previous book, *Gods and Thrones,* for a detailed
study on the topic of Genesis 6 and the "sons of God" coming unto the
"daughters of men and having children by them." In that work, I also
expand upon the question of "Can angels have sex?" since it is often

expressed as an objection that "angels are not sexual beings." That particular objection is often argued by using the statement of Jesus that angels are not "given in marriage"—as humans are (Matthew 22:30, Mark 12:25).

186. Augustine of Hippo (Author), Henry Bettenson (Translator), *City of God*, Penguin Classics; Revised ed. edition (January 6, 2004): 59, ISBN-10: 0140448942.

187. Clark, Heather. "Blasphemous Minister Who Supports Polyamory Claims 'Holy Trinity Is a Polyamorous Relationship'," Christiannews.net, 10-11-17, http://christiannews.net/2017/10/11/blasphemous-minister-who-supports-polyamory-claims-holy-trinity-is-a-polyamorous-relationship/.

188. Revelation 2:24, *Jamieson-Fausset-Brown Bible Commentary*, Biblehub. com, http://biblehub.com/commentaries/jfb/revelation/2.htm.

189. Revelation 2:24, *Vincent's Word Studies*, Biblehub.com, http://biblehub. com/commentaries/revelation/2-24.htm.

190. 1 Corinthians 6:18, *Barnes' Notes on the Bible*, Biblehub.com, http:// biblehub.com/commentaries/1_corinthians/6-18.htm.

191. 1 Corinthians 6:18, *Expositor's Greek New Testament*, Biblehub.com, http://biblehub.com/commentaries/1_corinthians/6-18.htm.

192. 1 Corinthians 6:18, *Cambridge Bible for Schools and Colleges*, Biblehub. com,http://biblehub.com/commentaries/1_corinthians/6-18.htm.

193. 1 Corinthians 6:18, *Ellicott's Commentary for English Readers*, Biblehub. com, http://biblehub.com/commentaries/1_corinthians/6-18.htm.

194. Romans 1:28, *Expositor's Greek Testament*, Biblehub.com, http://biblehub. com/commentaries/romans/1-28.htm.

195. Romans 1:28, *Vincent's Word Studies*, Biblehub.com, http://biblehub.com/ commentaries/romans/1-28.htm.

196. Romans 1:28, *Matthew Poole's Commentary*, Biblehub.com, http:// biblehub.com/commentaries/romans/1-28.htm.

197. Romans 1:24, *Ellicott's Commentary for English Readers*, Biblehub.com, http://biblehub.com/commentaries/romans/1-28.htm.

198. Romans 1:24, *Benson Commentary*, Biblehub.com, http://biblehub.com/ commentaries/romans/1-28.htm.

199. See this source for over one hundred Scriptures that refer to sexual sin, from Genesis to Revelation: https://www.openbible.info/topics/sexual_sin.

The sin of idolatry is often connected with the sins of sexual perversion (Revelation 22:15). Scripture (both Old and New Testaments) also frequently uses sexual terminology as metaphors for idolatry. As an example, Ezekiel 16 contains a harsh admonition against the nation of Judah for forsaking God for a love affair with pagan idols. God calls Judah a prostitute and describes her pagan worship ritual as fornication, adultery, and harlotry. The worship of idols consisted of ritual prostitution at pagan temples and shrines that blanketed the landscape of Israel's high places. See these NT passages as a few examples of the clear connection of idolatry and sexual sin: Ephesians 5:5; Colossians 3:5; 1 Corinthians 6:9–10.

200. CBS Atlanta. "CDC: 110 Million Americans Have STDs At Any Given Time," 10-6-14, http://atlanta.cbslocal.com/2014/10/06/cdc-110-million-americans-have-stds-at-any-given-time.

201. *Huffington Post*, "The Weinstein Effect: The Global Scourge Of Sexual Harassment And Exploitation," Nov. 2, 2017, https://www.huffingtonpost.com/entry/the-weinstein-effect-the-global-scourge-of-sexual_us_59fb02a8e4b09887ad6f3db9.

202. Newman, Alex. "Dr. Phil Interview Exposes Global Elite," 3-30-17, Pedophileshttps://www.thenewamerican.com/usnews/crime/item/25713-dr-phil-interview-exposes-global-elite-pedophiles.

203. United Nations, "'Act Now' to Help and Protect Trafficking Victims, UN Urges on World Day against the Scourge," 7-30-17, http://www.un.org/apps/news/story.asp?NewsID=57278#.WmCzI6inHIU.

204. FBI News, "The Scourge of Child Pornography," 4-25-17, https://www.fbi.gov/news/stories/the-scourge-of-child-pornography.

205. ABC News, "Porn Profits: Corporate America's Secret," 1-28-18, http://abcnews.go.com/Primetime/story?id=132001&page=1.

206. Nowak, Peter. "U.S. Leads the Way in Porn Production, but Falls behind in Profits," 1-5-12, http://www.canadianbusiness.com/blogs-and-comment/u-s-leads-the-way-in-porn-production-but-falls-behind-in-profits/.

207. Kupelian, David. "The Left's Ongoing Sexual Assault on America," WND.com, 1-30-18, http://www.wnd.com/2018/01/the-lefts-ongoing-sexual-assault-on-america/#SzjJsFUUh3p9SC4y.99.

208. Prager, Dennis. "Judaism's Sexual Revolution: Why Judaism Rejected Homosexuality," CERC— Catholic Education Research Center, accessed January 27,2018, Selected quotes were reprinted by written permission, https://www.catholiceducation.org/en/marriage-and-family/sexuality/judaism-s-sexual-revolution-why-judaism-rejected-homosexuality.html.

209. Ibid.

210. Farley, Harry. "UN Aid Workers Carried Out 60,000 Rapes in a decade." Feb. 14, 2018, https://www.christiantoday.com/article/un-aid-workers-carried-out-60000-rapes-in-a-decade/125803.htm.

211. MacLeod, Andrew. "The United Nations Is Turning a Blind Eye to Child Rape within Its Own Ranks," March 25, 2917, http://www.independent.co.uk/voices/united-nations-soldiers-paedophilia-un-child-rape-ngo-staff-a7648791.html.

212. Chay OT #2416, *Strong's Exhaustive Concordance*, Biblehub.com, http://biblehub.com/hebrew/2416.htm.

213. Chay OT #2416, *Brown-Driver-Briggs*, Biblehub.com, http://biblehub.com/hebrew/2416.htm.

214. Genesis 3:1, *McLaren's Exposition*, Biblehub.com, http://biblehub.com/commentaries/genesis/3-1.htm.

215. Genesis 3:1, *Jamison, Faucet, and Brown Commentary*, Biblehub.com, http://biblehub.com/commentaries/genesis/3-1.htm.

216. Genesis 3:14, *Keil and Delitzsch Biblical Commentary on the Old Testament*, Biblehub.com, http://biblehub.com/commentaries/genesis/3-14.htm.

217. Genesis 3, *Gill's Exposition of the Entire Bible*, Biblehub.com, http://biblehub.com/commentaries/gill/genesis/3.htm.

218. Several of the next chapters of this book will examine the personification of the "trees" in the Garden of Eden. You will see, in the Old Testament, what God Himself says about the matter, as well as three places in the New Testament where Jesus addresses the topic.

219. Naga OT #5060, *Strong's Exhaustive Concordance* and *Brown-Driver-Briggs* (Meaning #3), Biblehub.com, http://biblehub.com/hebrew/5060.htm.

220. Haptomai NT #680, *Thayer's Greek Lexicon*, Section 2b., http://biblehub.com/greek/680.htm.

221. Genesis 3:3, *Keil and Delitzsch Biblical Commentary on the Old Testament*, Biblehub.com, http://biblehub.com/commentaries/genesis/3-3.htm.

222. In Genesis 2:16–17, we find God's words to Adam regarding not eating from the tree of the knowledge of good and evil. Nothing is said in that text about God telling Adam not to "touch" the fruit. However, Eve had not yet been created. It is now Eve to whom Satan is speaking when the subject of "touching" is mentioned. In light of what we have discovered thus far, it makes perfect contextual sense that at some point Eve was given the additional warning: *Do not touch that "tree."*

223. Genesis 3:3, *Matthew Poole's Commentary*, Biblehub.com, http://biblehub.com/commentaries/genesis/3-3.htm.

224. Spurgeon, Charles H. "Christ the Tree of Life—No. 3251," Metropolitan Tabernacle Pulpit, accessed January 12, 2018, http://www.spurgeongems.org/vols55-57/chs3251.pdf.

225. Genesis 3, *Expositor's Bible Commentary*, (The last three sentences of the second paragraph from the top of the page), Biblehub.com, http://biblehub.com/commentaries/expositors/genesis/3.htm.

226. Dr. Strauss, Lehman. "Bible Prophecy (A Principle of Prophetic Interpretation; Isaiah's Prophecies; Micah's Prophecies)," Bible.org, accessed November 4, 2017, https://bible.org/article/bible-prophecy.

   Author's Note: A compound prophecy, or a compound reference, is one that either contains several layers of meaning and context, or one that begins as a reference to one thing, or person, but then shifts to a symbolic reference to something or someone else. See examples of this well-known biblical phenomenon in the above listed reference material by Dr. Strauss.

227. In my former book, *Gods and Thrones*, I take several chapters to deal with the comparisons of Isaiah 14 and Ezekiel 28. This section constitutes only a brief review of that study.

228. Delitzsch, Franz, *Biblical Commentary on the Prophecies of Isaiah*, accessed April 19, 2017, [Edinburgh: T. & T. Clark, 1875], 1:312.

229. Robert Jamieson, A. R. Fausset and David Brown, *Commentary Critical and Explanatory on the Whole Bible*, (Ezekiel 28), 1871, http://www.biblestudytools.com/commentaries/jamieson-fausset-brown/ezekiel/ezekiel-28.html.

230. Ezekiel 28:14-15, *Benson Commentary*, Biblehub.com, http://biblehub.com/commentaries/benson/ezekiel/28.htm.

231. Ezekiel 28:14, *The Bible Exposition Commentary: Old Testament*, accessed December 11, 2017, (Biblesoft PC Study Bible, copyright from 1988–2008) (**The Bible Exposition Commentary: Old Testament** © 2001-2004 by Warren W. Wiersbe. All rights reserved.)

232. Ezekiel 31:8, *Jamieson-Fausset-Brown Bible Commentary*, Biblehub.com, http://biblehub.com/commentaries/ezekiel/31-8.htm.

233. Ezekiel 31:8, *Pulpit Commentary*, Biblehub.com, http://biblehub.com/commentaries/ezekiel/31-8.htm.

234. Jewish Virtual Library, "Encyclopedia Judaica: The Garden of Eden," accessed December 3, 2017, http://www.jewishvirtuallibrary.org/garden-of-eden.

235. Aaron Blake and Frances Stead Sellers. "Hillary Clinton, Saul Alinsky and Lucifer, Explained," *Washington Post*, July 20, 2016,https://www.washingtonpost.com/news/the-fix/wp/2016/07/20/hillary-clinton-saul-alinsky-and-lucifer-explained/?utm_term=.641b05905a42.

236. Ezekiel 31:16, *Benson Commentary*, Biblehub.com, http://biblehub.com/commentaries/ezekiel/31-16.htm.

237. Ezekiel 31:16, "Commentaries," Biblehub.com, http://biblehub.com/commentaries/ezekiel/31-16.htm.

238. Dr. Ritenbaugh, John W. "Bible Verses about Egypt as a Type of Sin," (Forerunner Commentary), Bibletools.org, https://www.bibletools.org/index.cfm/fuseaction/Topical.show/RTD/cgg/ID/16607/Egypt-as-Type-Sin.htm.

239. Ezekiel 31:8, *Jamieson-Fausset-Brown Bible Commentary*, Biblehub.com, Biblehub.com, http://biblehub.com/commentaries/ezekiel/31-8.htm.

240. Jewish Virtual Library, "Encyclopedia Judaica: The Garden of Eden," accessed December 3, 2017, http://www.jewishvirtuallibrary.org/garden-of-eden.

241. Luke 13:19, *Wiersbe Bible Commentary: New Testament* (David C. Cook; New edition (November 1, 2007): 182, referenced at: https://godspeakyouth.files.wordpress.com/2017/09/wiersbe-nt.pdf (P. 182).

242. Dr. Collins, Martin G. "Bible Verses about Bird as Symbol of Demon (*Forerunner Commentary*)," (Parables of Matthew 13 [Part Four]: The Parable of the Mustard Seed), https://www.bibletools.org/index.cfm/

fuseaction/Topical.show/RTD/CGG/ID/3600/Bird-as-Symbol-of-Demon-.htm.

243. Matthew 13:33, *Cambridge Bible for Schools and Colleges*, Biblehub.com, http://biblehub.com/commentaries/matthew/13-33.htm.

244. Larkin, Molly. "Prophecy of Crazy Horse," Nov. 27, 2012, https://www.mollylarkin.com.

245. Revelation 2:7, *Adam Clarke Commentary*, accessed December 5, 2017, (Adam Clark's Commentary, Electronic Database. Copyright © 1996, 2003, 2005, 2006 by Biblesoft, Inc. All rights reserved.).

246. O'Reilly, Jennifer. "The Trees of Eden in Mediaeval Iconography." In *A Walk in the Garden: Biblical, Iconographical and Literary Images of Eden*, ed. P. Morris and D. Sawyer (Sheffield: JSOT Press, 1992), p. 170.

247. Revelation 22:2, "Commentaries," Bible Study Tools, accessed December 3, 2017, https://www.biblestudytools.com/commentaries/revelation/revelation-22/revelation-22-2.html.

248. Revelation 22:2, *John Gill's Exposition of the Entire Bible*, accessed December 2, 2017, https://www.biblestudytools.com/commentaries/gills-exposition-of-the-bible/revelation-22-2.html.

249. Genesis 2:9, *Gill's Exposition of the Entire Bible*, Biblehub.com, http://biblehub.com/commentaries/genesis/2-9.htm.

250. Spurgeon, Charles H. "Christ the Tree of Life—No. 3251," Metropolitan Tabernacle Pulpit, accessed January 12, 2018, http://www.spurgeongems.org/vols55-57/chs3251.pdf.

251. The Devil, "Devil Quotes," Good Reads, accessed Dec. 3, 2017, https://www.goodreads.com/quotes/tag/the-devil.

252. Ian Fleming Quotes, "Casino Royale Quotes," accessed December 4, 2017, https://www.goodreads.com/work/quotes/2503304-casino-royale.

253. Genesis 3:15, *Benson Commentary*, Biblehub.com, http://biblehub.com/commentaries/genesis/3-15.htm.

254. John 8:44, *Bengal's Gnomen*, Biblehub.com, *http://biblehub.com/commentaries/john/8-44.htm.*

255. *John 8:44, Pulpit* Commentary, Biblehub.com, http://biblehub.com/commentaries/john/8-44.htm.

256. John 8:44, *Meyer's New Testament Commentary*, Biblehub.com, http://biblehub.com/commentaries/john/8-44.htm.

257. John 8:44, *Jamieson-Fausset-Brown Bible Commentary*, Biblehub.com, http://biblehub.com/commentaries/john/8-44.htm.

258. Ephesians 2:3, *Benson Commentary*, Biblehub.com, http://biblehub.com/commentaries/ephesians/2-3.htm.

259. Romans 8:15, *Meyer's New Testament Commentary*, Biblehub.com, http://biblehub.com/commentaries/romans/8-15.htm.

260. Romans 8:15, *Gill's Exposition of the Scriptures*, Biblehub.com, http://biblehub.com/commentaries/romans/8-15.htm.

261. Merlin, Anna. "Oklahoma Removes Ten Commandments on Capitol Grounds, Which Sadly Also Means No Satanic Statue," 10-7-15, https://jezebel.com/oklahoma-removes-ten-commandments-on-capitol-grounds-w-1735155450.

262. Satan's Garden-Satanic Website, "Satanic Magic," accessed January 1, 2017, http://satansgarden.weebly.com/magic--ritual.html.

263. Rozsa, Matthew. "Arkansas Has Installed the Ten Commandments at its Capitol," 6-27-17, https://www.salon.com/2017/06/27/arkansas-ten-commandments-statue-monument-capitol.

264. The entire book of Hebrews, and especially the fourth chapter, is the definitive work proving that Jesus Christ's completed work of redemption is the ultimate fulfillment of the "law" of the Sabbath rest. The writer of Hebrews asserts that if you are "in Christ," you are keeping the law of the Sabbath. This is another reason Satan's profaning of Yahweh's creation was so despicable. Remember, the Garden paradise was created through the person of Jesus Christ (John 1:3; Colossians 1:16). The fourth commandment was ultimately about honoring Jesus, the Lord of the Sabbath (Matthew 12:1–8, Mark 2:23–28, and Luke 6:1–5). Satan desecrated the Sabbath by profaning the intent of the creation itself.

265. 2 Corinthians 11:3, *Expositor's Greek Testament*, Biblehub.com, http://biblehub.com/commentaries/2_corinthians/11-3.htm.

266. Romans 2:14, *Benson Commentary*, Biblehub.com, http://biblehub.com/commentaries/romans/2-14.htm.

267. Hebrew for Christians, "The Letter Shin/Sin, "accessed January 12, 2017, http://www.hebrew4christians.com/Grammar/Unit_One/Aleph-Bet/Shin/shin.html.

268. NSW Board of Jewish Education, "Shin (Hebrew Letter)," accessed January 12, 2017, http://bje.org.au/course/jewish-languages/hebrew-alphabet/shin-hebrew-letter.

269. Bargil Pixner (2010). Rainer Riesner, ed. *Paths of the Messiah*. Translated by Keith Myrick, Miriam Randall. Ignatius Press. pp. 320–322.

270. Opel, OT #6076, *Strong's Concordance*, Biblehub.com, http://biblehub.com/hebrew/6076.htm.

271. Zion meaning, "Etymology of the name Zion," Abarim Publications, accessed December 12, 2017, http://www.abarim-publications.com/Meaning/Zion.html#.WjwC69-nHIU.

272. Moriah, "OT: 4179," accessed Dec. 14, 2017, Biblesoft's New Exhaustive Strong's Numbers and Concordance with Expanded Greek-Hebrew Dictionary. Copyright © 1994, 2003, 2006 Biblesoft, Inc. and International Bible Translators, Inc.

273. Moriah meaning, "Etymology of the name Moriah," Abarim Publications, accessed December 12, 2017, http://www.abarim-publications.com/Meaning/Moriah.html#.WjwG1N-nHIU.

274. CMJ—USA, "Sibley," accessed Dec. 23, 2017, http://www.cmj-usa.org/content/sibley.

275. Wellman, Jared. "Wellman: Where on Earth Was the Garden of Eden?" OA Online, 1-3-15, http://www.oaoa.com/people/religion/article_7d948064-935d-11e4-90c2-4b09cc36f260.html.

276. Baker, Eric W. The Eschatological Role of the Jerusalem Temple: An Examination of Jewish Writings Dating from 586 BCE to 70 CE, (Andrews University -Digital Commons, 2014): 33–36, https://digitalcommons.andrews.edu/cgi/viewcontent.cgi?article=1012&context=dissertations.

277. Barker, Margaret. *The Gate of Heaven: The History and Symbolism of the Temple in Jerusalem*, (London: SPCK, 1991): 57, 63–64.

278. The seventy weeks of Daniel outlined in Daniel 9 refer specifically to end-time prophecy; as well as the fifty-day period from Jesus' resurrection until the giving of the Holy Spirit and the birth of the church in Jerusalem. Of course, that fifty-day period also relates specifically to the feast of Pentecost, the feast upon which the orthodox Jews, to this day,

commemorate the birth of Israel through the giving of the law at Sinai. Israel was "born" on the celebration of "fifty." So was the church.

279. Koenig, Bill. "2017/2018–5777," (Jubilee Year and the Capture of Jerusalem), January 12, 2018, https://www.watch.org/node/26631.

280. The Jerusalem Embassy Act, October 23, 1995, recognized Jerusalem as the capital of the State of Israel and called for Jerusalem to remain an undivided city. It also called for the US Embassy to be moved to Jerusalem from Tel Aviv. The law allowed the president to invoke a "national-security" waiver every six months. The waiver was repeatedly employed by Presidents Clinton, Bush, and Obama.

281. Landler, Mark. "Trump Recognizes Jerusalem as Israel's Capital and Orders U.S. Embassy to Move," *New York Times*, 12-6-17, https://www.nytimes.com/2017/12/06/world/middleeast/trump-jerusalem-israel-capital.html.

282. Radio Free Europe, "UN Votes 128-9 To Reject U.S. Recognition of Jerusalem as Israel Capital," 12-21-17, https://www.rferl.org/a/un-votes-reject-us-jerusalem-recognition-capital/28931789.html.

283. Author's Note: We cannot be dogmatically certain that the Garden of Gethsemane was the exact spot of the original Garden Sin. However, the spiritual connections between the Garden of Eden, the Garden of Gethsemane, the garden area of Calvary, and the garden tomb have been well documented for many years. For further research concerning that particular truth, the reader is encouraged to begin with the following excellent resources:

    a) Chaffey, Tim. "The Good Shepherd and the Three Gardens," Answers in Genesis, 4-9-13, https://answersingenesis.org/jesus-christ/resurrection/good-shepherd-three-gardens.

    b) Bradharte. "The 4 Hidden Meanings of Gardens in the Bible That Will Empower You," 7-6-15, https://ccsouthbay.org/blog/the-4-hidden-meanings-of-gardens.

    c) *Our Daily Bread.* "Two Gardens," April 17, 2006, https://odb.org/2006/04/17/two-gardens.

284. Scripture does not use the specific word "garden" for Gethsemane, although the word "garden" has traditionally been the common and

ancient description of that particular grove of olive trees that line the foot of the Mount of Olives. For example, *Strong's Concordance* says this about the word "Gethsemane": "Of Chaldee origin; oil-press; Gethsemane, a garden near Jerusalem."

285. John 19:41, *Pulpit Commentary*, Biblehub.com, http://biblehub.com/commentaries/john/19-41.htm

286. Hematohidrosis is a rare condition in which a human being sweats blood. You can read more on this condition at the website of the US National Library of Medicine, National Institutes of Health, under the article title: "Hematohidrosis—A Rare Clinical Phenomenon." See: https://www.ncbi.nlm.nih.gov/pmc/articles/PMC2810702.

287. Translated: "Tiberius Caesar—The Divine Son of God."

288. By Jewish reckoning, the first hour was roughly equivalent to our 6 a.m. The third hour would be 9 a.m. Noon would then be the sixth hour, and 3 p.m would be the ninth hour.

289. The Roman scourge, also called the "flagrum" or "flagellum," was a short whip made of two or three leather thongs connected to a handle. The thongs were knotted with a number of small pieces of metal and bones, attached at varying intervals. Scourging would quickly remove the skin from its victim. The criminal was made to kneel and then bend over. The hands would be lashed to a pole as the body was stretched towards the pole. This position ensured deeper lashes, especially from the shoulders to the waist. Under Roman law, there was no legal limit to the number of blows that could be delivered. Deep lacerations, torn flesh, exposed muscle and bone, and excessive bleeding would often leave the criminal at the edges of death.

290. According to John 19:23–24, the soldiers who crucified Jesus cast lots to determine who would keep His tunic because it was woven in one piece, without seam, thus making it extremely valuable and highly coveted.

291. Psalm 22:16–18.

292. *Jesus* is an Anglicized form of the Greek name *Yesous*. *Yesous* represents the Hebrew name *Yeshua*, or *Yehoshua* in its long form. The modern English equivalent of *Yeshua* is "Joshua." The name carries with it the idea that God delivers or saves, eventually, through His servant Messiah.